CW01084475

SOE

RECOLLECTIONS AND REFLECTIONS
1940–1945

SOE

Recollections and Reflections

1940–1945

J. G. BEEVOR

THE BODLEY HEAD
LONDON SYDNEY
TORONTO

British Library Cataloguing
in Publication Data
Beevor, John Grosvenor
SOE
1. Great Britain. *Army.*
Special Operations Executive
2. World War 1939–1945 – Secret service –
Great Britain
I. Title
940.54'86'41 D810.S7
ISBN 0-370-30414-4

Printed in Great Britain for
The Bodley Head Ltd
9 Bow Street, London, WC2E 7AL
by Redwood Burn Ltd
Trowbridge
Set in Linotron 202 Sabon
First published 1981

CONTENTS

INTRODUCTION

Resistance movements, including guerrilla warfare, continue to interest army commanders, staff officers, students and historians, revolutionaries and politicians. From 1939 to 1945, resistance movements and saboteurs were organised on an increasing scale in ten countries in Europe and three in south-east Asia, contributing to the success of Allied military operations to an extent which few could have foreseen. Such movements are the collective reaction by a people of character and spirit to total defeat in war or to occupation by an enemy of vastly superior power. With external help from co-belligerent allies, resistance to the enemy may lead to liberation within five years; otherwise it may last indefinitely. It is the response of moral outrage against the loss of independence, however mild the enemy occupation may initially be, or against the persistent brutalities of the occupying power.

Service in a resistance movement is a career that calls for intelligence, courage and dedication. There is a vast literature in several languages about such activities in the Second World War but after thirty-five years there is still no official published work on the part which the British (later joined by the Americans) played in the organisation and support of resistance as a whole in Europe and in Asia. An historical team from the American Office of Strategic Services prepared in 1948 an official report which was declassified in 1976, but it was not until 1980 that anything appeared in English on the history and performance of the British Special Operations Executive except as regards France mentioned below. In that year, three books were published on SOE generally; by David Stafford, a Canadian professor, and two former SOE officers, Patrick Howarth and Basil Davidson, but none of them have made an overall reappraisal of the contribution made by resistance movements to Allied military operations. And it is this which seems to me to be the key question which I have attempted here to answer.

[7]

SOE was created immediately after the fall of France by a War Cabinet minute in July 1940. It was wound up in January 1946. During this time SOE evolved from a centralised London-based organisation to a decentralised service with operational units responsible to Allied theatre commanders in different parts of the world.

I have written this account of the growth and evolution of SOE over thirty-five years after the events it describes and without access to the original archives because successive British governments have continued to withhold them from public access although an exception was made for Professor M. R. D. Foot's book on SOE in France published in 1966. A full and admirable work, it is the only official British history of any section of SOE or any branch of the resistance movement yet published, but it is limited to France alone.

General Sir Colin Gubbins, one of the true precursors, founders and moving spirits behind SOE and the head of it from 1943 to 1945, died in January 1976. It now seems impossible for a history to be written by any single author who combines first-hand knowledge, from having served throughout the war in a senior capacity with SOE, with the benefit of continued access over a long period to the official archives. Future historians are bound therefore to be imperfectly informed about the origins, achievements and disasters of the principal resistance movements and still less aware that SOE was their main supporting organisation.

I endorse wholeheartedly the statement by Admiral Earl Mountbatten of Burma in a foreword to *Operations Most Secret, SOE, the Malayan Theatre* by Ian Trenowden (Kimber, 1978): 'I must however emphasise that this book, like all books on SOE activities, has had to be written without full access to all relevant documents. Now that the thirty-year limitation on the publication of most wartime documents has been lifted I personally feel that it is a tremendous pity that those relating to SOE as a purely wartime organisation have not yet been released. It was Lord Acton who said, "The nation that keeps its archives secret has its history written by its enemies." It is now in the interest of our side of history that these documents should be made available subject only to a minimum of control.' It is good news that in 1980 approval was given for an official history of SOE's Force 136 in South-East Asia.

It is too early for a true and fair judgement to be pronounced on all the events of those war years and on the achievements and shortcomings of organisations responsible for the external encouragement and support of resistance; but surely it is high time that some account be made available in the compass of a single volume and with a background of some personal knowledge of the interrelation of resistance activities with Allied military planning? I therefore felt constrained, after reaching the age of retirement, to draw on my own recollections and on a selection of published works dealing with various countries by other authors with first-hand knowledge in an attempt to fill this gap.

General Gubbins asked me in August 1945, after I had returned to London for demobilisation, to go back to Italy briefly to help the official historians at Allied Force Headquarters in Caserta to start on the right lines with a history of SOE in the Mediterranean. Unfortunately I was unable to make any real progress in the short time available, as the historians had not then even begun to organise themselves or assemble material, and so my last SOE mission was frustrated. I had, however, had the fortune to hold several central posts in SOE which provided good background for this present book.

From January 1941 to June 1942 I was head of SOE mission in Lisbon where I had some responsibility for contacts in Western Europe and North Africa. In September 1942 I became assistant to SOE's second chief, Sir Charles Hambro. Later, from July 1943, I was a member of the newly formed SOE planning staff in London. From January 1944 to August 1945 I worked in Italy at the headquarters of Special Operations Mediterranean as General Staff Officer in charge of plans and operations.

Much of this book is based on personal recollections, refreshed by recent reading of books published over the thirty-five years since 1945. The staff of SOE, along no doubt with other secret organisations, were strictly prohibited from keeping diaries in wartime, for good reasons of security. I obeyed the prohibition and I did not attempt, while hostilities continued in Europe, to collect and retain any official papers for future use. I did, however, from May 1945 retain a few non-secret documents about SOE Mediterranean activities in Italy, the Balkans and Poland. Later when I returned to London in September 1945 for demobilisation and was asked to write a report on my Lisbon mission in 1941–2, I kept the manuscript copy of my report. The ancient Greeks had a saying that Memory was the mother of the Muses. While there is a continuing dispute whether Clio, the Muse of History, was truly entitled to be classified as a Muse at all, I have always, contrary to the more scientific Cambridge school, believed that she was. I realise that memories are often unreliable, but on the whole I have found that, where my own recollections can be checked against other sources, they are reasonably accurate. I hope that the test of publication will confirm this, but, if occasionally they are challenged, it will be no surprise.

Those of many nationalities who went into the field from Britain or the countries of the Commonwealth or the United States of America, whether in uniform or disguise, faced hardships and dangers of a special and exacting kind. They had missions to perform in secrecy, often in solitude, always in an atmosphere of stress, with the prospect of torture and death if captured. Conscious of the physical and emotional need for resisting attempts to force or beguile them into disclosures, many died under torture or were executed. Most have since been acclaimed for their endurance. Others, more numerous, two or more for every man or woman who went into 'the field', worked as staff or at training schools or on operational bases. They were not exposed to the same dangers and stresses of working in enemy-occupied territory, but the knowledge that their efforts were essential to the support of those in the field was a powerful and continual stimulus.

Obviously no one person can have first-hand detailed knowledge of events in nearly twenty countries over five years, and I am indebted to many sources for information and advice. First I acknowledge with gratitude the help which I have received from many of the books listed in the bibliography. I also acknowledge with thanks permission from the following sources to reproduce certain passages or documents: the Foreign and Commonwealth Office for résumés of Lord Selborne's memorandum of November 1943 (Appendix B); the SOE-OSS Agreement of June 1942 (page 82) and the Foreign Office-SOE Agreement of May 1942 (page 69); the Controller of HM Stationery Office for the extract of Lord Mountbatten's Report from South-East Asia Command to the Combined Chiefs of Staff of 1946 (Appendix D); Cassell & Co. for extracts from Sir Winston Churchill's *History of the Second World War*, Vol. VI, on the Warsaw rising; Macmillan & Co. for the quotations from pages 113/4, 125, 146/7 of Auty and Clogg's record on the proceedings of the London Conference on British Policy towards

Greece and Jugoslavia; Weidenfeld & Nicolson for quotations from *German Military Intelligence* by Paul Leverkuehn; Berkeley Publishing Co. for extracts from the *Secret War Report of the OSS* to the US Joint Chiefs of Staff, completed in 1948 and published in 1976, with annotations by A. Cave Brown; William Kimber for the quotation from *Operations Most Secret, SOE, the Malayan Theatre*, foreword by Admiral Earl Mountbatten, page 8; HM Stationery Office for the text of General Eisenhower's letter of 31 May 1945 to General Gubbins and for statistics and other facts in Professor M. R. D. Foot's *SOE in France* and to Professor Foot personally for his generous advice and factual corrections; Colonel H. M. Threlfall for the 1945 telegrams from the German Commander-in-Chief South-West, Bolzano, Italy, on the growing menace of Italian partisans (Appendix C) and much valuable advice. Special thanks are due to former colleagues General R. H. Barry, CB, CBE, Sir William Deakin, DSO, Sir Robin Hooper, GCMG, DSO, Colonel B. Sweet-Escott and Colonel Sir Peter Wilkinson, KCMG, DSO, OBE, who have read sections of the text or given me invaluable advice and criticism, and last but not least, to my wife, whom I first met on my SOE mission in Lisbon.

I

Origins

In setting out to review what SOE did, and failed to do, in support of resistance movements, what the underground movements themselves actually succeeded in achieving and how far these resistance movements contributed to Allied military operations in the Second World War, it is first necessary to examine what SOE was created to achieve, what were its restrictions and directives, how it functioned and what it could and could not do without impinging on other government departments. The guidelines laid down at its inception affected its role and limited its activities; they also affected its relationships with other countries, with governments-in-exile, with British government departments and with the armed forces, both British and, later, American. All these variables must be mentioned in order to make a fair assessment of SOE's achievements. I must also describe briefly how SOE evolved and grew, and finally, in the latter half of the book, I summarise SOE's activities in each country in turn in an attempt to show how successful or otherwise it was in encouraging resistance movements, guerrilla warfare, partisans and secret armies.

'And now set Europe ablaze' were Winston Churchill's words to Hugh Dalton upon the creation of the special operations executive. On 22 July 1940, during the dark days which followed the fall of France, a War Cabinet minute initialled by Neville Chamberlain was approved which created two new secret organisations: a security executive to co-ordinate the security services and a special operations executive to co-ordinate sabotage, subversion and black propaganda against the enemy overseas.

The security executive was set up under Lord Swinton to co-ordinate the activities of the various security services and counter-intelligence units of which the most important was known as MI5. The special operations executive was originally intended to comprise two separate departments, SO1 and SO2. SO1 was for black propaganda, misleading information which appeared to originate in enemy countries or enemy-occupied countries, and was responsible jointly to the Minister of Economic Warfare, the Minister of Information and the Foreign Secretary. By 1941 this department had changed its name and became a separate unit, known as the Political Warfare Executive. SO2 was set up under Hugh Dalton, then Minister of Economic Warfare, to co-ordinate all sabotage and subversion against the enemy overseas. By late 1941 this unit had also changed its name, to SOE, and I refer to it as such right from the beginning for the sake of clarity.

The two organisations, SO1 and SO2, were not the first of their kind. There had been others of a similar nature as far back as 1938; Electra House under Sir Campbell Stuart studying black propaganda; MIR headed by Colonel J. C. F. Holland and Major Colin Gubbins under the War Office, and another organisation headed by Colonel Lawrence Grand called Section D, which was an offshoot of the Secret Intelligence Service. In July 1940 these three merged into SOE.

Military Intelligence Research or MIR always seemed oddly named for it had been more concerned with operational ideas than research. It had the job of studying every aspect of guerrilla warfare, to find out what local freedom fighters would need in the way of supplies, training, equipment and communication networks. Its members worked closely with exiles and refugees, learning about the conditions in their homelands and keeping an eye out for any potential leaders amongst them who might be trained in underground resistance. On the whole MIR was staffed by army officers whose ultimate aim was to raise secret armies in enemy-occupied territory. They produced pamphlets called 'The Art of Guerrilla Warfare', 'The Partisan Leaders' Handbook' and 'How to Use High Explosives'. Gubbins visited Warsaw in 1938 and brought back Polish designs of time fuses and incendiary devices.

Section D specialised in secret operations such as sabotage and *coups de main,* two foreign phrases which indicated how unfamiliar such activities were to the British. Its members were interested in putting industrial factories, power stations, trains, rails and power supply lines out of action by selective destruction of key machinery – often one-man demolition jobs accomplished in urban areas. Most of the staff came from civilian backgrounds, and many had been engaged in industry or business.

MIR and Section D had occasionally co-operated before the 1940

[13]

merger but they had been responsible to different government departments. Now they were merged under one minister. I myself joined SOE five months after this merger took place and I was not normally conscious of who had belonged to which predecessor unit, but various colleagues would sometimes mention their earlier allegiance, which no doubt had some relevance to their outlook and some influence on SOE's later performances.

The first chief of SOE, Sir Frank Nelson, played a most important role in planning the organisation and recruiting key men for the staff and for overseas sections. He had a background of business and government and was an able, dedicated and conscientious man. He retired early in 1942 because of overwork and ill health and was succeeded by Sir Charles Hambro. In 1940, the chief was answerable to Hugh Dalton, a Socialist intellectual, who was imaginative, aggressive and not popular with Churchill. Dalton, being also Minister of Economic Warfare, had a small personal staff for SOE, his second and secret department. He selected Gladwyn Jebb, from the Foreign Office, to be his assistant under-secretary responsible for his contact with SOE and for supervising all its major policy aspects and relations with other departments and with the armed services.

SOE was conceived as a world-wide secret organisation directed by a single chief, based on London, despatching trained agents by land, sea and air to carry out specific missions assigned to them before they left. Obviously such a complex organisation could not be created overnight. Nelson had to find recruits of ability and experience and appoint directors or department heads to work out an organisation and establish its operating principles. His chief of staff, George Taylor, formerly of Section D, was an Australian of enormous energy and high intelligence, who set about his new job with enthusiasm. He concentrated first on Western Europe and then turned his attention to the Balkans and the Middle East, where Section D already had embryo organisations based on Belgrade and Cairo.

SOE missions set up in key neutral centres, Lisbon, Stockholm, Berne and Istanbul, were directly responsible to London; others were organised in Gibraltar and Madrid. Only Cairo, with its double role in the Balkans and the Middle East, had under George Pollock semi-autonomous SOE headquarters far removed from England. Special links with Africa, Australasia and the Far East were not made for some time.

This new secret organisation, SOE, was an experiment; its founders were unable to describe it with any clear vision of the future. It was an exciting, dramatic, secret venture which only evolved into an effective instrument of war after long trials, many errors and considerable controversy. Surprisingly at this early stage in the war the very words 'resistance movement' had not yet even been coined because as yet there was little resistance in conquered countries. General de Gaulle had used the word resistance on its own in his famous broadcast from London in the summer of 1940, but the two words 'resistance' and 'movement' were not regularly put together until late in 1942.

In 1940 few people really understood or foresaw how the nature and functions of a special operations executive would develop nor how resistance movements would be combined with and supplement regular military operations. Extreme secrecy made it difficult for outside officials to understand what was involved or why it was important enough to justify diverting a share of scarce resources to this unknown organisation which had yet to produce results. Many were jealous of its powers and privileges.

Dalton, with his qualities of imagination and ambition, was overoptimistic about the pace at which SOE and resistance activities could develop. He tried to persuade the chiefs of staff to treat SOE as a fourth service, additional to the Army, Navy and Air Force. He tended to give Churchill and other Cabinet ministers forecasts of resistance activities based on assumptions of a will to resist in excess of any realistic views before 1941, when first the Soviet Union and then the United States came into the war and gave the peoples of occupied Europe a real hope for an Allied victory. Resistance movements are only initiated when the people have some realistic hope of success.

The whole concept of secret warfare, embracing espionage, counter-espionage, guerrilla warfare, secret para-military and para-naval operations, was anathema to some. Such secret activities involved varying degrees of illegal or unethical methods which would violate normal peacetime morality and would not only be improper but often criminal; untruths, deceptions, bribery, forgeries of passports, permits or currencies, acts of violence, mayhem and murder. Just as the armed forces of any country in wartime are relieved by the laws and usages of war from any charge of murder when they kill a uniformed enemy in the course of armed combat – and many high-minded citizens have conscientious objections against that – so the secret agent, be he security officer at home or resistance organiser in enemy territory, must subject his conscience to his duties, always remembering that his activities are unacknowledgeable by his government and will be disowned if found out. In the words of Somerset Maugham:

> ' "One more thing," said the War Office colonel to Ashenden at the end of an interview in 1914, "if you do well, you will get no thanks; and, if you get into trouble, you will get no help. Does that suit you?"
> ' "Perfectly," said Ashenden.
> ' "In that case," said the colonel, "I'll wish you good afternoon." '

A secret service, especially in time of war, and especially one which operates aggressively in enemy territory, is endowed by Government with powers and privileges. High priorities for transport of all kinds, for communications, for recruitment, for protective 'cover' in other government departments or embassies abroad, for equipment and weapons and for non-accountable funds – all are indispensable for effective operation. Any suggestion, even if ill-founded, that any of these privileges are being misused naturally arouses strong feelings and antagonisms in official circles. SOE was fortunate to have a Director of Finance, John Venner, who with the background of an eminent and impeccable chartered accountant in the City of London combined an almost perfect balance between severe insistence on integrity and practical recognition of the need for delegation of authority and the impossibility of vouching secret funds beyond a certain point.

One of the first facts of official life for members of a secret organisation to remember is that other government departments and the armed services are, at a high level, on the watch for lapses and any apparent misuse of these privileges. They are also at times ambitious to assert their own control. Most secret services have both an inter-service element and also a composite side, part civilian, part military. We have already seen how SOE's own genesis involved the merger of one unit from the War Office and one from SIS, all put under the Minister of Economic Warfare.

Late in 1943, when Balkan guerrilla warfare began to play a major role in Allied strategic plans, Middle East Command made a determined bid to take over the Cairo section of SOE which masterminded the Balkan area. They nearly succeeded and indeed appointed the new SOE Commander in Cairo, General Stawell, who should in theory have been appointed by the Minister in London. Thanks to tenacity on SOE's part, to the understanding shown by the chiefs of staff, and in the last resort to the high esteem which the Prime Minister had for Lord Selborne, who by then had become Minister of Economic Warfare, SOE remained till the end an inter-service organisation responsible to a minister other than the Foreign Secretary and operating under directives received from the chiefs of staff or, as regards individual SOE units, under directives received from theatre commanders in the field.

Of all the non-service ministries, the Foreign Office was naturally far and away the most intensely interested in SOE activities. The Foreign Office, moreover, suffered most from developments in enemy-occupied countries which tended rightly or wrongly to be attributed to SOE. Sometimes, as in the growth of Communist-controlled resistance movements in the Balkans and in South-East Asia, they were in fact due not to SOE activities but to long-term Soviet subversion plans, which only came to official notice in London because SOE agents in those countries had discovered their existence and reported them to their headquarters as matters of operational intelligence.

There were three wartime categories of countries for the purpose of Foreign Office–SOE relations: neutral, conquered and enemy. In neutral countries Foreign Office interests were usually predominant. The British Government still had diplomatic relations, though SOE was intensely interested either in preparing for enemy occupation, as for example in the Balkans in 1941, or in using them as a base for communications with enemy-occupied or enemy territories, as happened in Lisbon, Stockholm, Berne and Istanbul. Then there were conquered countries, who were represented by either an Allied government-in-exile, usually based in London, such as Norway, the Netherlands, Belgium, Jugoslavia and Greece, or an Allied group aiming at government status as was the case with the Free French de Gaullists or the Free Thais. Finally there were the enemy countries themselves – Germany, Italy, Hungary, Rumania, Bulgaria and Japan, where it was free for all, apart from any questions of armistice terms or post-war conditions, which had to be reserved for discussion at the highest inter-Allied level.

Foreign Office relations with SOE over neutral and conquered countries were inherently difficult and were the source of much friction, especially in Greece and Jugoslavia. In retrospect friction is not surprising given the delays and uncertainties of secret communications with enemy-occupied and enemy territories and the difficulties which people in London had in comprehending the conditions which prevailed there. But there is no doubt that the friction was most acute when there was an exiled Allied government, to whom the British Government had feelings of gratitude and loyalty but to whom the embryo resistance movement on the spot was hostile. In the cases of both Greece and Jugoslavia there was a monarchical government-in-exile to which the British owed a real debt of gratitude for its loyalty and gallant resistance to Nazi invasion. In each case, largely unknown to the exiled governments concerned, a powerful resistance movement was growing up under the control of Comintern agents from Moscow. These two situations were both handled between London and Cairo at a time when communications were difficult. With the benefit of hindsight any student may conclude that they were not well handled by any of the parties concerned, the military establishment, the Foreign Office or SOE. The Foreign Office had a natural tendency to want to be consulted on any British-inspired act taking place in enemy territory, but, as one Cabinet minister said to Lord Halifax, Foreign Secretary in 1940, 'You should never be consulted. You would inevitably say no to everything, because you were not meant to be a bandit' (Dalton, 1957).

I mention these problems at some length in order to demonstrate some of the difficulties SOE had to face from the beginning. There were to be many early setbacks before SOE began to function effectively.

July 1940 saw Western Europe overrun from Narvik to Hendaye by an apparently invincible military machine, poised ready for its next offensive with the three obvious options of invading Britain, the Iberian Peninsula or the Balkans. If our planners despaired, as well they might, of defending either the Iberian Peninsula or the Balkans by conventional military means and sought inspiration in organising secret armies, they at least had the advantage of knowing that both areas had historically been the scene of frequent guerrilla warfare.

But no one, apart from those few who had participated in or studied the Spanish Civil War, knew how guerrilla warfare would succeed against bomber and fighter aircraft, tanks and other armoured vehicles. There was no foreknowledge in 1940 that two major techniques would develop, supply dropping by air and pinpoint navigation by night, which would eventually make it possible to transport, support and equip small groups either for special *coups de main* or guerrilla activities on a large scale.

Equally in 1940 there was little comprehension of the time which conquered countries were going to need to react against the enemy and how long it was going to be before the Allies could help them. In 1940 SOE could see various possible tasks upon which it could concentrate its energies: it could start to think up ways of helping countries already occupied to fight back and it could help them to create links with their exiled governments in London; it could initiate individual acts of sabotage and it could help countries not yet overrun to build up secret networks and communications against the day when the Germans might appear to be no longer invincible. With this end in view one of SOE's first acts was to send its own agents into Iberia and the Balkans.

SOE staff in neutral centres interviewed potential agents or helpers, collected information, papers and currency for use in adjacent enemy countries and received, helped and forwarded SOE agents. Sometimes, as in Lisbon and Istanbul, they prepared for a possible invasion. In the months I was destined to operate in Lisbon I also spent some time helping the Polish general staff in their secret movements of military personnel through France and Spain to Lisbon and Gibraltar. Overrun by the Soviet Union and the Nazis, the Polish government and army had re-created themselves in France in the winter of 1939, only to be scattered and disrupted when France itself was overrun by the Nazis in the summer of 1940. Indomitable, they proceeded with infinite effort and endurance by land and sea to reassemble yet again in England. In 1940 therefore SOE were already co-operating with one exiled government, which was in contact with an embryo secret army in its own country, with plans for organising and equipping it.

However, at this stage SOE did not have the use of any aircraft with sufficient range to drop supplies except to western Poland. It was unfortunate that the only country with a potential secret underground movement was at the extreme range for aircraft in 1940 and that to get there involved flights both ways over the powerful defence system of Nazi Germany. SOE did, however, manage to drop three Polish agents near Bielsko during a long dark winter night in February 1941.

After this first wave of activity, however, it became clear that before practical help could be offered to conquered countries SOE had to build up a reliable and effective headquarters staff and to establish recruiting and training programmes. Specialised equipment had to be developed and produced, especially explosives, shortwave radio transmitters and signal systems. Above all, resistance organisers and radio operators had to be selected, recruited and trained, a prolonged and continuing process.

During 1941 Gubbins requested his staff officers and directors of training to prepare a programme for the future. This resulted in a startling forecast. The preparation of a detailed programme for training key agents, resistance organisers and radio operators made it clear that secret operations on a substantial scale could not be mounted until the winter of 1942–3 at the earliest. Staff members with a civilian, as opposed to military, background found it hard to accept this forecast, but it proved correct. Training was paramount for the successful planning of resistance, whether sabotage or guerrilla warfare.

SOE's first major coup was in March 1941: it was, surprisingly, an outstanding success. Codenamed Operation Rubble, it involved hi-jacking some British freighters in Gothenburg harbour in Sweden and then bringing them back through the Skagerrak and the Kattegat to the North Sea where they were able to be escorted home by the Royal Navy. These British freighters were loaded with Swedish special steels, mostly ball bearings, urgently needed for armament manufacture, but had been immobilised in a neutral port without means of getting home when the war broke out. This project was being discussed at morning meetings when I first joined SOE in December 1940, for it was SOE who infiltrated agents and crews into Sweden to take over the freighters and bring them out under the command of Sir George Binney. SOE also liaised with the Navy for them to escort the boats once they were outside neutral waters. This operation was repeated later in 1941 under code name Performance.

Operation Rubble was a wholly untypical SOE project, but it illustrated the principle that SOE's role included executing any operation which for any reason could not be openly carried out by

Army, Navy or Air Force because it violated neutrality or was an illegal or irregular action. Of course both Navy and Air Force were able to co-operate when the freighters reached the North Sea, but they could not initially enter Sweden's neutral waters. Late in 1941 SOE also helped in another para-naval operation, by seizing a 10,000-ton Italian liner from Fernando Po, an island off West Africa.

Two early SOE sabotage targets in the Balkans were the Iron Gates on the Danube, the deepest gorge in Europe, and the oilfields at Ploesti in Rumania. Much thought and planning were put into these demolition projects before the German invasion of Jugoslavia in April 1941 and the simultaneous take-over of Rumania; indeed Gubbins himself reconnoitred both sites in 1938; but no effective action proved possible because of defensive enemy measures. Even in the subsequent years of guerrilla warfare in Jugoslavia no successful action was ever taken against the Iron Gates. Ploesti continued to be a main source of oil to the Nazi–Fascist powers until 1944 when the US Air Force inflicted damage in a costly daylight bomber raid after the German air force had been practically eliminated in the Mediterranean.

The German staff intelligence service, the Abwehr, were well aware of the vulnerability and importance of these two Balkan targets. Paul Leverkuehn, a senior Abwehr officer, says that Admiral Canaris, chief of the Abwehr, had assumed that the British Secret Service would initiate sabotage acts against the production centres of oil and against its means of transportation; and that why nothing of the sort was in fact ever attempted remained a mystery (Leverkuehn 1954). One of the reasons undoubtedly was that the Abwehr alerted the Sigurantca, the Rumanian Security Service, to the need for counter-sabotage measures; and, since the Allies had succeeded in the First World War in putting the Ploesti oilfields out of action, the advice was very naturally heeded. Moreover, as Leverkuehn says, in war the perpetration of any considerable act of sabotage is among the most difficult of any of the tasks of a secret service.

Created in 1940, what had SOE accomplished by the end of 1941? It had set up recruiting and training organisations in Britain and the Middle East for the future and it had established missions and agents in all main neutral centres in Europe. Operationally it had dropped three Polish agents in western Poland, and a few agents, mostly Frenchmen, in France; it had organised blockade-running operations out of Sweden and had captured some enemy ships in West Africa; but it had not managed to demolish the Iron Gates nor to sabotage the Rumanian oilfields.

In retrospect there is no cause for surprise that results achieved in its first year by so novel an organisation were small. Time was needed to recruit and train the diverse staffs of an inter-service organisation involved in liaison with Army, Navy and Air Force, as well as civilian departments. Time was needed to design, develop and produce specialised equipment and to establish by research, aided by trial and error, the methods by which they should be used. Experience in the field, and that mostly meant in enemy-occupied territory, was vital to create confidence and aptitudes to face emergencies. Above all the first two years of SOE were years when the Allied cause was in dire straits; one year when Britain had no European ally except Greece – and the mere thought of victory was an act of faith – and one year when first the Soviet Union and then the United States were added unwillingly as co-belligerents, but were themselves struggling to muster their resources. It was not until after mid-1942, two years after the creation on paper of SOE as an organisation, that the peoples of occupied countries could expect help in establishing resistance movements, secret armies or partisan groups. And it was, with rare and courageous exceptions, only at about that period, mid-1942, that conditions began to make it possible to create clandestine organisations, with all that is implicit in that process; the selection and training of leaders, organisers and couriers, the establishment of communications, safe houses, the distribution of arms and explosives, the provision of secret finance, and above all the imposition of the security measures without which clandestinity is a short lived and suicidal affair.

2

Recruitment

Several British organisations of an essentially secret or mainly secret nature existed by 1940. There was the Secret Intelligence Service for overseas intelligence; MI5 which covered home security; MI9 which helped British escapers, evaders and prisoners of war. There was a unit specialising in radio communications (RSS) and another solely concerned with codes and ciphers (GC & CS). It was reasonably clear from the outset that SOE should not trespass on these fields. There were many cases, however, where the line of demarcation was difficult to draw; for example, an SOE agent in enemy territory might use as his escape route an underground line established by MI9 for evaders and prisoners of war or *vice versa*; or an SOE agent might bring back useful secret intelligence reports, essentially the field of SIS. Information was an inevitable and sometimes important by-product to be gained from any agents or group of resistance movements recruited or organised or supported by SOE.

With these exceptions, SOE might be involved in many forms of secret warfare, whether physical or psychological, para-military or commercial, technical or scientific. Those who worked for SOE in the field must be trained to be versatile and those who recruited, trained and organised them at home bases had to cover a wide range of possible activities. SOE could advise, equip, organise and even influence resistance movements, but it was not itself able to direct or control them; so its own ideal recruits needed to be subtle in their leadership and apt at handling resistance leaders inspired by national enthusiasms. SOE could offer to set up communication networks for underground movements, to arrange parachute drops and pick-up operations, and to select and plan acts of sabotage; it could send in officers or agents to encourage and to guide resisters; it could give moral as well as logistical support, but its agents had always to remember that the size, scope and success of its activities would be governed by the nature of the local resistance movement in any given country. SOE was a catalyst rather than an initiator and for this reason it needed recruits to direct its training centres in Britain, recruits inside foreign countries who were known leaders or potential leaders, and recruits who would act as go-betweens and agents.

To do its varied work effectively, SOE needed to run its own organisation from top to bottom and to train all its own agents so that they were capable of action, as well as survival, in enemy-occupied territories. Training schools were a major key element in SOE and were one of the most conspicuous contributions made by General Gubbins to SOE's effectiveness. It was a cardinal doctrine of SOE right from the beginning, inherited through Gubbins from MIR, that the training of resistance organisers was of the first importance and was essential if there were to be results of any military value.

It was clear that 'in the field', in enemy territory or enemy-occupied territory and, with certain obvious exceptions, in neutral countries secretly used as bases, SOE personnel would need training in security, self-defence or unarmed combat, use of hand weapons and explosives, wireless communication, codes and cyphers. In most areas parachuting would be the only form of operational transport. In mountainous areas suitable for guerrilla warfare, training in handling rifles, machine-guns, mortars and hand grenades, as well as other guerrilla activities, such as movement across country at night, should be added. In coastal or riparian areas such as Denmark, Norway, the Netherlands, France, Greece, Jugoslavia and South-East Asia, marine and para-naval experience would be essential, and a small para-naval training unit was set up on the Helford River in Cornwall. To provide for all these and other training facilities country houses and institutions would have to be requisitioned as training centres. Holding stations would also be needed because Allied personnel would have to be held in special secret hideouts before being despatched into the field, for security reasons, and these stations would preferably need to be near to the take-off airfield. In the end SOE had taken over in Britain some sixty properties in all for training centres and holding stations.

Early schools included a demolitions course at Stevenage in Hertfordshire, fieldcraft training at Loch Ailort in Argyll, black propaganda at Watford jointly with SO 1, and industrial sabotage at Huntingford. Fieldcraft, guerrilla warfare and demolitions were taught at Arisaig in Argyll; there was a special school for the Poles at

Briggens near Ware, and another for the Czechs at Chichley in Surrey. As the war progressed and SOE moved into wider fields, overseas schools were opened in Palestine, Australia, Canada, Algiers, Ceylon and India. There was even a ski school for SOE operators in 1944 near Rome.

The special training schools covered a wide range of activities. Most courses naturally included physical training to promote fitness and endurance, including running, swimming and sometimes rope-work on cliffs and crossing of rivers. There were specialist schools for all the obvious para-military subjects: training in the use of small arms; demolitions and the use of explosives including destruction of roads and bridges and the different techniques requiring cutting charges (dynamite or plastic explosive) and lifting charges such as ammonal; industrial sabotage in the selection of the vital and vulner-able parts of machinery and the best forms of attack designed to cause lasting or permanent damage in different targets such as railway engines, power stations, electric pylons or ships; movement across country by night together with personal camouflage and other systems and techniques needed for guerrilla warfare; unarmed com-bat and the various methods of silent killing.

In the field of clandestine work and underground existence, there were schools dealing with numerous less military and less physical subjects, such as security principles and precautions, concealment of papers and weapons, the picking of locks and methods of escape from prisons, and essential background on the agent's intended country, including ration cards, passes, traffic regulations and cur-fews. Last but not least (for all agents except those going into the field by sea or overland or by Lysander pick-up operation) was the parachute school, which involved learning to jump, controlling within the possible limits the direction of descent, methods of land-ing, and procedures to be followed immediately after landing.

Radio operators of course had separate technical training, both in operating and maintaining their sets, in code and cipher procedures and security checks. Candidates for operators were normally given a ground exercise, being sent to a town where they were to find themselves a lodging, set up their set and establish contact with some radio station, and finally when 'arrested' to undergo interrogation by a 'policeman' or security officer.

From the day he joined SOE in November 1940, Colin Gubbins directed and supervised the directorate of training as well as the directorate of operations. He had unique qualifications for the task. He had studied guerrilla warfare whilst at MIR; he had gained experience with the Poles in Warsaw in 1939 when he helped them to plan their underground army; he had been in Norway in 1940, and he spoke several languages including French and Russian. He was a qualified parachutist and had an excellent command of the needs of intelligence work. Gubbins recruited men and women for a highly diversified range of activities; SOE needed agents with linguistic or other qualifications for operating in specific countries, who would also have to be trained in security rules and para-military activities, probably also in parachuting. Training instructors were required in all these disciplines and qualifications, and not only specialist instructors but supporting staffs for the administration and security of the training establishments. SOE also had to find supply staff, including high-powered scientific and technical experts for inventing and designing new or improved explosives, weapons and radio equipment, and commercial and administrative officers for organising manufacture and delivery. Last but not least, directors and staff were needed who would be responsible for policies, administration, finance, security liaison and intelligence, air and sea operations, supply and procurement, and training.

One of the most arduous administrative jobs was the handling of recruitment, pay, promotions, welfare and manpower planning. The process of recruitment was delicate and exacting; security demanded that neither the name or even the existence of SOE, nor the nature of the work be disclosed to the candidate until he had been both accepted as suitable and cleared for security.

SOE operated under the cover title of Inter Service Research Bureau with offices at 64 Baker Street, London; it also had token cover offices with the three service ministries of which the most used was the War Office with the cover title of MO 1 (SP). All that could be disclosed to the candidate was the cover title ISRB, that it was engaged in research and other activities of common interest to the three armed services, but its exact nature could not be disclosed unless and until the candidate was accepted and sworn in. Though invited by one of my pre-war law partners to come to London from an artillery unit to which I was attached pending a course at the Staff College, Camberley, I was so unenlightened by my official interviewer that I only decided to accept an invitation to the unknown by reason of an accident. I stayed that night in London with a friend working in the War Office, and also in his house was another guest, General Beaumont-Nesbitt, who had been director of Military Intelligence, and of course knew about ISRB. Conscientiously he declined to disclose to me the nature of its activities, but he was prepared to go so far as to say that for a wartime soldier it should be more interesting than a conventional military career.

SOE recruited from both sexes and from civilian and military sources. The part played by women proved to be greater than anyone could have foretold. Not only was there the obvious need for secretaries and cypherenes both in London and also in major units and missions abroad, but women with language qualifications had remarkable records of achievement in the field of certain occupied countries, especially in France. Much has been written, rightly, on the heroic exploits of the many women agents who performed operational roles; many were captured, tortured and executed, or spent their last days in the appalling conditions of concentration camps, especially Dachau, Ravensbruck and Torgau. The roles which they played in the resistance movements of which they became a part were vital to success. Among many outstanding figures a few deserve special mention, having achieved lasting fame: Countess Krystyna Skarbek, (alias Christine Granville) who during 1940 organised escape lines from Poland through the Balkans to the Middle East, and in 1944 in the south of France browbeat and bribed the local Gestapo into releasing the famous captured British organiser, Francis Cammaerts; Noor Inayat Khan (Madeleine), a radio operator executed in Dachau concentration camp, and Diana Rowden (Paulette), executed in Natzweiller concentration camp.

A vivid picture is given by Professor G. H. N. Seton-Watson, a Balkan expert, who worked in Rumania in 1940, Jugoslavia in 1941, Cairo and Istanbul from 1942 to 1944 and who was one of the leading figures in SOE Cairo in spite of his youth.

'SOE was an upstart organisation, inevitably viewed with suspicion and jealousy by all existing departments . . . The first recruits in 1939 and 1940 were a mixture of widely different types from different places, bankers and business men, mining engineers and journalists from the Balkans . . . These were later joined by volunteers from the armed forces, some impelled by special knowledge of and special concern for Greece and Jugoslavia. Nearly all the earlier recruits lacked the habit of subordination to a regular hierarchy; were disciplined by no mandarin ethos; and were impatient or even contemptuous of the bureaucratic conventions of the diplomatic service and its auxiliaries. To the diplomats they often appeared brash, ignorant of things which diplomats were trained to regard as important and at times a positive menace. Often neither side made much effort to understand the other' (Auty and Clogg, 1975).

Surprising people found themselves involved in underground warfare and chosen as agents, because a foolproof cover was essential if a man was to justify his presence. SOE's representative in Tangier early in 1941 was a genuine expert dealer in green tea, a commodity frantically sought after by the Moslem inhabitants of Algeria and Morocco because of the British blockade to which French territories became subject after the Franco-German armistice of June 1940. A Danish dentist in Copenhagen was also a key agent. He played a leading role in the resistance movement with a clientele who could be genuine dental patients or undetected saboteurs. Obviously the best cover was the genuine kind with a real background of practical knowledge. The green tea dealer would not have lasted a week or even a day if he had no more background than a few lectures in Baker Street; and an unqualified dentist would have been unmasked at the first application of the drill.

Those men and women who went into the field in enemy-occupied territory and those resisters who received them and worked with them, whether in clandestinity or in open guerrilla warfare, faced dangers, hardships and torture. Their casualties were heavy. Others have written of their endurance and heroism. Their chances of survival and success depended above all on three factors: first, the fortunes of war, such as how and when their country was liberated – contrast for example the histories of Belgium and Poland; secondly, their own skills and endurance and survival capacity; thirdly, the ability of those backing them up at headquarters in terms of foresight, planning and the interpretation to those in high command or in government of what resistance movements could and could not do. For instance, they could harass regular army forces in rough and mountainous terrain but could not resist heavily armed regulars by holding prepared positions; they could attack and run away but not try to hold.

Resisters in the field came from all classes and occupations in their own country. Peasants and aristocrats, civil servants and priests, businessmen and merchants, lawyers and bankers, engineers and teachers; and last but not least from the armed services. In Poland the Peasants' Freedom Organisation provided most of the reception committees for air-supply sorties from England and most of the internal communications for the Home Army. In France Jean Moulin, ex-Prefect and first head of the Gaullist National Resistance Council, managed a picture gallery as cover for his activities. Others found bookshops a cover for meetings and the distribution of propaganda. In Thailand the head of the resistance movement was the Head of State and one of his right-hand men was Chief of Police.

SOE also recruited, in several countries, a great many packers who made up the containers and parcels which were dropped to partisans to provide them with equipment. The main supplies were carefully packed in long cylindrical steel containers so that they could be parachuted in. Unbreakables such as boots, clothing and certain rations were often dropped 'free' in packages without parachutes, but main supplies such as rifles, sten guns, light machine-guns, ammunition, hand grenades, explosives and detonators, radio sets and medical supplies had to be extremely carefully handled. Many containers were made up into standard packs which contained rifles, sten guns and ammunition, but others had to be made up specially to meet specific demands from the field. Gold sovereigns were small but most important as a source of funds to resistance movements in the cities or guerrillas in the hills. It has been estimated that between 1942 and 1945 40,000 tons of material was parachuted into Europe alone (ERM, 1960).

At its peak SOE probably employed on its own payroll, in terms of British manpower, over 7,500 people in the United Kingdom, 4,000 in the Mediterranean and 1,300 in South-East Asia, a total of nearly 13,000 (ERM, 1960). These figures do not include packers and other labourers of local nationalities. In comparison with the figure of 1,300 British personnel for South-East Asia, the total ration strength of SOE's Force 136 was over 6,000 (Sweet-Escott, 1965). The total figure of 13,000 does not of course start to include those who worked in their own countries within the various resistance movements, many of whom SOE had recruited through their own agents.

3

An Amateur Learns his Job

All but a handful of SOE personnel started as amateurs with everything to learn. Some were trained for work in the field at successive courses in the special training schools. Later they had to learn in enemy-occupied territory how to survive in underground warfare. Others worked at headquarters in England or elsewhere; they learned their roles and procedures from colleagues more experienced or by the process of trial and error; when possible they went on courses, but for staff officers vacancies were few. A third category, of whom I was one, were sent abroad to neutral countries, or Allied bases, with little preparation and briefing depending on the urgency of the mission. The process of learning to be a secret agent in the field, or a staff officer or head of a secret mission in a neutral or Allied country, is infinitely varied depending on circumstances. There are, however, certain features common to all. First, there is the need for calm, caution and common sense. Second, there are the operational elements of all clandestine activities: the choice and use of cover; the use of cut-outs; communications, security and speed; and a cell structure to limit the damage done by enemy penetration or arrest of any member of a group.

In my first SOE assignment I had one variety of experience in Lisbon from January 1941 to June 1942. I had no previous knowledge of secret activities, but had the advantage of legal training and practice, which at least develops discretion, analytical thinking and care in the use of words. I had three weeks in Baker Street in December 1940 absorbing the objectives of SOE and meeting principal colleagues. I studied the chances of the Iberian Peninsula being invaded by the Germans, and read all available material on Portugal and on SOE's plans for activity in Western Europe and West Africa. I paid one visit to a training school, where in three hours I was exposed to some of the latest techniques in demolitions and small arms. I was told that I must ensure sound liaison between the embryo

SOE team in Lisbon and the well-established SIS teams. In the event of a German invasion of Portugal (then considered probable in April 1941) and the overwhelming of the government and armed forces, I was to be prepared to demolish the oil installations in the Tagus estuary as Target No. 1 and any other major targets to be agreed. It was recognised that time was desperately short. I was also directed to keep in close contact with SOE Gibraltar, especially on the subject of North Africa and German invasion prospects. I was also to render all help possible to other SOE European country sections in view of the sudden importance of Lisbon as an international centre.

I had no role in Spain, where the British Ambassador, Sir Samuel Hoare, was opposed to any secret activity which might provoke Franco to join the Axis, although Hoare himself had had secret intelligence experience in Russia in the First World War and was not opposed to secret activities of which he knew and approved. I was, however, to maintain close contact with the Naval Attaché in Madrid, Captain Alan Hillgarth, who on behalf of the Ambassador supervised secret activities in Spain. During 1941 he was reinforced by two young SOE officers who handled the movement of SOE personnel going into or coming out of France and Gibraltar through Spain.

I had visited SIS in London for interviews with the chief and his deputy. Not surprisingly they urged me to keep in close touch with their top man in Lisbon, who knew the country and had long experience in clandestine activities; and to do nothing and recruit nobody without consulting him. This advice would obviously have given him an effective veto on any SOE activity. I replied cautiously that having as yet no experience in this field, I should be most grateful for competent advice. Within a month of my arrival in Lisbon I had occasion to remember their words of wisdom. In London both the chief of the secret service and the director of military intelligence at the War Office asked me – with remarkable courtesy to a junior officer but of course to test my reaction – what I would do about the Iberian Peninsula if I were in Hitler's shoes. I said that first one must consider the Battle of the Atlantic; the Luftwaffe had, since the fall of France, based their long-range Focke-Wulf Condor bombers at Mérignac near Bordeaux, from which they could cover as far as the Azores; and it would be a tremendous advantage if they had bases seven hundred miles further south in Portugal. The second consideration would be the neutralisation of

Gibraltar and the closing of the Mediterranean, a colossal gain to the Axis; but the decision must depend on Franco's willingness to grant free transit through Spain.

Neither of them, and therefore nobody in London, knew that Hitler, after his meeting with Franco at Hendaye on 23 October 1940 several weeks earlier, in a fury about Franco's numerous conditions, had decided to turn his back on Spain and Portugal and postpone Operation Felix for the invasion of Portugal and the capture of Gibraltar. London apparently had no knowledge of that fateful decision until much later. On 16 December 1940 Churchill himself still believed that a German invasion of Spain was more likely than an invasion of the Balkans (Hinsley, 1979, p. 257). However, when Hitler invaded Jugoslavia and Greece in April 1941, it looked less likely to happen and it soon became still clearer from Ultra and other sources that his real objective was the Soviet Union. We now know that, while keeping his other options open mainly for the sake of cover, Hitler decided on 11 December 1940 again to postpone Felix, which he only cancelled later and that he decided on 18 December 1940 to invade Russia, as appears from his directive No. 21 of that date (Lewin, 1978, p. 103). According to R. V. Jones (Jones, 1978, p. 205), the Joint Intelligence Committee appeared only to have come to the conclusion that Hitler would attack the Soviet Union on 12 June 1941, although the Bletchley code-breakers and Churchill had both reached that conclusion earlier.

My cover had been arranged as Assistant Military Attaché to the Lisbon Embassy. This had been agreed by the Ambassador, Sir Ronald Campbell, when one of my colleagues had been visiting the Peninsula in November, and had later been officially approved by the War Office. The cover was admirable because in the normal course of my duties I was destined to interview scores of men and women of every nationality, who called on the Military Attaché on leaving Europe or North Africa on their way to Britain or America. Much of their information was of value to SOE and they sometimes also volunteered their personal services. Having no previous knowledge of Portugal, I was able to explain to Embassy colleagues, naturally curious, that my main job was to relieve the Military Attaché, himself a fluent Portuguese speaker and fully occupied with Anglo-Portuguese affairs, of some of the burden of military intelligence about other countries, especially France, Belgium, the Netherlands, Poland and North Africa.

My briefing in Baker Street had included being told about the early stages of an incident which had happened to a former Spanish agent of the British. This man, whom I will call L. M., was a member of a left-wing organisation, with whom all contact had been dropped in 1940 as a result of the Hoare policy of keeping Franco neutral at all costs. In about September 1940 L. M., on his own initiative, assisted two important persons, one French and one British, to cross Spain and escape into Portugal by its northern frontier. When crossing the River Minho at night they were caught by the Portuguese police and imprisoned in Oporto. Then after a decent interval the Briton and the Frenchman were released unobtrusively to their respective consuls and went their way, leaving L. M. alone in the Oporto gaol. It was recognised in London as a serious danger that, if the Portuguese secret police handed him, a Spanish citizen, back to the Spanish Seguridad, he could be publicly exhibited as evidence that, in spite of Hoare's assurance to Franco, the British had maintained their sinister contacts with the Spanish Republican underground. London had decided that any action required to prevent him being handed back to Spain would be the responsibility of SOE. Obviously any such action could involve violence or other irregularities in a friendly neutral country and should be avoided if possible. Obviously, also, if SOE acted and failed, it could create a public scandal, which hostile critics of SOE and Britain could exploit.

A week after my arrival in Lisbon I had an urgent cable from Baker Street saying that the Portuguese police were proposing to hand L. M. over to the Seguridad and that I should spare no cost and use all means to prevent this. As a new arrival I had no funds, no equipment and no organisation. All I could do was study the situation, think and reflect. I came to a surprising conclusion. Both the Foreign Office and SOE had led me to believe that the Prime Minister of Portugal, Dr Salazar, though running a dictatorial regime, was in his heart loyal to the ancient Anglo-Portuguese alliance and was anti-Nazi. It was well known that his considerable influence on General Franco was always in favour of keeping Spain out of the war. I concluded that the L. M. affair, with the risk of a Nazi-inspired anti-British political trial in Madrid, was important enough for the Ambassador to take up with Salazar, and that the prospects of Salazar seeing the point were good.

Fortunately, an old friend, David Eccles from the Madrid Embassy, was in Lisbon. I told him confidentially about the problem, and he agreed to join with me in persuading Campbell, the British Ambassador, to take on an assignment which was obviously distasteful. I gave Campbell the background story. Eccles, who ranked as Counsellor both in Madrid and Lisbon, confirmed that the Madrid Embassy were expecting just such a political trial to be concocted under Nazi pressure to discredit the British in Franco's eyes. With great reluctance the British Ambassador agreed to tackle Salazar. When he did so, the result was remarkable. To his great relief Salazar was most grateful for the information; he knew about the man in question but had no idea that his police were proposing to hand him over to Spain; he would put a stop to it at once, and the man would stay in a Portuguese gaol for a long time to come. I cabled London that the problem was solved and reported by diplomatic bag the surprising method I had used. I thus had the good luck at the outset to acquire credit both with SOE London and with my Ambassador. My own contribution had been to analyse the situation correctly and then to persuade Campbell, with help from David Eccles, to do what was needed. It was a solution uncharacteristic of SOE in its early days.

My first step on arrival in Lisbon was obviously to get to know my nominal boss, the Military Attaché, and establish an understanding about work responsibilities. He was a highly sensible and broad-minded man who recognised that I was only nominally on his staff and was essentially responsible to a secret organisation, not to the War Office. We agreed that I must carry out certain formalities, such as calling on the Portuguese Major-General do Exercito and the Secretary to the General Staff, and also that in the Embassy I should interview as many as possible of the refugees and visitors from other countries not concerned with Portugal. French citizens wishing to go to Britain or America naturally avoided their own Vichy Embassy and added to the volume seeking help at the British Embassy, where, incidentally we had a Free French attaché working in our office. Shortly afterwards the Military Attaché recruited as his assistant a British resident in Portugal to help him on his Portuguese work, which in view of requests for arms and secret staff talks was considerable.

Only three people in the Embassy had been informed of my real SOE function; the Ambassador, the head of Chancery and the Military Attaché. I soon sensed that the Air and Naval Attachés were also in the know, but I took, rightly, all evasive action possible to prevent the list being enlarged. Embassy staffs are inevitably inquisitive and every serious and ambitious diplomat believes that he (or she) is so discreet and security-minded that he is entitled to know everything. My main difficulty came when I recruited a small staff of two because they were given cover under the guise of Ministry of Economic Warfare officials. It took some devising to explain this incongruity. I dropped hints that one of my special functions was to liaise with the Ministry of Economic Warfare over the purchase of wolfram, Portugal's most important strategic mineral, heavily competed for by the belligerents. Another quasi-cover which I used to disarm inquisitive colleagues was interest in prisoners of war, escapees and evaders. Of course, in reality that was the function of another secret organisation, MI9, whose representative in Lisbon was Donald Darling, but it was so new that probably nobody except the SIS and service representatives knew about it.

I also had a windfall because of the Ambassador's mistaken idea of the range of my SOE duties; he said to me in my first week, 'We need a Security Officer in this Embassy, and, as I gather you will have nothing to do unless and until the Germans cross the Pyrenees, I want you to take this in hand.' He wanted my duties to include prevention of the abuse of diplomatic bag facilities, especially transmission of currencies. I naturally refrained from confessing that I had no training in that kind of formal security duty. After all, I had had eighteen months in the army and some recent briefing on certain security matters, and anyway a lawyer is supposed to be able to turn his hand to most things. Nor could I then foresee how much I should have to use bag facilities for purposes which, though certainly official, such as sending currencies for meeting the operating expenses of Allied representatives in Madrid, Gibraltar and elsewhere, including the cost of transporting personnel, whether escapers or agents, might not have been approved by the Ambassador had he known. So I initiated in January 1941 a regular night-patrol, visiting all offices to ensure that filing cabinets were locked and no important papers were left lying around. On the first night I had the satisfaction of impounding the Ambassador's credentials to the Portuguese Government.

When I was told in London that I was to ensure close liaison between the embryo SOE organisation in Lisbon and the SIS, I asked what the SOE group comprised. I found that it consisted of two well-known journalists and one financial expert. The two journalists were experienced and engaging characters. One was a veteran Catholic with valuable sources of information from the Cardinal Patriarch downwards. The other mainly engaged in black propaganda, for which at that time, before the formation of a political warfare executive, SOE had certain responsibilities. Both were useful sources of local information but no more. The financial expert was Michael Terestchenko, who under Kerensky had been the last Finance Minister of Tsarist Russia before the Bolshevik revolution, fluent in eight languages, known in financial circles in every country in Europe and a man of great wisdom. There was, of course, a security problem in meeting such collaborators regularly, without some watchful eye drawing conclusions and passing them either to the Secret Police or to Von Karsthoff, the Abwehr chief at the German Embassy. I never saw the journalists at our Chancery (where the head porter was, as always, inevitably a source of information to the local police) but at the British Club; not in the dining-room or the bar, where sooner or later the frequency of contact would have been noticed, but usually in the billiard room.

Terestchenko, however, always came to see me at the Chancery. After his first visit I decided, in order to avoid comment on our frequent meetings, to introduce him as an unrivalled international expert to a lady who was wrestling in the Chancery with problems of forwarding Red Cross parcels to prisoners of war. Needless to say, she found him invaluable. After his brief meetings with her he then came along to my room without having to inform the hall porter. He was often helpful to me on financial matters; but once, to my surprise, he gave me information about a newly erected transmitter in a German-owned house close to his own at Estoril. I passed this news on to a close friend who headed Section V, the Counter Intelligence Section working for MI5 and SIS. Months later my friend told me that it had completed a link in the invisible chain with which Section V were surrounding 'Eins Marine', Department No. One of the Abwehr, the German naval intelligence section in Lisbon engaged in tracking the routes of British convoys. When I left Lisbon in June 1942, I heard that Kuno Weltzien, the Lisbon head of Eins Marine, had no longer any agent who was not under the control of the British Section V, who then fed him such information as they thought suitable. This was a triumph in miniature on the same lines as the XX Committee in London, which from 1941 to 1945 had effective control of all German agents in Britain.

British seamen coming ashore in Lisbon were one of the Abwehr's best sources of information in the U-boat war. The Abwehr financed or controlled a few brothels, where the girls were briefed on extracting and memorising the details of routes and dates of convoys and so forth. The British Shipping Office, part of the Consulate, was not idle and had good relations with certain other houses, which somehow were specially cleared for security. One day one of my colleagues in the Embassy presented me with a specimen invitation card in perfect English: 'Madame A cordially invites you to her home on ... at ... pm to have a jolly good time and dancing too.'

SOE's first directive to me had been to be ready to demolish the numerous Tagus estuary oil installations in the event of the Portuguese Government being overwhelmed by a German invasion. By April, when the time factor ceased to be important as Hitler had moved south-east into Jugoslavia and Greece, certain plans were ready, though some others had to be left till the USA became a belligerent. The main security problem, however, of planning any post-occupational organisation or any local demolition teams was the excessive enthusiasm of the Portuguese. The 700-year-old alliance and Peninsular War memories of Talavera and Torres Vedras meant that those Portuguese who were pro-British, and the large majority were, were so thrilled and elated if asked to do something active that few were able to keep the secret to themselves. I soon decided that I would never personally have any talks with potential Portuguese organisers of demolitions or guerrilla warfare, but on security grounds would always work through a cut-out. Moreover, my ignorance of the country made it essential to operate through British residents fluent in the language, preferably bi-lingual and in full sympathy with the best of that most delightful people.

Soon I had three regional organisers; two of them employees of large British companies in the north and south, and one a foreigner long resident in Lisbon. I paid one visit to Oporto to meet and brief the northern organiser, and I stayed with some old friends, whose family had been rooted in Oporto for over a century. I was met at Oporto railway station early one morning by my hostess, who said quite seriously that her husband had had a great shock and I must treat him with care. Asked how so, she said he had just heard that he had been downgraded from No. 1 to No. 3 in the Nazi black list of the British residents of Oporto. My three organisers all had merits, but they were all, as this story demonstrated, too well known for their pro-Allied activities. As a result of a police drive, mainly against distributors of British propaganda, they were all forced to leave the country by the end of 1942. But by then the North African landings had proved a turning point of the war, and there was no longer any serious risk of a Nazi invasion, whatever doubts the Foreign Office or the chiefs of intelligence might harbour.

Unexpectedly, I was able in about August 1941 to include in our demolition plans the installations of the government oil refinery SACOR in the Tagus estuary. A senior Portuguese military captain told one of my colleagues, Commander Glen, that in case of a sudden invasion certain high officials felt they ought to have a contingency plan to deny the oil to an invader, but they needed technical help and advice. This we were able to provide, but I was careful to keep in the background, in case this was an attempt to penetrate the British services and find out who in the Embassy was in charge of such matters. Unfortunately Glen, who was a member of SOE then, although he often claimed to be straight Navy, and who had joined me in Lisbon after service in Jugoslavia up to April 1941, was ordered back to London that July for other duties. I then had to expose myself, explaining to the Portuguese captain that this was a special matter which I was taking over as a favour to Glen. I later succeeded in providing the captain and his radio service with a radio set and operating instructions for communication to Gibraltar in case of need. The radio link was tested at regular intervals.

I went three times to Gibraltar in February, April and July 1941 for liaison purposes, to talk with a senior SOE colleague, the Governor, the Defence Security Officer, Colonel Medlam, and two or three other staff officers, a natural proceeding for an Assistant Military Attaché. In April, going by sea, I was asked to take charge of Brigadier-General Roy S. Geiger, an American who was to be the first US military observer to the Eighth Army in the Western Desert. At that time, before America or the Soviet Union were involved in the war, there was a tendency in British circles to wishful thinking, to imagine that the RAF could win the war by bombing or that political warfare experts would devise some miraculous propaganda which would cause the Nazi regime to collapse. 'No,' said Geiger, 'you've got to chase them back to Berlin with bayonets.' How right he was! As we approached Gibraltar and the Rock loomed up on our port bow, he asked wistfully if I thought it would be in order for him to put on his army uniform – we were, of course, both travelling in civilian clothes. As I had the good fortune to know both the Governor, General Sir Clive Liddell, and the Defence Security Officer, Colonel Medlam, from my February visit, I warmly encouraged this technical breach of neutrality. The Security Service, who at that date had probably never seen a US army uniform, welcomed him; and in no time he was having lunch at Government House. British morale was greatly lifted and as April 1941 coincided with the Nazi invasion of the Balkans, it was an uplift much needed.

The Nazi invasion of Russia in June 1941 seemed to me in Lisbon a sure sign that an invasion of the Iberian Peninsula was out of the question for at least a year if not for ever. I wrote to London in July that my directives of December 1940 about preparatory action in Portugal were out of date and, as the most important work of the Lisbon mission now clearly related to other countries, especially Belgium, France and North Africa, I would like to return for consultation. In September 1941 I spent a few days in London and in addition to colleagues in Baker Street I had talks with senior members of the Foreign Office and the Joint Planning Staff. I stressed the delicate nature of organising demolitions and the nucleus of à resistance movement in a neutral country, which not only had a formal and ancient alliance but was also engaged in secret staff talks with our War Office. The answer was, as I feared, indecisive and for me wholly unsatisfactory. 'Hitler might be in Moscow by the end of 1941 and if so he might switch forces back to Iberia in 1942. So continue as before but with the utmost discretion.' I said of course I was already using the utmost discretion of which I was capable; but this was a dangerous game, where something might go wrong for reasons beyond my control, and the result could be awkward.

So I returned to Lisbon and told our three regional organisers to go slowly and even more carefully. I never provided them with any arms or equipment, though of course they needed funds to build the framework of a regional organisation which was to stand ready for further action should circumstances require it. Early 1942 saw a Portuguese police drive to suppress pro-Allied propaganda, which after the USA came into the war in December 1941 was having an inflammatory effect on the Portuguese. One or two of those arrested, when asked what contact they had with any British, mentioned the names of two of our regional organisers, and the police no doubt reported to Salazar that there were signs of an underground British organisation engaged in something more serious than open propaganda.

Around February 1942 I was asked by a highly respected British resident working for SIS, well known to me and often in the Embassy, if I could do him a favour. He needed an apartment or room somewhere to interview a man, whom he did not want to see in the Embassy. I had a short-term lease of an apartment for exactly the same purpose for the use of SOE staff, though I had never used it myself. In the interest of good relations I agreed to his seemingly harmless request. Weeks later the man interviewed, whoever he was, was arrested and when asked if he had any contact with the British said he had once met my friend (whose name he did not know) at this address. The police soon found that there was a lease in my name and naturally drew a wholly erroneous conclusion. On 4 March Salazar raised with the Ambassador in veiled terms the question whether, while the secret staff talks were proceeding, there was another British organisation and a member of the Embassy making unilateral preparations to resist a possible German invasion.

The Ambassador returned, highly embarrassed, and told me that, as his relations with Salazar depended on total mutual candour, he did not see how he could avoid disclosing my name; but he would reflect on it. Two or three days later he told me he had concluded that he must disclose my name as responsible for these activities. I urged that such an admission about a member of his Embassy staff with diplomatic status would aggravate the situation rather than improve it. I said that, if he did nevertheless take an action which led to my withdrawal, I was responsible for many people in occupied countries and must have good time to arrange a hand-over to a successor. I cabled London urgently to secure Foreign Office support to prevent such an ill-conceived disclosure. Unfortunately the Foreign Office telegram advising against it arrived just after Campbell had left the Embassy to see Salazar. As might have been expected, Salazar was furious and asked for my immediate withdrawal. Campbell gave some assurance but insisted that there should be a decent interval so as to prevent undue publicity.

I had already decided that, if my withdrawal were requested, there were two actions I ought to take. First, I had to prepare my own report to the Ambassador on my directives and activities which were essentially in the interests of Portugal, if an invasion occurred, and this report must be in a form which he could show to Salazar.

Second, I must prepare with help from SIS, if I could persuade them to co-operate, a report on illegal German activities in Portugal, which were by now far more illegal and extensive than anything I had done or contemplated. The Germans had infiltrated and penetrated government departments, they had bugged the Ministry of Foreign Affairs and possibly the Prime Minister's own office; they had also bribed officials on a considerable scale. Fortunately, thanks to good relations with the SIS heads of intelligence and counter intelligence in Lisbon (the latter an old friend of over twenty years' standing), it was found possible to prepare such a report, after clearance with London. It was finally edited by the head of Chancery, an extremely able diplomat, and, together with my personal report, it was accepted by the British Ambassador who, at the next opportunity, delivered the two documents to Salazar. Some three weeks passed before Salazar told Campbell that he was impressed by my report as *'sincero e leal'*, he was grateful for the report on German activities, some of which were obviously a shock to him, especially the penetration of certain government departments, and that he had seriously considered whether to cancel his request for my withdrawal. On the whole, however, he thought it best that I should leave Lisbon but he left it to the Ambassador to decide at his discretion on the date.

This solution was good news. Plans for my successor were already well advanced in London, and the staff of our mission would at least have a leader, which was essential. The man in question was already familiar with Iberia and North Africa. Personally I wanted to get back to London for some new assignment as soon as possible, so I was delighted when, in the second week of June, I was allowed to return.

I was pleasantly surprised to find in London that there was no evidence that any of the enemy services, German, Italian or Japanese, had any knowledge of my activities or of the existence of SOE. Two months after my return, when I started work as assistant to Charles Hambro, now chief of SOE, I had the experience of reading a decrypt of a signal from the Japanese Military Attaché, Lisbon, to his War Office in Tokyo. He reported that the recent rumours of diplomatic troubles between Portugal and Britain were now explained and that an assistant military attaché, a certain Major Beevor, had left the country.

Thus ended my apprenticeship in clandestine activities. I had learnt a number of useful lessons. One of them was never to do an unnecessary favour to a member of another organisation, such as lending an apartment for an interview, which might have any possible risk. A high degree of self-regarding interest is a condition of survival. I should, of course, never have taken the lease in my own name; if I had been more security-minded and more unscrupulous, I should have used either a false name or even the name of a member of another embassy. But I had also learned another lesson about relations with other secret organisations, or rather I had been confirmed in an instinctive feeling which I had had before arriving in Lisbon. In a moment of crisis another secret organisation can be of great value if your previous contacts have been serious and constructive.

A subject requiring study by any secret agent, whether as operator or supervisor or in the more defensive role of security officer, is bribery. The word has, of course, unpleasant connotations in normal private or public life, implying corruption and criminal liability. But in secret work in wartime it may include the giving of a secret and well-deserved reward for important services, which may be praiseworthy or patriotic but would have fatal consequences if disclosed in the wrong quarter. It is essential in this field, as in other forms of secret activity, to consider closely and to analyse with care the nature of the proposed operation, whether illegal or improper or merely risky. Above all one must use whatever discretion or powers of imagination one may possess in order to introduce modifications or changes, which may remove any criminal aspect or at least put the transaction into a different form, and so reduce the risk of exposure and punishment.

One classic example was carried out in Portugal with apparently complete success. A certain important official, whom I will call 'the Captain', was reputed to be pro-British and the Germans decided that he must be at least temporarily converted. So one day Herr A, a local German resident, came into the Captain's office and said that he had been recalled at short notice to Germany, that he happened to own a large car in good condition with four new tyres – an important asset in wartime – and that he had got to find a buyer urgently in the next two or three days; he was willing to accept a very modest price, which he mentioned, by instalments over a period; he wondered if the Captain could possibly think of a potential buyer. The Captain, after a decent period of reflection, thought he could and the deal was soon clinched.

Three days later a wholly different German, Herr B, came to the Captain's office, introduced himself as having just arrived from Germany and in need of a large car in good condition, with four new tyres; he needed it urgently and was prepared to pay a substantial price, which he mentioned, cash down. He wondered if the Captain possibly knew anybody who might have such a car and be willing to sell. The Captain after a decent period of reflection thought he could and the deal was soon clinched.

Nobody had paid a bribe and the Captain had not received a bribe. His *amour propre* was not at stake and he could not be punished or even criticised by his superiors. Breaking down what was in substance one transaction into two wholly separate transactions made all the difference.

In another case I was able to help a British colleague, who was under pressure to provide some financial help in a harmless form to a senior Portuguese officer. The Major, as I will call him, was in a position where he had access to a good range of military intelligence in Spain and Portugal, and he used to pass some selected items on to a representative of one of the British services, probably with the full approval of his superior officer, though off the record. None of the material I saw seemed to me of great interest, but obviously the Major was a source worth preserving. He often complained with growing gloom of his low income and the high cost of living but he made it clear that as a matter of honour he could never accept any payment for the intelligence which he was providing solely because of the ancient Anglo-Portuguese Alliance of 1374. But the lamentations increased and clearly another form of payment had to be devised. We discovered from conversation with the Major that he had an interest in the income of a small trust fund in England. I advised my British friend that I could arrange for a payment to be sent from London to the Major, ostensibly a bonus payable on the fund. In due course the Major was pleasantly surprised to receive through the mail a printed letter with an official cheque. He told my friend of this happy event next time they met and proceeded with the usual task of handing him some more items of information. As my friend left and went down the stairs the Major called out a cordial farewell with a broad wink. He appreciated the way it had been done and the flow of intelligence continued.

4

Evolution

Up to now I have sketched in the beginnings of SOE and one or two aspects of its early activities. I should like now to outline how SOE, as I saw it, evolved and grew after 1941. Then I propose to discuss in Chapter Five its relationships with other British governmental departments, including the Foreign Office and the armed services, and in Chapter Six to describe relations with the United States of America, their Office of Strategic Services and their achievements in the support of resistance. After that I shall summarise SOE's activities in each country in turn.

In April 1941 the Balkans were overrun by Hitler's armed forces and SOE Cairo was reorganised into two main divisions, Balkans and Middle East. In June the Nazi invasion of the Soviet Union resulted in left-wing elements in occupied territories in Europe becoming for the first time more positively pro-Ally.

It will be remembered that before August 1939 the Soviet Union and its Communist Party had been engaged on an active programme of subversion and sabotage throughout the capitalist countries of Europe and North America; that they had been active in the Spanish Civil War and had been bitterly opposed to Nazism and Fascism both in Germany and in Italy. When in August 1939 Molotov and Ribbentrop had signed a non-aggression pact and created a Soviet-German relationship which was little short of an alliance it completely and utterly reversed everything that had gone before. Communists in all countries were dumbfounded, both parties and individuals, to find themselves on the same side as the Nazis. Many felt constrained to avoid anti-Nazi activities even if they were unable to give positive open support to their former bitterest enemies. Many continued to denounce capitalism, disrupted the Allied war effort, hampered the work of munitions factories and even exercised subversive influence over the armies in imperialist or capitalist countries, such as France. Only when the Nazis invaded Russia did the obedient Communist organisations begin to join in the work of resistance. The countries where this change-about was most noticeable were Jugoslavia, Greece and Albania.

From the second half of 1941 onwards, therefore, conditions became much more propitious to infiltrate occupied territories in Europe and to restore old contacts. In September 1941, for instance, two royal Jugoslav officers and an SOE officer, Captain D. T. Hudson, were landed by submarine in the Gulf of Kotor off Montenegro to make contact with General Mihailović in Serbia.

In December, the Japanese attack on Pearl Harbor brought the Americans into the war. This event stirred the hearts and hopes of the prostrate peoples of occupied Europe; it was much needed, for 1942 began harshly. The Wehrmacht, having survived with great endurance their first Russian winter, drove on to Stalingrad and the Caucasus, while in North Africa the Afrika Korps under Rommel thrust as far as El Alamein in Egypt and threatened the whole Middle East with a giant pincer movement. In 1942 American and British naval and military disasters at the hands of the Japanese in the Far East opened up new theatres of operations for resistance movements and *coups-de-main* operations in South-East Asia.

In Western Europe in 1942 the preparatory work of infiltration and establishment of underground lines was beginning to produce networks; at the same time progress was being made with the new techniques of dropping men and supplies to a pinpoint by night and the development of reception committees. New secret weapons, the concealed uses of plastic explosives, new secret radio transmitters and improved security methods began to make it possible for secret agents to survive and to operate in occupied countries in Western Europe. Various sorties were made across the English Channel at this time, to land and take off agents. SOE managed one of its best coups late in 1942 when it destroyed a special German-designed infra-red station set up in Tangier to guide U-boats through the Straits of Gibraltar. But as yet the concept of 'resistance movements' on any scale was uncertain and the phrase was not yet in general use.

In 1942, when I became assistant to the second chief of SOE, Sir Charles Hambro, I found that an odd event had occurred in Stockholm. An SOE officer working in the British Embassy had been blown and discredited by the thoughtless action of a colleague. This colleague had told a visitor that he himself as an attaché could not discuss a proposal for sabotaging ships in Swedish waters but that

Mr T (the SOE officer) was responsible for any enquiries involving sabotage. Mr T was of course compromised and had to be withdrawn from Sweden. I found it odd that SOE was adopting an apologetic attitude to the Foreign Office when it should have been aggressive and criticising the thoughtless action of the attaché concerned. This episode, reminiscent of episodes of which I had had personal experience in the Lisbon Embassy, led me to conclude that there was a pressing need for a confidential briefing of senior diplomats and service personnel on the functions of SOE and the part it was intended to play in the war effort. Previously its existence was so secret that anybody could be excused for ignorance of its functions. Moreover, some senior people in official positions, especially in British embassies in neutral countries, badly needed lessons in elementary security when approached by individuals wanting to talk about secret intelligence or secret operations such as sabotage.

Most of the senior men concerned in embassies and consulates, counsellors, first secretaries and service attachés, were – as would be expected – reliable, mature and security-minded when dealing with secret and highly sensitive matters. There were occasional exceptions, such as one eminent and most intelligent minister I recall, whose sense of humour was prone to overcome his sense of security. But in wartime embassies there are temporary wartime officials, some of whom are not always aware of the risks of even the mildest indiscretion. Perhaps the most dangerous type, however, was a career diplomat who, brought up in a more gentlemanly peacetime atmosphere, sometimes tended to regard his career diplomatic colleagues, not only British but Allied or even neutral, as wholly reliable repositories of secret information.

So, with the approval of Charles Hambro, I drafted late in 1942 a paper on the origin and functions of SOE. After revision and approval by the SOE Council and subsequently by Lord Selborne, the new Minister of Economic Warfare, it was circulated in November 1943 as a War Cabinet paper by Lord Selborne for the secret information of all ambassadors and commanders-in-chief. It is impossible to say what effect it had in the diplomatic and service circles for which it was intended; but certainly from 1943 onwards there seemed to emerge a better understanding in senior official circles of the functions of a complex secret organisation, carrying out a wide range of unacknowledgeable operations (other than intelligence and security) which could not be carried out openly by one of the armed services. A *précis* of this paper has been made available by the Foreign and Commonwealth Office and will be found in Appendix B.

Somewhat earlier in 1942 commanders of various Allied forces in London, brooding over the growth of resistance movements in their home countries, submitted to General Brooke, then Chief of the Imperial General Staff, a proposal for a combined Allied staff on resistance matters. The CIGS replied briefly that there was no need for any such action, because it was precisely for this purpose (co-ordination of efforts by the various underground armies) that the Special Operations Executive had been set up. This factually correct reply left the Allied commanders breathless; SOE was so secret that its name and existence had never been disclosed to them. Norwegians, Dutch, French, Poles and Czechs thought they were dealing with different officers at the War Office, Colonel A, Major B and so on. At that time, in the middle of 1942, all of them certainly were in contact with General Gubbins whom they thought re-presented the War Office. When in Lisbon I myself had always used my War Office cover as Assistant Military Attaché whether in deal-ing with colleagues in the Embassy (with only four exceptions) or with Allied representatives. I think we were right in the early period to treat the very existence of SOE and its name as a secret, but certainly the result of the CIGS letter to the Allied commanders in 1942 multiplied several times over the number of people who shared the secret. Although it could have been handled with more imagina-tion, it was a correct decision, and was an important milestone along the road by which SOE gradually arrived at the intermediate posi-tion of a semi-secret organisation.

Extreme secrecy had its problems, however: it caused jealousy and ill-feeling. There were also fears that money was being squandered. By the summer of 1942 the organisation was expanding rapidly at great expense, but was not yet in a position to show results. Some top civil servants were probably worrying that funds were not being used correctly. A special enquiry was held by Sir John Hanbury-Williams and Sir Edward Playfair at the request of the Treasury. They found every sign of vigorous growth but rightly insisted on more attention to organisation and administration. They paid high tribute to the work of John Venner, the Director of Finance, in controlling the massive use of non-accountable funds in difficult circumstances.

For SOE was now embarking on the most expansive and expensive phase of all, the support and supply of large numbers of underground workers in several countries simultaneously. Up to now, as I have mentioned earlier, SOE was constricted in its activities by lack of trained staff and a desperate shortage of aircraft. Much of its work had consisted of sabotaging railways, power stations, factories and canals, but now the concept of 'secret armies' in enemy-occupied territories was not just a hopeful thought in Gubbins's mind but an actual possibility. Gubbins and his colleagues had been thinking in such terms since the pre-war MIR days before SOE had even been thought of, but it was only now, as 1942 progressed, that they would have a chance to put their old ideas into practice, first in a limited and most clandestine way in Poland and then more conspicuously in France.

From November 1942 onwards the Allied landings in North Africa had a major effect on SOE, whose signals station in Gibraltar carried most of the important traffic for these landings. Morocco and Algeria now became a theatre of Allied military operations and ceased to be covered by SOE's Iberian Section, whose role henceforth was much reduced; an SOE mission was established in Algeria to enable men and supplies to be landed in Sardinia, Corsica and southern France; operations into Italy, previously directed from London through a high-powered SOE officer in Switzerland, became directed more and more from the Mediterranean.

SOE Cairo continued to operate into the Balkans, a fast growing and more openly military unit much dependent on General Headquarters Middle East. A new SOE mission was established in Meerut near Delhi, later moving to Ceylon (Sri Lanka) to operate into South-East Asia; and finally SOA (Special Operations Australia) was established in Queensland operating into New Guinea, Indonesia and Singapore. The role of SOE in Baker Street became more an administrative co-ordinating and supply base. It was dealing, of course, with issues of policy and liaison with the chiefs of staff, service ministries, and the Foreign Office, but was mainly responsible for the efficiency of its subordinate units, which around the world were operating in support of (and always in advance of) the plans of the respective theatre commanders. American military doctrine stressed the autonomy of the theatre commander; and after Pearl Harbor in 1941 this doctrine prevailed.

After the enemy surrender in North Africa in May 1943, huge quantities of small arms and ammunition were captured, useful for guerrillas in the Balkans but not suitable for the Allied armies who had different small arms of different calibres. At one time Churchill had directed the War Office to offer them to Turkey, which he still hoped to tempt out of its neutrality into joining the Allies. Fortunately, SOE heard of this situation in time, and were able to bring strong arguments to bear at the ministerial level. This, combined with a recent upsurge Churchillian interest in the gallant Jugoslav partisans led to him reversing his own directions in a characteristic minute beginning 'A rifle is of value only in the hands of a man who is prepared to use it.'

1943 saw the Allied capture of southern Italy and the overpowering of the Luftwaffe in the Mediterranean, so that massive supply droppings by air became possible for the first time. The mountainous terrain of large areas in the Balkans encouraged the build-up of bands of partisans who, given arms, communications and supplies were able to develop into major guerrilla warfare units. Air bases in southern Italy transformed the sending of supplies not only to the Balkans but to a lesser extent to north Italy and to Poland and Eastern Europe. The dominating factor, however, was the availability of aircraft. The growth and even the survival of resistance movements or regional groups proved to be dependent on air supply. No movement could achieve its own aims or make its contributions to Allied military strategy without reliable, secure radio communications which called not merely for more radio sets but for trained operators, as well as the obvious requirements of arms and explosives and other stores. Hence the relations, good or bad, of SOE with resistance movements and with the Allied governments-in-exile (if any) depended in large measure on availability of aircraft to assure vital supplies.

Air transport was also essential for sending key men into occupied territory, trained officers who could carry instructions from Allied headquarters and who could direct or at least influence policy or strategy in the field. Transport out was in a different way almost as important as transport in. In France a unique landing service developed, using first the small Lysander aircraft and later the larger and longer-range US Hudson. This service proved of immeasurable value in bringing out key agents or leading political figures. By contrast, in Belgium and the Netherlands the terrain and high-density population made Lysander pick-ups too risky to the point of impossibility; and other forms of transport out, such as by boat, were also impracticable, so that the direction and control of resistance was far more difficult. This fact undoubtedly contributed largely to the disaster in the Netherlands, when the Abwehr in early 1943 succeeded brilliantly in penetrating the embryo resistance without being detected for many months and inflicted heavy casualties.

Thus the scale of operations and the consequent requirements of arms, equipment, containers, parachutes and personnel all depended heavily on the availability of specialised supply-dropping aircraft known in the Air Force as special duty aircraft. With two exceptions these aircraft were bombers, whose allocation to SOE work was at the expense of the bomber programme and was inevitably resisted by the bomber commands and the air staffs at all levels up to the highest. The exceptions were, first the Lysanders used mainly in France but also in Italy and Burma, and second the US transport Dakotas (unarmed C47s) which were used over Jugoslavia and Greece and Poland in 1944, when enemy fighters could virtually be ignored.

The opposition of the air staffs to increasing the allocation of bombers could only be overcome at the top level, not merely at chiefs of staff or commanders-in-chief level but usually at War Cabinet level, if some special event occurred or some strategic need of over-riding importance became apparent. On 22 June 1943 Churchill initialled a minute saying that SOE's demands for aircraft had priority even over the bombing of Germany (Auty and Clogg, 1975, p. 17) and in July 1943 the chiefs of staff authorised SOE's air-craft allocation to be increased to thirty-six.

This sudden increase in the availability of supply-dropping air-craft was an immense stimulus to SOE's growth, which needless to say involved severe growing pains. This was most vividly ex-perienced in the Middle East and the Mediterranean in 1943, when more C47s became available for supply droppings and landings in Jugoslavia and Greece. This meant an immediate multiplication of many requirements which could not possibly be satisfied at such short notice: on the air side parachutes and containers; on the supply side small arms and ammunition (even captured enemy supplies in North Africa had to be transported to new airfields in south Italy), explosives, medical stores and radio sets. More radio operators and cypher staff were needed to handle the greatly increased traffic, so were quartermaster staff and air operation control staff, as well as the recruiting and training of additional operational officers for the field and for general staff at headquarters.

Some time in the second half of 1943 when the future command set-up in the Mediterrranean was being planned, the truth dawned. SOE's structure and organisation, as well as its forward operational planning, had to be adapted to the new Allied military structures of the immediate future. It was no longer just a secret service, based on London and executing plans or projects conceived by its chief and his staff in the secret recesses of their London offices in Baker Street. It was a secret operational service trying to handle as many as possible of the para-military activities, which the regular services were for whatever reason unable to handle themselves – in other words supplementing their activities in their various theatres of operation. It could never succeed in so doing unless it was constantly informed with the latest up-to-date information on relevant future strategic plans. For example, it was vital for SOE to know top-secret material such as the dates and areas of Allied assaults on Sicily, south Italy, Normandy and the south of France, as well as embryo ideas for crossing the Adriatic into the Balkans or striking north-east from Italy through the Ljubljana gap, which were never more than ideas in the thoughts of the planning staffs, always destined to be stillborn because of global strategy or inter-Allied policies. It was also most important for the high commands of the three services to know, or to have means of rapidly discovering, what special operations could and could not do in a given area at a given time. It takes many months to build up a secret army or resistance group in selected key areas, with arms, equipment, supplies and communications, and – not least important – some beginnings of local knowledge.

By the middle of 1943 the SOE structure and set-up at Baker Street consisted of Sir Charles Hambro as chief with two deputies, Sir John Hanbury-Williams, who was then in charge of administration, and General Gubbins, who ran the operational division. Soon after Hambro and Hanbury Williams resigned and were succeeded by Gubbins with Sporborg as his only deputy chief. There was also an SOE Council which consisted of the chief and his two deputies, all directors of departments, and special advisers from the Foreign Office and the Air Ministry.

The Planning Department headed by Colonel R. H. Barry endeavoured to forecast the main needs and demands which would be made for personnel recruitment and training and for supply, especially for parachutes and supply-dropping aircraft. These demands would have to be worked out for a year in advance to enable the SOE operational units to carry out the directives of their theatre commanders or the British chiefs of staff.

There were also technical and liaison directorates for service liaison, security, technical research and supply, signals and ciphers, training, finance and administration. Seven separate operational directorates were organised for Western Europe, Iberia and North Africa, the Balkans and the Middle East, South-East Asia, the Far East and Australia, Africa (other than North Africa) and the western hemisphere.

The Western Europe directorate was from 1943 organised under Brigadier Mockler-Ferryman and was based on Norgeby House in Baker Street. A series of country sections covered Western Europe, including Scandinavia, France and the Low Countries, which for reasons of communications and escape routes needed unified direction, and Germany, which remained throughout the war an isolated section, restricted by the ferocious security system of the Third Reich. This Western European directorate was from January 1944 responsible to the Supreme Headquarters Allied Expeditionary Force under General Eisenhower for co-ordinating resistance movements in France, Belgium, Luxembourg and the Netherlands to give maximum support to the cross-Channel Operation Overlord. It was also responsible for resistance movements in Norway and Denmark which carried out continuous acts of sabotage so as to tie down German divisions which would otherwise be available for defensive roles in France.

In December 1943 the Mediterranean theatre was unified under an Allied force headquarters and SOE was responsible to them with a Special Operations Mediterranean which was based on southern Italy. This SOE Mediterranean division consisted of several units: from Cairo Force 133 operated into Greece, the Aegean and Bulgaria; from Bari Force 266 operated into Albania under the Balkans Air Force, and Force 399 supplied Tito's Partisans in Jugoslavia in co-operation with the British Military Mission No. 37. From Monopoli Number One Special Force under Commander Holdsworth with Colonel R. T. Hewitt as his deputy supported the Italian partisans and resisters in northern Italy. At the western end of the Mediterranean in Algiers, ISSU 6 operated into southern France and was busy preparing for the August 1944 Allied landings which were originally codenamed Anvil, but which the security system services changed at the last moment to Dragoon.

Force 139 under Colonel Threlfall operated into Poland and Czechoslovakia, and Number Six Special Force into Austria. Operations which involved air sorties from southern Italy into Poland, Czechoslovakia and Austria did not come under the Allied force headquarters in the Mediterranean because they were to countries outside this area; instead, SOE had a direct responsibility to the chiefs of staff in London.

In the Far East the SOE unit named Force 136 was based in Ceylon, responsible to South-East Asia Command and expected to organise resistance movements and *coups de main* in Burma, Thailand, Indo-China, Malaya and the East Indies.

SOE operated a small joint unit with the Australians, responsible to the South-West Pacific Area headquarters of the American commander, General MacArthur. This unit worked into New Guinea, Netherlands East Indies, Singapore and the Philippine Islands.

By the end of 1943 (when I had to leave the London planning staff under orders from General Gubbins to proceed to Cairo as SOE's General Staff Officer in charge of planning in the Mediterranean Area under General Stawell) we had prepared a paper for the chiefs of staff in London on SOE aircraft requirements for 1944. These requirements were our estimates of the aircraft necessary to meet our directives from the various theatre commanders concerned, in Europe, the Mediterranean, Middle and Far East, plus requirements for Poland and Czechoslovakia. This paper showed a peak requirement in 1944 for 350 aircraft. This huge figure astonished everybody in SOE, apart from the chief and the planning staff, and reduced our air adviser to a state of speechless rage because he regarded it as irresponsible and unjustifiable. Having myself drafted this paper, I was happy to defend it tooth and claw with chapter and verse against the invectives of our internal critics. Later, after I had arrived in the Mediterranean theatre, I was delighted to hear that it had in substance been approved by the chiefs of staff, thanks to the support of the theatre commanders. So 1944 was the first year when SOE had the resources necessary to perform the tasks imposed upon it.

After the surrender in Europe in May 1945, more aircraft and other supplies became available to South-East Asia Command, and Admiral Mountbatten, the theatre commander, having had previous experience of the value of special operations, was willing to allocate aircraft to support guerrilla operations in Burma, Thailand and Malaya.

The liquidation of SOE started in 1944 on an internal and unofficial basis with the object of releasing resources, especially in manpower, from Europe to the Far East. By the end of 1944 the Germans had withdrawn from France and Belgium and from Greece, Albania and most of Jugoslavia, and all the British liaison officers who had been operating there and acquiring valuable operational experience were available for transfer elsewhere. Prompt decisions were obviously required at all levels, to avoid delay in releasing manpower no longer needed and to accelerate the run-down or close-down of installations, such as packing stations and local headquarters, which became unnecessary almost immediately after victory in Europe in May 1945.

Soon after the Teheran Conference in November 1943 and the Allied decision to unify the Mediterranean theatre under AFHQ, Churchill had written a characteristic and prescient minute, which I happened to see, saying: 'A strong hand will be needed to curb and prune those vast establishments which have embedded themselves in the Nile Delta.'

Colonel Franck, then Commander of SOE in the Mediterranean in succession to General Stawell, paid heed to these words and put Colonel Henry Benson in charge of Force 133 Cairo from early 1945 as chief liquidator. This was a task for which Benson as an eminent accountant and a forceful personality was singularly well equipped. In addition to outposting British officers and other ranks with refreshing speed, he unearthed in the suburbs of Cairo various specialists, such as Cretan cobblers, who if left to themselves could have gone on for years producing Cretan boots or other wares for the benefit of non-existing liaison officers. The liquidation of Force 133 and the redeployment of its manpower proceeded with speed.

In 1945, before the Labour Government took over in Britain in August, Anthony Eden as Foreign Secretary had decided that SOE should be formally liquidated as soon as possible. The formal decision was taken in January 1946 by his successor, Ernest Bevin. That the bulk of its records were then destroyed is evidenced by a Foreign Office statement of 14 December 1949 prepared for a Netherlands Parliamentary Committee of Enquiry. As mentioned in the bibliographical note, an official history was drafted in 1946–8 but has never been completed or published.

5

Relations with British
Government Departments and Services

If the subject of SOE's relationships with other government departments and with the armed services and other organisations were to be covered in full, it would make a book in itself. All I can do here in one chapter is to sketch in some of the many problems which arose and explain the changing areas of conflict and goodwill. Inevitably in so doing I shall mention some SOE activities which will be mentioned again more fully in the sections on the different countries, but these relationships are an important subject, which has created considerable controversy.

From the beginning there were inter-service rivalries and jealousies. Specialist intelligence departments such as MI9 and operational units such as the commandos were all chasing recruits at the same time as SOE: each wanted people of high calibre. Moreover, SOE was dependent in different ways on all three services; it had cover offices with the three service ministries; it made good use of them and in particular had to liaise ceaselessly with the directors of military operations and personnel at the War Office. It also had to liaise with exiled governments and their armed services. To transport agents into foreign countries it had to seek help from the Royal Navy and Royal Air Force. Both these services wanted to be sure that what they were being asked to do was of crucial importance and was not unduly risking men, craft or machines. But since all was top secret, it was hard to convey the necessary assurances with complete conviction.

There was a naval liaison officer at Baker Street and SOE had a cover address at the Admiralty, NID(Q). There was a small para-naval unit, based on the Helford River in Cornwall for sorties to the French coast, especially Brittany, to land or take off agents. The enemy coastal patrols and security measures progressively tightened up from 1941 onwards, and after 1943, when the cross-Channel Operation Overlord was universally expected, the sea routes to the

Breton coast became more and more difficult, although they continued to be operated with good results.

Individual naval projects were limited to the obvious areas; Lerwick harbour in the Shetlands, for instance, provided a base for ships operating to and from Norway; there was the blockade running of ships loaded with ball bearings from Gothenburg in Sweden in 1941, Operations Rubble and Performance; the hi-jacking of an Italian ship from Fernando Po in 1941, Operation Postmaster; numerous para-naval operations in the Middle East and Adriatic; landings of men and supplies in Corsica, the Adriatic coasts of Italy, Jugoslavia and Albania in 1943 and 1944; the evacuation of the captured General Kreipe from Crete in 1943; and operations in South-East Asia Command from Colombo to Burma, Thailand and Malaya. The most spectacular individual para-naval operation, Jaywick, was Major Ivan Lyon's feat with three Australians in 1943 of sailing a native boat over two thousand miles through enemy-controlled waters from North-West Australia to Singapore, sinking 37,000 tons of Japanese shipping and returning safely to base. Major Lyon, whom I met in Cairo in January 1944 on his way to London to get improved equipment for a repeat operation, was captured and shot on his second attempt.

Perhaps the most productive naval-SOE coup was the destruction in the neutral territory of Tangier in late 1942 of a special German-designed infra-red station set up to guide U-boats through the Straits of Gibraltar. Sea transport largely supplied Norwegian, Corsican and Malayan resistance movements, but elsewhere air transport was vital.

For air transport in Western Europe bombers were needed, two-engined or preferably four-engined, for parachute drops of personnel or supplies, plus small Lysander reconnaissance aircraft for night landings and pick-ups; in the Balkans, bombers and C47s, two-engined unarmed Dakota transport aircraft for drops or in some areas landings and pick-ups; in South-East Asia four-engined bombers or long-range Catalina seaplanes and Lysanders for pick-ups in Burma. One of SOE's main recurring problems in its relations with the Air Ministry was the need for bomber aircraft. This was clear competition with the bomber offensive which the Air Force believed was a certain winner.

By 1942 SOE was confident that the task of putting out of action a small target in enemy-occupied country could be carried out better by a small team of well-trained agents with light arms and high explosives than by a hundred-bomber raid. The bombers might easily miss the target and kill or injure scores of our friends and allies. This confidence was justified by two important SOE operations, one on a railway bridge in Greece in November 1942 and the other on the heavy water factory in Norway in February 1943. Both targets were attacked with complete success in spite of being heavily guarded. These two successful operations and the upsurge in resistance activity in 1943, especially in France and Jugoslavia, combined to enable SOE to present the chiefs of staff in late 1943 with an overwhelming case for the allocation of over three hundred aircraft at the peak period of 1944.

Professor R. V. Jones, working in Air Intelligence as well as SIS, was a powerful critic of the Air Ministry thesis that Britain could win the war by night bombing:

'Through 1941, so long as the myth of our bombing accuracy persisted, he [the Chief of Air Staff] pursued the policy of attacking oil installations on the argument that, if the German armed forces could be deprived of fuel, their fighting ability would be destroyed. Then had followed the realisation that we could not even hit towns, let alone individual factories; and yet Bomber Command was the only weapon we had which could reduce the German war potential' (Jones, 1978, p. 303).

In Germany itself there was never a true resistance movement, least of all one capable of attacking a factory, but it was otherwise in Norway, Denmark, France, Italy (after 1943), Jugoslavia and Poland. The slow painful growth of resistance movements in certain countries was largely due to their being starved of air supply until the time when their strategic value was at last recognised. This phenomenon is displayed statistically in a striking manner in France and is also prominent in different ways in Jugoslavia and Italy.

Naturally the best type of aircraft for special operations at night was the long-range bomber, designed to carry heavy loads, easily adapted for parachuting personnel as well as heavy containers of arms and other stores, and with light defensive armament for use against night-fighters. But this same type was obviously most in demand by Bomber Command, so that the air staffs could usually argue with some justification that allocation to special operations could only be at the expense of the bomber offensive.

Long-range aircraft were also essential for reaching from British bases to southern France, north Italy or Poland, or from Middle East bases for reaching the Balkans. They were not essential from United Kingdom bases to northern France, Belgium or the Netherlands, or from south Italian bases to the Balkans. But up to 1944 there were no surplus medium-range aircraft available with a worthwhile lifting capacity and defensive armament. The distances from Ceylon to South-East Asia were so great that for most sorties only the super long-range Catalina seaplanes or B24 Liberators were suitable.

It was only in 1944, when Allied air supremacy in the Mediterranean theatre was complete and the liberation of south Italy made suitable air bases available on the Adriatic coast from Brindisi up to Foggia – whether for bomber squadrons or supply droppers – that it became possible for SOE to use the great American aerial workhorse of the Second World War, the unarmed medium-range communication and transport aircraft, the C47 or Dakota. They were available in quantity and could even land without difficulty on temporary landing grounds in occupied territory, thus eliminating the need for parachutes, which were often scarce, and making it possible to bring men out (including wounded) as well as taking men in.

Whatever aircraft were being used, it usually happened that in every squadron one or more would be unserviceable on a given day. This added a further element of uncertainty to the overriding uncertainty of weather conditions over the target area. And, of course, it made life still more dangerous and difficult for the brave and tenacious men and women who were to assemble in occupied territory around midnight to form the reception committee.

An air base for supply-dropping operations could be in theory simple and rapidly organised, if it were only designed for one operation or a few operations. But this never happened. The base had in practice almost always to provide a continuous seven-day week, fifty-two weeks in the year, airborne operation for men, weapons, equipment and sorties of a wide range, with good telecommunications. Every sortie had its own individual needs, which had to be scrupulously observed, failing which the time and effort and risk of men and machines – and the men most at risk in the field – could be totally wasted. Essential needs included good access roads, hard stands, good weatherproof storage facilities for hundreds of tons of

diverse stores, a parachute-packing station and a separate equip-
ment-packing station, where long tubular metal containers could be
packed securely with arms, ammunition, radio sets, explosives, gold
coins, medical stores and innumerable other items – once even
folding boats to cross in winter a mountain river, the River Drava on
the southern borders of Austria. All these facilities must be adjacent
to an airfield and linked to it by transport. At one time, in 1944,
we had a packing station near Bari where hundreds or sometimes
thousands of Jugoslav Partisans were working round the clock to
meet the needs of their compatriots on the other side of the Adriatic.
A good description of the urgent creation of a temporary air base at
Protville, Tunisia, will be found in Hamilton-Hill's *SOE Assignment*
(1973).

Air sorties were governed not merely by weather conditions over
the target area but also by the phases of the moon. The feat of
navigating to a pinpoint by night and dropping personnel to a
reception committee identified by a few torches or sometimes
bonfires was only possible during the full-moon period of ten or
twelve days every month. If bad weather coincided with moon
period, drops for that month were out, and radio waves crackled
with the outrage of the deprived men in the field. Often, too, weather
reports at base were bad, when actual weather conditions over the
reception area were clear. 'Tell MAAF to sack the Met man and
hang out the seaweed', signalled an infuriated British liaison officer
from north Italy one fine night in June 1944, a signal which I am glad
to say was read out at one morning MAAF meeting at Caserta where
I happened to be present.

SOE air supply operations, being clandestine, nocturnal, inter-
service and the reverse of routine – indeed every operation was
individualistic, if not unique – were complex affairs, difficult to plan
and control. They involved the co-ordination of movements to the
air base of one or more agents with their conducting officer from a
holding camp together with one or more – or many – carefully
packed containers of equipment and supplies, every one prepared to
meet the pre-arranged needs of the recipient in the field; and then the
co-ordination of the SOE units responsible for all these activities
with the Air Force units responsible for the preparation and briefing
of the air crews concerned, and the operation, checking, fuelling and
loading of the various aircraft. Often one aircraft would be making
two or more sorties to different places in the same country or in two

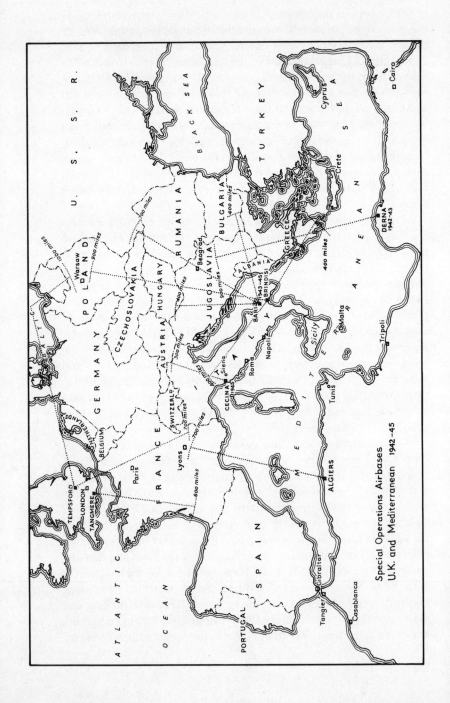

Special Operations Airbases
U.K. and Mediterranean 1942–45

or more countries. I recall a night near the Brindisi base, when Charles Villiers, who was due to be parachuted into northern Jugo-slavia – the sortie was made on three consecutive nights before it succeeded – was asked by the aircraft commander when in flight to help in off-loading over another area in Jugoslavia bundles and bundles of Allied propaganda from the political warfare people. He was outraged to find that it was all written in Albanian, meaningless to the Croats or Slovenes, an error at the packing station undetected by anybody!

For the guidance of both sets of staffs involved, both SOE and Air Force, it was vital to have instructions which spelt out clearly the responsibilities of all concerned. In the winter of 1944, with the advantage of seeing past errors and past attempts at definition, I helped the air operations staff to prepare an improved and expanded version of instructions for all those using the Cecina airfields near Siena.

Pick-up operations played an important and super-secret role in SOE operations in France and to a much lesser extent in Burma, Jugoslavia and Poland. The RAF used single-engined Lysanders, so-called 'Army co-operation' aircraft with a range of 600–700 miles, capable of taking up to a maximum of three passengers, or twin-engined Hudsons, with a range of a thousand miles, capable of taking between eight and ten passengers. These two types of RAF aircraft from 1941 to 1944 flew over 320 sorties to France, of which over 210 were successful, taking in over 440 passengers and bringing out over 630 at the cost of six pilots killed in the course of opera-tions. The large majority of these sorties were flown in 1943. In addition, in 1944 USAAF C47s did twenty pick-up sorties for SOE (apart from what they did for OSS), taking in over sixty and bringing back over a hundred passengers.

In Asia, Lysander pick-up operations played an important role for SOE's Force 136 in Burma – Group Captain Verity, an outstanding pick-up pilot and commander, mentions one RAF pilot, Arkell, who did no fewer than thirty-five Lysander pick-ups there (Verity, 1978, p. 195). And in Poland, C47s operating from Brindisi in south Italy, made three important pick-ups in July–August 1944, bringing out to London via Italy important military and political figures and selected parts of one of the secret V2 rockets. There were also a number of landing operations by C47s in Jugoslavia and Greece, in areas liberated, even if only temporarily, by guerrilla action. They were especially valuable in Jugoslavia, where heavy equipment and supplies were taken in and large numbers of sick and wounded brought out. For further details on the allocating of special duty aircraft see Appendix F.

Although, on the whole, relationships with the Air Force can be said to have been cordial, there were individual airmen who were not always enthusiastic. Air Marshal Tedder was acting as deputy to Eisenhower just before the invasion of France. Even as late as 14 April 1944 he protested, in a memorandum to the American General Bull, that the last-moment allocation of twenty-five extra American aircraft to the support of the French resistance, whose value he doubted, was 'quite unjustified'.

The British Army staff did not at first believe that guerrillas or secret armies would be of much use to them in their operations, but in the last months of the war the undisputed achievements of SOE and OSS became clearer. Balkan guerrilla warfare, the demolition of the Gorgopotamos bridge and the sabotage of the Rhône-Saône canal and the Norsk Hydro heavy water plant became known and the Army staffs at high level began to show more enthusiasm. Eisenhower himself was always receptive to the value of resistance movements as a supplement to regular military operations, perhaps because he learnt early on in November 1942, during the North African landings when much of the most important signal traffic went through the SOE signals network, just how helpful a special operations organisation could be.

I remember that when I was asked by Hambro, then chief of SOE, late in 1942 to draft a recommendation to the War Office for the promotion of Gubbins from brigadier to major-general, because of his record and abilities and because he was having to give directions to officers of exiled governments or Allied armies who were sometimes of general rank, that Hambro's recommendation encountered some opposition which was only overcome with difficulty. The War Office attitude towards SOE was sceptical at best.

Surprisingly, SOE had no official relationship with the Ministry of Economic Warfare, although we shared the same minister. Dalton kept his two departments, the one secret and the other open, strictly separate. As mentioned earlier, Dalton, a brilliant but temperamental left-wing intellectual, had the disadvantage of being uncongenial to Churchill, who was usually reluctant to see him on SOE affairs. Captain Hillgarth, the Naval Attaché in Madrid, told me that when

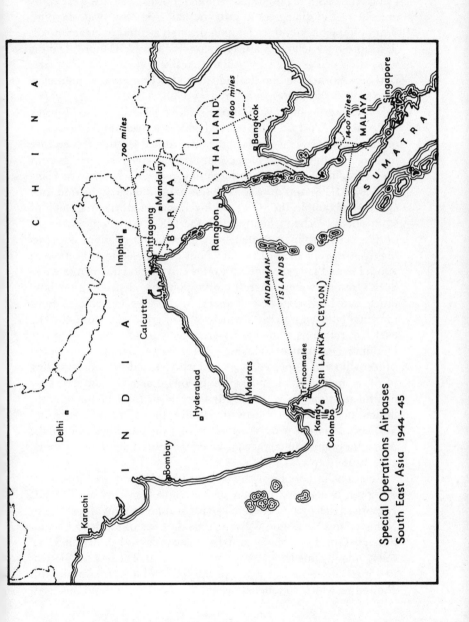

Special Operations Airbases
South East Asia 1944–45

summoned to the Prime Minister's country house at Chequers one evening early in 1942, on returning from Spain, he arrived just as the Prime Minister and his guests, including Lord Vansittart, were coming out of the dining-room into the hall. Churchill was slapping 'Van' on the back and exclaiming through a cloud of cigar smoke, 'Extraordinary fellow, Van! He actually likes Dr Dalton!' Dalton was succeeded in 1942 by a diametrically opposed character, the Earl of Selborne, a methodical and orthodox Conservative politician who was liked and respected by Churchill.

While responsible organisationally and politically to the Minister of Economic Warfare, SOE worked under the operational directions of the chiefs of staff as heads of the three armed services. It therefore had regular contact with their committee and constant dealings with the subordinate units in their hierarchy, particularly the Joint Planning Staff (JPS) and occasionally the Joint Intelligence Committee (JIC). For example, the SOE monthly progress report to the chiefs of staff would be channelled through the JPS, with whom we would discuss periodically its contents and format. Our relations with this highly intelligent and professional body of inter-service officers were good; I would say excellent but for the early period up to 1942 when SOE's results were meagre or disappointing, depending on how much had been expected of them. We always felt able to have informal talks with the JPS which were of great value to both. The excellent relations from 1943 were largely due to the head of our Planning Department, Colonel R. H. Barry, a first-class career officer who was respected by all and who had a deep understanding of SOE, its potential and its limitations. Later I found a similar helpful relationship with the Mediterranean Joint Planning Staff, limited only by the problems of distance; they were at Caserta and SOE headquarters was at Mola di Bari on the other side of the Apennines until January 1945, when we moved up north to Siena, even further away.

Relations in London with the Joint Intelligence Committee were different, being less constant and at times less cordial. The JIC comprised the directors of intelligence of Admiralty, War Office, Air Ministry and Economic Warfare, plus the head of SIS with a senior Foreign Office chairman, usually Victor Cavendish-Bentinck, an outstandingly intelligent and shrewd diplomat. The head of SIS was of course an important figure in the JIC, and it was naturally this committee which conducted the enquiry late in 1943 into the disaster of the Abwehr penetration of the Dutch resistance movement. This disaster not only led to the capture and death of over fifty gallant Dutchmen, but was also used by critics to cast doubt on the authenticity of resistance movements in other countries. Fortunately any doubts on major penetration elsewhere were soon dispelled, though individual groups, particularly in France, were occasionally penetrated and in due course written off, a recurring risk of underground warfare. Lord Selborne's paper of 11 January 1944 Do (44)2 to the War Cabinet Defence Committee dealt fully with this prob- lem, and also restated the case for SOE continuing as a single organisation responsible to a minister but guided by operational directives from the chiefs of staff or theatre commanders (Stafford, 1980, p. 138).

Relations between SOE and the chiefs of staff organisation natur- ally took place at two different levels. SOE would be represented by our own chief or his deputy when invited to attend a COS meeting, a relatively rare event. But when attending meetings of JPS or JIC, or more often informal meetings with individual staff officers, SOE would be represented by an officer of the SOE planning staff, headed by Barry and in 1943 including Peter Wilkinson, Charles Villiers and myself.

From the date of the American entry into the war in December 1941 a Combined Chiefs of Staff Committee (CCS) was set up in Washington DC. The USA already had its own Joint Chiefs of Staff (JCS) with supporting staff set-up for planning and intelligence. The British already had a top-level military mission there headed by Field-Marshal Sir John Dill, who had established close and cordial relations with their Chiefs of Staff Committee chairman General George Marshall.

There was already a senior representative of British Security Co- ordination with headquarters in New York and a liaison officer in Washington, namely William Stephenson, a Canadian who was in the unique position of co-ordinating British security, intelligence and special operations in the western hemisphere. British security liaison with the combined chiefs of staff was handled on the SOE side mainly in Washington, where separate staff for the three activities were maintained. In London OSS/SOE liaison started early in 1942 when Colonel David Bruce was in close touch with Hambro and Gubbins, and Stacey Lloyd of OSS started working with SOE's Central European Section. In Washington Colonel Franck and later

Colonel Pleydell-Bouverie handled liaison with the planning staffs of the combined chiefs of staff.

Representation through British security co-ordination in Washington was important for SOE, especially through the part which it was enabled to play in the Anglo-American arrangements for establishing theatre commands and for giving and revising directives from chiefs of staff to theatre commanders. It was the responsibility of the combined chiefs of staff to formulate and recommend to the War Cabinets of the two governments the areas and boundaries of each command, the nationality and identity of the theatre commander and his deputy and the objectives and duties to be imposed with all the consequences as to priorities of allocation of equipment, supplies and personnel. This inevitably meant for SOE a transition period in which directives from Anglo-American combined chiefs or theatre commander would replace directives from the British COS in London. It was always helpful if the British security staff in Washington could find out from the CCS–JPS what they had in mind when drafting directives for setting up a new theatre command, so that they could get from SOE London any suggestions or comments affecting the support of resistance movements in the area, including the establishment of air-supply bases and instructions to the RAF and USAAF commanders for air-supply operations. A high standard of liaison and exchange of ideas was achieved in this field. Telegrams from the CCS to the theatre commander on matters affecting special operations became by 1944 frequent and of growing importance to service departments and others, especially the Foreign Office and State Department. For instance, SOE could and did help with advice when problems arose after the invasion of Italy. At one stage, in spring 1943, the joint planners became acutely conscious of the tactical and geographical difficulties of 15th Army Group fighting its way up the Italian peninsula from south to north with reduced personnel and equipment because of priority given to Overlord Normandy landings for 1944. They felt constrained to consider, as an alternative, stopping short at a line somewhere north of Naples on the west coast and the vital air bases round Foggia on the Adriatic coast, and mounting some limited trans-Adriatic operation into southern Jugoslavia or Albania. The strategic justification would be firstly to tie down German forces in the Balkans as well as north Italy and thereby keep them away from the defence of the Channel ports and France, and secondly to establish a Balkan bridgehead through which massive supplies could be provided to the Jugoslav Partisans and other resistance groups. Obviously such an idea (which proved abortive) was of vital interest to SOE and one on which SOE was uniquely qualified to advise.

Foreign Office relationships with SOE were bound to be difficult, for every resistance movement had political motives and aspirations seldom identical with those of the governments of the country whether at home, under enemy occupation or abroad in exile. The Foreign Office were a party to the War Cabinet minute of July 1940 to set up SOE as a new secret department under a minister who was also the Minister of Economic Warfare. They were strongly represented in the new SOE by seconding a Foreign Office man of high calibre, Gladwyn Jebb, as chief executive and right-hand man to the Minister. By July 1940 Poland, Denmark, Norway, Holland, Belgium and half of France were already under enemy occupation and, except for Denmark and France, were then already represented by exiled governments in London, to be followed in April 1941 by Jugoslavia and Greece. So it was obvious that if SOE did anything within the ambit of its charter – call it sabotage or subversion or secret armies or resistance movements – there would be a conflict of jurisdiction between the British Government and the exiled Allied governments.

It was also obvious that, except in the event that all three agreed, the conflict would be between the exiled government, the Foreign Office, who would be under pressure to take account of the exiled government's views, and SOE, who were acting under directives from the chiefs of staff, who were responsible to the Minister of Defence, who happened also to be Prime Minister.

In SOE's early years, the Allied war situation seemed desperate. Everybody in Britain tended to pray for the miracle that the unarmed, unorganised, prostrate peoples of conquered Europe would rise up and destroy or at least frustrate the all-conquering Nazis. John Steinbeck wrote a vivid novel on this theme entitled *The Moon is Down* (Steinbeck, 1942) and Churchill read it. As a result, he saw massive uprisings all over Europe and became over-enthusiastic about the potential of spontaneous, unorganised resistance movements using explosives dropped at random over the landscape. He misunderstood the difficulties which would-be resisters faced from ruthless, heavily-armed occupation forces, he did not recognise the need to parachute in trained organisers and the need to drop arms and explosives to pre-arranged points for reception. We had to brief Lord Selborne to convert the Prime Minister from his attractive heresy.

We often tend to forget that to a great many people in Europe in 1940 and 1941 the German occupational forces in their countries appeared likely to stay for ever. Even anti-Nazis accepted that the *status quo post bellum* might remain for decades, and there was strong German propaganda to back up this concept of a 'New Order' for Europe as a great benefit for Europeans. Resistance seemed futile at first and even later it seemed a very long shot. The chances of Britain being able to free the whole of Europe single-handed seemed, and was, a fantasy. Resistance-minded people held their hand until they saw which way the wind would blow. It took much longer than anybody could understand for SOE to come into effective operation, and for secret communication systems and the core of resistance movements to be created. All concerned hoped against hope that SOE would somehow do something at an improbably early stage in its existence, but it was not possible to initiate resistance in a country unless the movement had some convictions and native aspirations of its own. Then contact had to be established with the newly formed underground, if it existed, or someone had to be dropped blind to find and train organisers. It was not until the end of 1941, when America and the Soviet Union, the world's largest and strongest powers, became allies of Britain, however involuntarily, that the conventional war outlook ceased to be desperate and ultimate victory became more than an act of faith.

This transformation also caused Allied leaders and senior officials to think in terms of conventional warfare and over a period caused all of them, and SOE itself, to think more in terms of supplementing normal military operations than of spectacular sabotage operations in conjunction with subversion. It is worth recalling at this point the request of certain Allied military leaders in London in June 1942 for an inter-Allied staff to co-ordinate underground warfare, resulting in the first deliberate disclosure to them of the existence of SOE.

Early in 1942 it was considered desirable to record the basis of collaboration between the Foreign Office and SOE. The Foreign and Commonwealth Office have made available to the author the following résumé:

MEMORANDUM ON FOREIGN OFFICE-SOE AGREEMENT

At the suggestion of Dr Dalton, Minister of Economic Warfare, a Memorandum was drawn up by Mr Gladwyn Jebb, setting out the basis on which the Foreign Office and the Special Operations Executive should collaborate. It was approved by Sir Alexander Cadogan and became operative on 23 May 1942 when it was circulated to all SOE Directors and Regional Heads.

First the Memorandum lists SOE's main tasks, namely:
  (a) to promote disaffection and, if possible, revolt in all enemy and enemy-occupied countries;
  (b) to hamper the enemy's war effort by sabotage and partisan warfare in these areas;
  (c) to combat enemy interests and Fifth Column activities by unacknowledgeable means in any other part of the world where SOE may be permitted to do so.

3. SOE would have to obtain the Secretary of State's prior agreement to any of their operations likely to affect foreign policy. For their part the Foreign Office would make available to SOE all information affecting, or likely to have a bearing upon, SOE operations and plans.

4. The degree of interest taken by the Foreign Office in SOE's activities varies in different areas. Thus in enemy and enemy-occupied territories SOE will work under the directives of the chiefs of staff or the responsible commander in chief. All acts of sabotage and the creation of disaffection against the enemy can, in general, be undertaken on the initiative of SOE though they will have to keep the FO informed by periodical reports of any developments of political significance. If, however, any organisation in touch with SOE is found to be in a position to exercise political influence in the country SOE will at once consult the FO and chiefs of staff as to the line to be adopted by SOE in its dealings with any such organisation.

5. As the FO have a special interest in unoccupied France and its unoccupied overseas territories SOE agrees not to conduct operations in them except with FO consent.

6. In Allied countries SOE interests are chiefly the recruitment of agents and co-operation with the governments concerned in subversive operations. Provided the Allied authorities are in

agreement with SOE about these the FO need not be consulted about recruitment though they should be kept informed on general lines of co-operation in subversive matters. The same applies in regard to SOE relations with the exiled Allied governments.

An example of the Foreign Office-SOE relationship occurred at the end of 1942 soon after the North African landings. Talking over future prospects one day with Hambro, we considered the next steps. We knew that although Overlord had overriding priority, Churchill and his chiefs of staff favoured exploiting the opening up of the Mediterranean. If so, by early 1944 the Allies might have occupied south Italy; air bases and packing stations there would transform the supply-dropping prospects in the Balkans, just as our new base under construction near Algiers would transform the supply-dropping position in the south of France. So SOE should for the first time be able to consider special operations on a serious scale in enemy countries hitherto thought too remote – Italy, Hungary, Bulgaria and Rumania. We knew, or thought we knew, the broad political thinking about the future of Italy, and soon afterwards at the Casablanca Conference a public announcement was made stating unconditional surrender of the Nazi and Fascist regimes as an Allied war aim. But there had been no occasion to review the position of Hungary, Bulgaria and Rumania since they declared war against Britain in June 1941. So Hambro wrote to the head of the Foreign Office, asking for political guidance in relation to these three countries. In due course he received replies, broadly on the lines we expected.

Britain had traditional links of friendly relations with Hungary, though they were enemies in the First World War, but no great commercial interests except freedom of navigation on the Danube. However, Britain obviously had a political interest in the future of a country which bordered on Western Europe. Britain also had traditional links of friendship with Rumania and had had considerable pre-war commercial interests – but it was hard to see that Britain could play a significant role in an enemy country bordering on Russia, whose interests would obviously be predominant. In Bulgaria, traditionally linked with Russia, Britain had virtually no commercial, political or strategic interest, except that it bordered on the territory of our ally Greece.

MI5, the home security service, and the secret intelligence service responsible for external security, known variously as MI6 or SIS, had nominally clear lines of demarcation. The so-called three-mile limit (which was then the normal limit of national sovereignty out to sea) was the limit of MI5's jurisdiction, anything beyond that being the zone of SIS. Obviously and inevitably friction and uncertainty arose if an over-simplified geographical formula was used to define a complex relationship. If MI5 discovered that an enemy agent A in country X was about to visit Britain or to send a sub-agent there on a mission, MI5 had no right on its own to take any action in country X to watch or discredit or mislead agent A; its only proper course was to ask SIS to help it by taking action in country X. To this course MI5 might well have objections. Likewise, SIS might well have objections to using its own staff in country X on a mission, possibly of a dangerous or compromising nature, on behalf of another independent organisation. So early on in the war a special section was set up responsible to MI5 and SIS jointly, to cover cases which involved both security, counter-intelligence and intelligence or involved action both inside and outside the British three-mile limit. Fortunately for me this joint section was represented in Lisbon by an old friend of mine, and our mutual confidence was helpful. SOE from 1941 had a senior director of immense experience and stature, Air Commodore Boyle, a former director of intelligence at the Air Ministry, responsible for both security and intelligence and for liaison with MI5, SIS and service intelligence departments.

SOE had its own security department, mostly staffed from MI5, headed by a well-known barrister, John Senter. This was an important and responsible department in many ways. First, for security clearance of candidates; second, for security briefing of new recruits; third, for maintaining surveillance of all headquarters staff and staff at stations, training schools and overseas missions, and ensuring observance of proper security standards, and fourthly, for watching any visible progress of agents in the field, judging by reports and signals traffic, and in the light of any information from other sources. All SOE agents had to be cleared with MI5.

One serious case of breach of security by a staff officer in Baker Street occurred in 1943 and was reported in the press, though naturally without any mention of SOE. Captain O. Uren, a member of SOE's Eastern European Section, fluent in Hungarian, had contacts with a British Communist who was a Soviet agent. In the course of several meetings he handed over a number of secret documents about SOE's activities and plans in Eastern Europe and, as I was told, a list of all SOE's head office staff, with the symbols allotted to them for communication purposes. This serious and deliberate breach of security involving delivery of most secret documents to the agent of a country which was then an Allied power, did not of course amount to treachery or communication with the enemy.

It so happened that with twenty or thirty other members of the Headquarters staff I was attending in September 1943 a course at an STS in Hampshire and one of the others present was Uren. After a few days he disappeared and we or some of us were informed by a member of the Security Directorate that he had been arrested for a grave breach of security. Later on return to London I was told by John Senter, Director of Security, seconded to SOE from MI5, the nature of the breach. This was the only case of its kind known to me, but inevitably there were cases of a different kind, mostly already publicly reported, of SOE agents in the field or members of resistance movements supported by SOE who, after being arrested and tortured or otherwise threatened or coerced by enemy security officers, gave away secret information to the enemy.

To label relations between MI5 and SOE as good or bad or indifferent would be irrelevant and misleading. The function of a security service is to exercise eternal vigilance over other departments – and of course individuals – and to suspect everybody at all times, not necessarily of treason or disloyalty but of indiscretion or lack of judgement or principle. Particularly when there is a question of protecting colleagues or subordinates under suspicion, there is a painful conflict of loyalty, which may have disastrous results, as witness the saga of Burgess, Maclean and Philby over the period 1930 to 1960. But every staff member of SOE, as a top secret organisation with a high risk wartime role, knew he was a major target for penetration by enemy counter-intelligence, and he could not fail to think every hour of every day of the compelling need for observing security regulations. MI5 was therefore SOE's best friend, as well as a stern and constant critic. And there was no element of competition in their respective roles.

There were other factors which favoured good relations. Apart from a handful of staff who had come from other secret departments and had had the benefit of formal training and experience in top security, all the staff recruited by SOE were initially amateurs in terms of a secret organisation. Those who had experience in the three armed services had some experience of discipline and elementary security; those with legal and other professional education in civil life had some grounding in professional secrecy, sometimes developed to a high enough degree for immediate secret work in wartime. But to the majority, secrecy was something novel and unnatural. All were conscious of the pressing need to learn the rules of security, not only the elementary negative rules, refraining from discussing secret matters in the presence of an unauthorised person, but the more sophisticated rules: how to throw an inquisitive busybody off the scent or how to discuss important secret matters in the presence of a third party without his knowing it.

SOE relations with SIS were a major liaison problem. Part of SOE, Section D, had originally been an offshoot of SIS. All or most of SOE's procedures and practices were derived from it. SIS in the first year or more provided signals and cipher services, radio sets and forged documentation, none of which SOE provided initially for itself, vital though they were. Since neither the Foreign Office nor SIS on its behalf had succeeded in July 1940 in getting formal control of SOE, which was shared between the Minister of Economic Warfare and the chiefs of staff, they naturally wanted to maintain control through technical means as long as possible. When I went to Lisbon in January 1941, all my signals traffic in and out was handled by SIS. It was only several months later that I had my own cyphers and staff to handle my own traffic.

It is probably a mistake to suppose that the inherent differences between secret intelligence and special operations (which are substantial in spite of their many common features) can be easily overcome by grouping them together within a single ministry or under the command of a single chief, but see Chapter 15, p. 235. Certainly the American senior men whom I knew in OSS maintained that their secret intelligence and special operational branches had constant friction and fierce disputes, although they were ultimately responsible to the same director, Donovan. One should start discussion of this problem by analysing some of the main elements of inherent difference between these two forms of secret service.

Secret intelligence demands long-term results and continuity of sources, which means maximum emphasis on security. It may take years to establish the vital contacts for a key agent and to perfect his cover. Any action which risks exposing him may destroy the work of many years, and is to be avoided at almost all costs. He should never be put in contact with another agent who may put him in jeopardy. His communications and local supervision must be wholly separate and not shared with another agent. But the special operations man may be charged with a single violent act in an urban area and he may be withdrawn to his home base immediately thereafter. He may, if properly housed by a local resident of long standing, even be a foreigner with no knowledge of the country or the language, though obviously some such knowledge is desirable. He may be destined, if he escapes, never to visit that country again. To him success is more important than long-term security, even though security is vital for a short period.

Alternatively, the special operations agent, if engaged in organising secret armies or guerrilla warfare, may be best located in a remote rural or even mountainous area, as opposed to an urban area. He may even be in uniform. In order to rouse the population, he may carry out an order or an armed attack or an act of sabotage in the knowledge that it will lead to reprisals in that area and thereby provoke resentment and further rebellious acts regardless of reprisals. This was certainly the policy of Communist-led movements in Europe from 1942–5. The essential and unavoidable difference therefore is that secret intelligence work demands long-term security to the ultimate degree of permanent invisibility, whereas SOE involves a physical para-military act, which apart from minor sabotage, such as sand in the axle boxes, must rapidly or immediately be detected by the enemy. There are, of course, grey areas, when a resistance movement is operating – as it must – its own local intelligence service; and then intelligence and operational manoeuvres tend to overlap. It is a platitude to say that secret intelligence is one of the by-products of a resistance movement.

Another big difference is the scale of operations. Secret intelligence is highly concentrated with a relatively small number of trained agents (though each will be recruiting, training and using his own sub-agents) and probably a limited amount of subjects though unpredictable in both numbers and nature. But SOE people operated in areas where resistance developed on a massive scale and were engaged in a form of underground warfare, involving movements of men and materials and major problems of forward planning for personnel – especially signals personnel both at base, and, if parachute-trained, for the field – and supplies, above all parachutes and radio sets.

At least twice in the Mediterranean SOE was on the verge of breakdown, and was certainly running below any acceptable level of efficiency, because the volume of signals traffic, especially that to and from the field, had expanded suddenly for operational reasons to an unpredictable level, with which the signals staff and cipher staff were unable to cope and were running several days behind schedule. SIS were thus fortunate in losing to SOE the massive burden of handling its expanding signals traffic which achieved, by 1944, a level which nobody could have believed in 1941. General de Gaulle's right-hand man in his secret service, Colonel de Wavrin (alias Passy), is on record as saying that 'on the signals side the technical services of SOE showed themselves to be much more comprehensive and competent than those of the Intelligence service' (de Wavrin, 1947, p. 185 footnote). In the Mediterranean SOE's secret map room at AFHQ Caserta showed in the summer of 1944 over 150 missions each with its own radio operator in the areas served from Mediterranean bases. These areas were southern France, north Italy, Jugoslavia, Albania and Greece, but excluded Poland, whose radio communication was handled mainly through London though partly through Monopoli in southern Italy. The volume of Mediterranean signals traffic in and out was immense. London's traffic with Western Europe was as great or greater. The combined total at the peak was over two million words a week (Barry, 1960).

SIS resented the creation of SOE as a new secret organisation operating in enemy-held territory independent of SIS's control. When another secret service – MI9 – for escapers and evaders came into existence, SIS secured effective control of its operations (see Langley, 1974). The resentment against the creation of an independent SOE undoubtedly was the main reason for the abrasive relations between SIS and SOE. These intrinsic differences between the two secret units were to some extent obvious and predictable from the creation of SOE, but they increased as time passed and as the dynamic growth of SOE became, during 1943, a real and serious factor in the Allied war effort. Meanwhile, SIS was having its own difficulties as a result of having been starved and run down during the inter-war period, and was the object of considerable criticism in top service circles. Thus the background to the relationship between the two was highly unpropitious.

Malcolm Muggeridge, who worked for SIS, wrote: 'Though SOE and SIS were nominally on the same side in the war, they were generally speaking more abhorrent to one another than the Abwehr was to either of them' (Muggeridge, 1972). There were exceptions, as his wording implies. My own relations with the two top SIS men in Lisbon were fortunately such that when I returned to London in 1942 they said they wished I could get a transfer to their organisation, so that they were responsible to somebody they knew well and somebody who knew the local problems. Away from London, men of good sense and good will could overcome the mutual hostility between their headquarters. In London itself, when I was Hambro's assistant, I found that a friend was performing the same services for the head of SIS. We arranged to lunch together at monthly intervals to identify and try to compose the main subjects of discord between our masters.

Another Muggeridge comment deserves a quotation: 'Intelligence work necessarily involves such cheating, lying and betraying, which is why it has so deleterious an effect on the character. I never met anyone professionally engaged in it whom I should care to trust in any capacity' (Muggeridge, 1972). An exaggeration no doubt, but a viewpoint which deserves mention. In the early years of SOE an adjective often in use was 'SOE-minded', a term of praise which connoted ingenuity, playing the cards close to your chest, capacity for an oblique approach to conceal your true objective. No doubt this was not surprising and in some degree necessary for a secret service in war time. But I recall some difficulty in explaining it to Sir John Hanbury-Williams, my deputy chief, an eminently upright straightforward man of the highest morality and probity, who found secret service work almost incomprehensible.

In Britain in the Second World War, SIS was subject to some exceptional forces – some adverse, some favourable. At the beginning of the war, starved of vital finance during the years of peace, it had too few first-class operators and too many run-down old professionals. It suffered inevitably from Hitler's conquest of Western Europe in only two months of *blitzkrieg*, but there was one priceless asset: the head of SIS was also the head of the government code and cypher school who handled the Enigma machine at Bletchley, and he had control of the distribution of Ultra traffic. The top men at SIS thus had the benefit of the top-secret inside knowledge which Ultra bestowed, covering not only the plans and activities of the Nazi armed services, but also much of the activities of their secret organisations, especially the Abwehr, in so far as they were transmitted on the air. The dominant position conferred by Ultra obviously gave the possessor considerable power in comparison with other organisations denied that privilege. The London chief of SOE and his deputy used to see a weekly folder of selected Ultra material relevant to SOE work, which the director of SIS had received from Bletchley. In the Mediterranean in 1943 the SOE director of operations in Cairo had been personally allowed some access to Ultra material relating to Balkan resistance movements and enemy counter measures. From January 1944 the SOE commander in the Mediterranean (first General Stawell and later Colonel Franck) were 'permitted recipients', to use the official phrase, of Ultra material in relation to resistance in Italy as well as the Balkans. But, as will be seen later, the exclusion of SOE from Ultra material relating to Tito's Jugoslav Partisans, at least up to January 1943, and the use which a senior SOE officer in Cairo then made of Ultra in persuading Churchill (by-passing General Headquarters Middle East, the Foreign Office and SOE London) to authorise contact with and support to Tito, had explosive effects not only on Anglo-Jugoslav relations, but also on SOE Cairo and on SOE's relations with the Foreign Office.

6

The American Office of Strategic Services

In May 1940 Churchill appointed William Stephenson, a Canadian air ace from the First World War, a successful radio manufacturer and a business tycoon, generally known as 'Little Bill', to be head of British Security Co-ordination (BSC) in the western hemisphere. He based himself in New York and combined under one roof security, intelligence and special operations. Stephenson soon discerned that President Franklin D. Roosevelt, who had a highly efficient security organisation in the Federal Bureau of Investigation, felt the need for a secret intelligence organisation for overseas, and that he was beginning to have private talks on this delicate and difficult subject with Colonel William J. Donovan. On Stephenson's advice, the British gave Donovan great help and encouragement, so that five months before America entered the war he had already achieved an official position with the title of Co-ordinator of Strategic Information.

It was a piece of great good fortune for Britain – while giving all due credit to Stephenson for perception and judgement – that the first American head of an American wartime service for secret intelligence and special operations should be well disposed towards Britain, although of Irish descent. 'Wild Bill' Donovan was by profession a Wall Street lawyer with a big practice in corporate, anti-trust and political matters. He was in politics a Republican; a man of outstanding courage, physically and morally. He had a wide network of personal friends in the political and business world and above all a close friendship – remarkable for a Republican – with the Democrat of Democrats, Franklin D. Roosevelt.

The main official source for detailed information is the *Secret War Report of the OSS* to the US Joint Chiefs of Staff, prepared in 1948 by a team headed by Kermit Roosevelt, grandson of President Theodore Roosevelt. This report was declassified in 1976 and published in the same year with official deletions.

As a result any historian of American support for resistance movements or American secret intelligence and black propaganda now has a great advantage over historians of British activities in these fields.

In July 1940 the American Navy Secretary, Knox, proposed that Donovan should visit England to study what was going on, including the recent work of German Fifth Columnists in Europe. He returned on 4 August having made valuable contacts; he reported to Knox and then to the President. That December he returned to England and then spent three months touring the Mediterranean and the Balkans. In March of 1941 he reported back to the States on the problems and dangers for shipping posed by U-boats, on the need to deny French North-West Africa to the enemy and on the importance of psychological warfare. The American Cabinet committee reviewed his suggestions for an overall intelligence agency with propaganda and subversive attributes and decided to draft a Presidential order on 25 June 1941. This established as an official agency the Office of Co-ordination of Strategic Information and was finally issued by the President in his capacity as commander-in-chief.

Vigorous opposition was immediately mounted by the war and navy departments, so it was decided to make this new agency a direct part of the executive office of the President.

In December the Japanese attacked Pearl Harbor, which made America a belligerent, and the following June, in 1942, the Office of Co-ordination of Strategic Information was converted into the Office of Strategic Services and was 'designated as the agency of the joint chiefs of staff charged (outside the western hemisphere) with the military programme for psychological warfare'. (Shortly before this, Donovan had lost the function of open propaganda to the Office of War Information.)

Donovan immediately set up a special operations department for physical subversion of the enemy, known as SO. Its functions included sabotage operations and the support and supply of resistance groups whose main task was to keep up a flow of sabotage acts. Inevitably these activities came almost exclusively under the control of the military theatre commanders. Hence special operations in Washington (like their London SOE counterparts after 1943) soon became in the main a servicing activity, building up, maintaining and reinforcing the operational efficiency of its units in the various theatres of war. Like SOE, this American department also had to suggest and recommend to each theatre commander the ways and the areas in which special operations or resistance movements could be expected to contribute to strategic plans. The theatre commander, as an orthodox regular officer, usually with no experience of special operations and no knowledge of the country behind the enemy lines, could not well judge either the potential or the limitations. Above all he had to be persuaded that guerrilla forces with light arms and explosives should be limited to ambushes and attacks on communications, and had little chance of survival in holding fixed territory against heavily armed regulars.

Donovan also set up 'operational groups' who were authorised by a joint chiefs of staff directive of December 1942 and established in May 1943. They were highly-trained foreign language speakers, trained parachutists, skilled in sabotage and small arms and designed to operate in small bands behind the enemy lines, in some way similar to the British Special Air Service but with more emphasis on foreign languages. Separate recruiting programmes were established – Company A for Italy, B for France, C for the Balkans and later, one German group. These operational groups were a force which took advantage of the large numbers of Americans who were bi-lingual or nearly so because of foreign-born parents, and undoubtedly they achieved much valuable work. Reading the American *War Report* for the first time in 1979, I received a stronger impression of achievement by these operational groups than seemed possible for 1944. In Greece, in France in 1944 and in Italy in 1945, the number of operational groups in action and the range of their activities was substantial. However, it is often not easy to distinguish operational group activity proper from special operational units working with local resistance groups, or even from secret intelligence units. For instance, the American *War Report* says that there were 'over seventy-five Office of Strategic Services teams behind the enemy lines in Italy in May 1945'. Then twelve pages later it states that there were 'over three hundred operational groups, secret intelligence, morale operations and special operations agents infiltrated to Greece in 1943–4'.

Impressed by the successes of Nazi propaganda and Fifth Column activities which he had seen in Europe in 1940, Donovan attached great importance to psychological warfare as a weapon to be linked to subversive activities. He set up a special 'morale operations' branch for black propaganda, which he felt should deal with contacts with underground movements, bribery, secret subsidies, black-mail, counterfeiting of ration cards, currency, passports, rumour-spreading and chain letters. He considered that all these activities should be conducted as part of SO, his special operations unit. However, it will be remembered that the British had split off their 'political warfare executive' black propaganda unit in 1940 when SOE was formed. This early separation now caused complications, for the British political warfare executive did not wish to work with the American equivalent of SOE. In order to avoid getting tangled up in this British controversy, Donovan separated his own 'morale operations' branch from his special operations section.

The Americans founded another special operational group which handled the development of secret weapons, radio and guided miss-iles. They also had a maritime unit to deal with landing operations, rubber boats, kayaks, seamanship, navigation and underwater swimming. Another special research and development group handled weapons and such devices as pocket incendiaries, delay devices, limpets and silencers. And there was also a communications branch to cope with codes, ciphers and radio equipment.

On the one hand Donovan welcomed and acknowledged all the help he had received from SOE, but on the other he insisted that his American set-up should establish its own identity and stand on its own feet. There are now two versions extant of the negotiations in June 1942 between SOE and the Americans and I give them both to show some of the problems. First I quote from the American *War Report* and then I give a Foreign Office version. SO in the first quotation refers, of course, to Donovan's special operations organisation.

OSS War Report of 1948 (Chapter II). 'Negotiations by Donovan and Goodfellow [Deputy Director of Operations] and Sir Charles Hambro for SOE were in progress in London when COI became OSS in June 1942. They resulted in the SO/SOE agreement of 26th June. The agreement, which set forth the basic elements of co-operation in every theatre of war, was based upon the general principle that Americans would control areas specifically desig-nated as spheres of American influence, while SOE would control special operations in areas dominated by the British. India, East Africa, the Balkans and the Middle East were to be the province of SOE with American liaison and assistance. SO was to control special operations in China, Manchuria, Korea, Australia, the Atlantic islands and Finland. Several vital areas were subject to special consideration. It was agreed that Western Europe, where SOE was already operating, would continue under its supervision. However, American units were to begin operations on the Continent under general SOE control, preserving the independence of separate unit commands. Special procedures were also established for North Africa including Spanish Morocco. This area was regarded as predominantly an American sphere of operations and the chief of SO in North Africa was to co-ordinate the activities of SOE and SO. (Gibraltar, however, was an exception to this arrangement since it was to remain outside the sphere of the American SO mission in North Africa.) West Africa was to have an American mission working through the British SOE office there.'

Although the details of this Agreement have been published in the USA, the Foreign and Commonwealth Office, pursuant to the policy of embargoing SOE archives, decline to make it available to the public or researchers in London. The following résumé was however made available to the author following a formal request:

Foreign Office Summary of the SOE-OSS Agreement. 'The Office of Strategic Services (OSS) was officially established in Washington on 13th June 1942 as an operating agency under the command of Colonel (later General) William Donovan appointed by the President. One department of the organisation, designated SO, was to deal only with operations, whilst another – SI – dealt with intelligence. Within a fortnight of its foundation two American SO officers arrived in London, and from 16th to 22nd June 1942 discussed with leading members of SOE the principles of world wide SOE-SO collaboration. The result of these negotiations was laid down in a draft agreement which by common consent would become operative only after it had been approved on the one hand by the Foreign Office and the British Chiefs of Staff, and on the other by the State Department and the American Joint Chiefs of Staff. These approvals were obtained during July and August whereafter the provisional agreement reached in June was formally ratified by an exchange of letters signed by Sir Charles Hambro on 8th September and by Colonel Donovan on

12th September 1942. Attached to each was a "summary of agreement between British SOE and American SO". This was based on the result of the June discussions. The summary established the principles of liaison work between SOE HQ in London and SO in Washington. It also determined the areas in which only SOE could carry out operations and those allotted to the SO Branch of OSS for their operations. Thirdly, a joint area was agreed in which both organisations could operate by mutual consent as and when deemed advisable, but keeping each other fully informed.'

There is no difference of substance between these two versions, but they naturally reflect the different positions of SOE, established in 1940 with two years' experience of at least embryo underground activities in the resistance field, and OSS, newly created in 1942 with no record of experience and only the first beginnings of an organisation. The OSS version spells out the allocation of areas of activity, including some areas of joint activity especially in Western Europe and North Africa, and the underlying reasons, whilst the British version puts more emphasis on the procedure for obtaining governmental approvals and says little about responsibility for different areas.

The first and most interesting area of American–British collaboration over special operations was North Africa. After the fall of France in June 1940, the French Government under Marshal Pétain established itself at Vichy in the unoccupied zone and broke off relations with Britain. The USA, however, maintained diplomatic relations with Vichy and had an embassy there. In 1941 a team of twelve US vice-consuls was established in French North Africa, headed by Robert Murphy, a senior diplomat from the US Vichy Embassy. Its function was officially to supervise the distribution of American imports, especially cotton, sugar, tea and petroleum, but it also provided a consular information network to watch over any German or Italian penetration and tried to strengthen the French will to resist. This was an important US move, and the consular network was destined to play an important role in the Allied landings of November 1942, Operation Torch. No British representatives were allowed in North Africa after the British fleet shelled French naval ships at Mers-el-Kebir in July 1940, when they refused to accept any of the alternatives offered to them, including sailing across the

Atlantic to a French port in the Caribbean. When Donovan's special operations unit came into existence it sent a first-class representative to Tangier from the autumn of 1941, Colonel William Eddy, an Arab expert with long experience in the Middle East. The Americans and SOE now co-operated to set up a clandestine radio network by July 1942 between Tangier and Gibraltar with Casablanca, Algiers, Tunis and Oran, so as to ensure communications in case of a US diplomatic break with the Vichy government. Radio sets and parts were smuggled in from British supplies in Gibraltar.

Thus the first major operation in which OSS/SO and SOE collaborated was in an area where the Americans were well established. The British by contrast were officially excluded, apart from the all-important base of Gibraltar and the neutral international zone of Tangier where a British legation was maintained. Preparations were secretly put in hand to assist an American (or Allied) landing and to organise resistance to any German counter-invasion, a constant source of anxiety though it never materialised. Combat groups were organised in the main ports, Oran, Algiers, Casablanca and Port Lyautey. Arms and light equipment, sten guns, .45 pistols, ammunition, flares and explosives, were provided from SOE supplies in Gibraltar, shipped to the British legation in Tangier and then transferred to the US legation for distribution. Hand grenades were obtained from a Moroccan Riff leader who had access to a large supply left over from the Spanish Civil War. In reply to a request from Washington for a guide who knew the harbour, the chief pilot from Port Lyautey was brought out through Tangier and Gibraltar and sent to the USA. Deception rumours were circulated that an Allied invasion of Dakar was imminent and that an exceptionally large British convoy was about to pass the Straits of Gibraltar with supplies for the relief of Malta, then desperately hard pressed. In some miraculous way secrecy was maintained and Operation Torch was a complete strategic surprise.

While relations between OSS/SO and SOE at the working level in North Africa were close and cordial, relations at the top level between Washington and Baker Street had a serious setback in October 1942. Talks took place in Washington, where George Taylor of SOE was visiting, about the establishment of bases in North Africa, assuming that Operation Torch was successful (Sweet-Escott, 1965, pp. 138–40). Donovan himself participated. The conclusion was that there should be a base in North Africa for operations into

France and Corsica, Italy and Sardinia, and that a common OSS/
SOE establishment should be set up, to include training schools and
a radio station. The SOE team sent off a long telegram to London
reporting the result, addressed personally to a very senior officer in
Baker Street. He unfortunately, whether due to absence from
London or absence of mind, failed to circulate it to his colleagues. By
chance some of his colleagues had been having similar talks with
Colonel Gunther, then the senior OSS/SO officer in London, and came
to the opposite conclusion; namely, two separate bases. Donovan
was furious. He could not believe that it was due to first-class
muddle and thought he had been double-crossed. So after Operation
Torch took place in November 1942, OSS and SOE each set up their
separate base in Algeria with some inevitable duplication and waste
of resources. Moreover, when a year later in December 1943 the
Mediterranean was unified and the General Headquarters Middle
East came under Allied Force Headquarters (based first in Algiers,
later in Caserta) and the combined chiefs of staff in Washington
directed the Supreme Commander to set up a single Special Operations Mediterranean, SOM, intended to combine SOE and SO in
one, OSS tacitly declined to participate. Special Operations
Mediterranean was officially designated Anglo-American, but the
American element was never made effective. OSS, while always
welcome at SOM, located near Bari, maintained its own separate
headquarters under Colonel Ed Glavin called the 2677th Regiment
near Naples. Glavin nevertheless wrote me a most cordial letter of
thanks and farewell in the summer of 1945 (see Appendix E).

Under the agreement of June 1942 the American OSS was entitled
to priority, if not exclusive rights, to all special operations in North
Africa itself ahead of SOE. But the German surrender in Tunisia in
May 1943 came only six months after Operation Torch, and there
was not time for any local special operations of importance.
American–British relations in North Africa remained on the whole
harmonious, thanks largely to the commander of the SOE base,
Colonel Douglas Dodds-Parker. Later, when the command of the
Mediterranean theatre was unified, he performed a valuable role as
SOE Mediterranean Liaison Officer with AFHQ and to some extent
with OSS also. He was later succeeded by Colonel B. Pleydell-
Bouverie and later still by Colonel Lord Harcourt. Each of them
performed at Caserta indispensable services by keeping Allied Force
Headquarters (especially its Staff Section 'G3 Special Operations')

informed about the activities and plans of SOM units in the theatre, and *vice versa*.

Italy was the scene of one of OSS's major contributions to the war. The American *War Report* of 1948 lists numerous missions, starting with a team dropped into Sardinia in September 1943 and teams operating in support of Operation Avalanche (the Salerno landings) in the regions of Naples and Amalfi, and concluding with activity in 1944 and 1945 on the Swiss–Italian border including liaison with Allen Dulles, the OSS chief in Berne, on the German surrender negotiations in April 1945. 'In spring 1945 OSS (SI and SO) had more clandestine radio circuits in operation and active liaisons with a greater number of effective resistance groups than did its British intelligence and operations counterparts.' During 1944 the American OSS headquarters in Italy moved with 15th Army Group to Siena, and was known as 'Company D'. At that date OSS had twenty-eight teams totalling sixty-three agents in north Italy. This information comes from the *War Report* which presumably adds together the SI and SO missions.

American SO and SOE had problems over the air-supply organisation until October 1944, because there were too few aircraft available. From late 1943 RAF bases and SOM packing stations were set up in Apulia, near Bari and Brindisi. At first, sorties were mainly concentrated on the Balkans, where the resistance movements were older and far more developed than the infant Italian groups, who only began to come into existence after the Italian armistice of September 1943. From October 1944, when the German withdrawal from the Balkans was far advanced and after the suppression of the Warsaw rising, supply-dropping airlift, in spite of heavy losses over Warsaw in August, began to increase to the benefit of the Italian partisans. Also from October 1944 the US 885th Bombardment Squadron under Brigadier General Monro Maclosky was moved to Brindisi. They attempted mass supply drops, which proved uneconomic as the margin of error (92 tons recovered out of 223) was too high. But from then onwards the available airlift for Italian resistance began for the first time to equal demand. Unfortunately weather conditions in the winter of 1944–5 were exceptionally bad, but successful sorties delivered tonnages of 149 in November, 350 in December, 175 in January and 592 in February. A new forward air base and packing station was organised at Cecina, south of Pisa, and 885 Squadron moved there in March 1945, in which month OSS sorties delivered 890 tons.

OSS and SOE both maintained contact with the high command of the Italian resistance (CLNAI), and in September 1944 a special operational mission established permanent liaison with them in Milan. In November a CLNAI delegation came out via Switzerland to Caserta for discussions with Allied headquarters, in which OSS and SOE played leading roles. The result was a tripartite agreement between Supreme Allied Command, the Italian Government and the Italian CLNAI for provision of funds to cover 90,000 partisans at 1500 *lire* per month plus other expenses, totalling 160 million *lire* per month, provided in equal shares by OSS and SOE (this total was raised by agreement in March 1945 to 350 million *lire*). It was also decided that the Italian CLNAI would control their own partisans and co-operate with Allied forces. In April 1945 OSS had over 75 groups in occupied Italy all in radio communication with Company D or with its detachments at Fifth Army and Eighth Army.

OSS/SO helped SOE in the Balkans with resistance groups. OSS personnel inevitably became involved in political issues and often disagreed with British policy. In Jugoslavia the first OSS officers were dropped to Tito's Partisan headquarters and Mihailović's Chetnik headquarters in August 1943. The first British liaison officers had been with Mihailović since October 1941 and with Tito since May 1943. Under the June 1942 agreement OSS gave SOE the right to co-ordinate special operations in the Balkans; and so American liaison officers had to use British SOE communications and ciphers. In November 1943, however, Donovan, on a visit to Cairo, established the Americans' right to independent communications. In October 1943 after the Italian surrender, when the partisans got temporary control of the Adriatic coast, OSS organised shipments of stores and equipment from southern Italian ports to the Adriatic island of Vis under Partisan control. By January 1944, when the British, who had contributed all the military supplies, took over the operation, 155 voyages had been made, shipping 2000 Partisan troops and 11,000 tons of supplies to Vis and evacuating 700 Partisan wounded and 20,000 refugees. American operational groups, along with British command units, made frequent attacks on the Dalmatian islands after the German forces had reoccupied them. When in 1943 the British decided to support Tito's Partisans, in spite of the protests of the royal government-in-exile, and to give the

Chetniks one last chance before withdrawing all British liaison officers, the US Government decided to send a team to Chetnik headquarters to help with the rescue and transport of US airmen shot down on bombing missions and to collect intelligence. This mission, under Colonel McDowell, was sent against British advice and, as anticipated, aroused serious suspicion and hostility on the part of Tito. In September 1944 an independent American military mission was sent to Tito under Colonel Ellery Huntingdon, soon succeeded by Colonel Charles Thayer, and took command of the fifteen OSS teams in the field. Shortly afterwards the Germans evacuated Belgrade in their withdrawal from the country, and the American military mission established itself there, until the summer of 1945, by which time a US embassy had been organised.

Between August 1943 and November 1944 over three hundred OSS agents of various kinds were infiltrated into Greece and the Greek islands. Agents were recruited principally in and around Cairo, where there was a large Greek community, some of them from the USA. Training in parachuting and demolition was given at the British school at Ramat David in Palestine. The chief obstacle was the shortage of operational transport, from which SOE and SIS were also sufferers, though OSS felt they were unduly low on the ladder. The American operational groups organised two important sabotage operations in May 1944 to cut the flow of chrome ore from Turkey to Germany by demolishing two bridges at Svilengrad and Alexandropolis on the Greek–Bulgarian border. The final stage in the Greek resistance movement, Operation Smashem, included enthusiastic sabotage activities by OSS groups, one of whom claimed to have blown up 7400 yards of railroad track, an act which must have delayed post-war recovery in Greece to a considerable extent. As in France, Italy and elsewhere, there was a conflict in the final stages of enemy withdrawal between destroying enemy facilities for movement and preserving transport facilities vital to post-war recovery.

Because of civil war in Albania, no American special operations units were sent there, though secret intelligence sent in five teams. The SOE mission in Albania refused to co-operate unless British command and radio communications were accepted.

In August 1944 a two-man American team was dropped into Bulgaria near the Greek border and they joined Greek guerrillas in harassing German troops in their withdrawal. The team moved in on

Sofia but were unable to get there until mid-September, joining forces with another OSS team arriving by road from Istanbul. They helped arrange the evacuation of over three hundred airmen, mostly American. On 24 September the Russians, having taken control, ordered both OSS and SOE missions to leave Bulgaria under pain of imprisonment.

In August 1944 after an anti-Nazi *coup d'état*, an OSS team of twenty-one landed at Popesti airport in Rumania in 15th Air Force B17s and evacuated over thirteen hundred American airmen.

Twenty-two American personnel with light arms and stores were landed in September and October 1944 at Banska Bystrica in Czechoslovakia to support a premature and ill-planned rising in Slovakia which was encouraged by the Red Army advance. In October the Russians independently flew in two Czechoslovak brigades, lightly armed and poorly equipped. German counter-measures soon broke up the rising and the resisters and their American allies took to the mountains, where most died of starvation and exposure. A few escaped to the Russian lines over fifty miles away, and only two of the OSS men survived. One other OSS agent was dropped near Prague in February 1945 and contacted a small resistance group.

Attempts were made through American contacts in Istanbul and Berne to persuade the Horthy government in Hungary to turn against the Nazis and to accept the need for unconditional surrender. No success was achieved, however.

SOE, having supported resistance groups in Norway and Denmark for two years, played the leading role there, but a joint organisation, Special Force Headquarters, was set up by SOE and OSS in London and Stockholm from 1943. In Norway, resistance was centralised under a section of Norwegian High Command in London controlling a group known as Milorg. OSS helped greatly by supplying in 1943 three US submarine chasers to strengthen the fleet of fishing boats based on Lerwick in the Shetlands and six long-range B24s of the USAAF based in Scotland for the flights to Norway during the short summer nights. In Denmark SOE and OSS organised sabotage campaigns against the transport system at the request of SHAEF to block or delay the southward movement of German reserves to the battlefields in northern France in 1944.

For OSS, as for SOE, the support of the French and, closely associated, the Belgian resistance movements was the supreme task, because of the obvious strategic importance of co-ordinating resistance activities with military operations in the final assault on Nazi Germany in 1944. There were constitutional problems over the 'legitimacy' of the Vichy government and the corresponding lack of status of General de Gaulle's Free French movement until the liberation of France in September 1944. There were also complications because special operations in France were based partly in England and from 1943 partly in Algiers; moreover, it was necessary to put tripartite teams of US, British and French officers under a French general heading a staff section of SHAEF working under the directions of the Supreme Allied Commander, General Eisenhower. I have mentioned all these problems in more detail in Chapter Nine.

Belgium had experienced occupation in 1914–18 so there was a tradition of underground activity. The volume and quality of intelligence collected and transmitted by the Belgians, especially in relation to air defence installations, receives a special tribute from Professor R. V. Jones (Jones, 1978, pp. 266–77). In the co-ordination of resistance in support of Overlord's military operations, occupied Belgium was organised jointly with northern France. The greatest achievement of the Belgian resistance was in frustrating German plans for demolition of the port of Antwerp.

Special mention should be made of Allen W. Dulles. He has already gone down in history for his work as an American intelligence officer in Switzerland in the First World War, as an international lawyer in Sullivan and Cromwell between the wars, and as the first director of the Central Intelligence Agency after 1946.

Dulles and his second in command, Max Shoop, another international American lawyer, arrived in Switzerland by train in November 1942, a few hours before the news of the Allied landings in French North Africa broke through to the Nazi frontier police, who promptly closed the French–Swiss frontier. Both of them told me after the war, Shoop in Paris and Dulles in Washington, how narrowly they escaped being captured and interned before ever reaching Swiss territory. Once in Berne, Dulles's cover was to be special assistant to the American Minister. Under this guise he carried out many activities. He initiated some American black propaganda successes in Germany, including the OSS contribution to the effective British-organised *Soldatensender* radio broadcasts. He had valuable contacts with political circles in Germany, and was not inhibited by any previous experience of being double-crossed by members of a phoney German resistance group.

In 1943 he established contact with a well-placed German Foreign Office official, codenamed Wood. Another important contact was Gisevius, a high Abwehr representative in the German consulate in Zurich, who was in touch with the group, codenamed Breakers, who were planning the coup against Hitler which was tried and failed at Rastenburg on 20 July 1944. Gisevius was one of the few who survived. In February 1945 Baron Parilli, an Italian industrialist, on behalf of SS General Karl Wolff, informed Swiss intelligence, for transmission to OSS Berne, that the General sought to establish contact with the Allies to seek special surrender terms for the German army in Italy. Allen Dulles was in charge of the negotiations, which were reported to and controlled from Washington and London, complicated by Moscow's suspicions of its allies and Berlin's suspicions of its top officers in Italy. In the course of negotiations two German commanders-in-chief, first Kesselring and then von Vietinghoff, were relieved of their command and Wolff himself was summoned to Berlin by his master Himmler. As the *War Report* says: 'With OSS personnel in Berne operating under cover, preliminary dealings could take place clandestinely without risking embarrassment to the US Government. At the same time OSS had the advantage of prompt access to the White House, the Joint Chiefs of Staff, the State Department and high military authorities in the Mediterranean theatre. Moreover, the facilities and techniques of a clandestine service were readily available.' As a result of these negotiations, the German army in Italy unconditionally surrendered on 2 May 1945, a week before and quite independent of the overall German surrender on Luneburg Heath.

In the autumn of 1944, after the liberation of France and Belgium, scores of OSS men were redeployed to South-East Asia and the Far East. In China neither the Chinese Government under Chiang Kai-shek nor General Stilwell, his Deputy Supremo, seemed in need of their services (Harris Smith, 1972, p. 284). In SEAC (ribaldly interpreted in US circles as 'Save England's Asiatic Colonies') the American Eifler of OSS received from Mackenzie, who was the SOE commander of Force 136, an assurance that 'You can count on all possible co-operation from me and my organisation.' Harris Smith says that 'OSS and SOE co-operated in Burma in some of the most successful irregular military operations of the war.' He also welcomed the establishment by Lord Mountbatten and General Donovan of a Joint Division under command of a British officer with a US deputy. But he concluded pessimistically that 'the relatively cordial relations soon reverted to their original and in a sense normal state of rivalry and suspicion'.

Thailand was the exceptional case in that the two organisations were backing different local groups. OSS had established a link-up with one part of the Free Thai movement, working overland from China in 1943. SOE with its Force 136 had other contacts with the Free Thais. Andrew Gilchrist wrote an illuminating book on the operational work and policy problems of Force 136 in Thailand and in it he records another serious misunderstanding due to an error by an unnamed staff officer, which resulted in the OSS feeling double-crossed (Gilchrist, 1970, pp. 189 *et seq.*). The OSS asked for help in arranging a reception committee in the north of Thailand near Chieng Mai. SOE thought that the Free Thais were weak in that area and asked if OSS would care to suggest another area. This was put in a form which by accident, not by design, made the suggestion appear to emanate from Pridi, the head of the Free Thais. OSS then arranged without consultation a blind drop in central Thailand. Their party was captured and finished up in the same gaol in Bangkok as some Force 136 agents. Fortunately, the police chief was also a top member of the Free Thais, so both sets of agents, OSS and Force 136, were well treated and in due course released.

SOE and OSS relations were inevitably complicated by the OSS developing views, occasionally exaggerated, about alleged British political ambitions. Inevitably the issue of monarchy versus republicanism raised its head in Greece, Jugoslavia and Italy. Two Italian illustrations from R. Harris Smith's *OSS* (1972, pp. 105, 112) are worth noting: '... Disagreements with the British, who were reluctant to arm the Italian resistance forces, were rife,' and '[Italian] resistance leaders usually blamed the lack of assistance on London's devious foreign policy and its servants at the British Theatre Command.'

But these criticisms related to the early period of Italian resistance, which was negligible at the time of the armistice in September 1943 but was beginning to attain serious proportions after the capture of Rome in June 1944. The SOE No. 1 Special Force was inhibited not by any 'devious foreign policy' but by the practical operational necessities of building up communications, radio and otherwise, contacting resistance groups and training organisers, and establishing supply-dropping procedures including dropping zones; all of which took months of preparation.

After the upheaval caused by the Delegation of Six (See Chapter 7) visiting Cairo in August 1943, Harris Smith also describes some Greek problems which he felt had political overtones: 'The PM [Churchill] replaced the SOE Brigadier [Myers] with his twenty-six-year-old second in command [Woodhouse], a baron's son whose political conservatism was more in line with London's thinking.' But Woodhouse at all times said loud and clear that there were no differences between Myers and himself on the handling of the policy problems thrust upon them by the circumstances and political ambitions of the various Greek resistance movements. Harris Smith also says: '... they [OSS officers] showed that they took a stand directly opposed to that of the British [*viz* in supporting the King of Greece]; they made no secret of the fact that the USA were not interested in political objectives but only in finishing the war quickly.'

After Churchill had decided personally to send a British mission to Tito, Harris Smith reports that: 'Roosevelt wanted to send US missions to both Partisans and Chetniks. But SOE Cairo went to great lengths to prevent OSS infiltration into the Balkans. Plans to land OSS men on the Jugoslav coast were constantly blocked by the British Navy which requisitioned every small vessel that OSS requested.'

Whatever the justification for this complaint, both OSS missions got there in the end.

7

Greece, Albania and Jugoslavia

Greece, Albania and Jugoslavia were all monarchies up to 1939. All then suffered the double miseries of enemy occupation and civil war. In all three the nucleus of a hidden Communist network had long been created by the Comintern from Moscow, ready to be activated when needed. All the kings escaped into exile abroad but only King Zog of Albania did not play any active or significant role as leader of a government-in-exile and so SOE's relations with the Albanian government were not a problem. For Greece and Jugoslavia the position was exactly the opposite.

The British Government were grateful to both Jugoslavia and Greece for their gallant resistance to Nazi invasion: they recognised the exiled governments, both of which were royalist and right-wing. The best organised elements in the local population, however, proved to be Communist or Communist-controlled and anti-monarchical, which created a prominent and divisive political issue. Political and diplomatic relations between the British Government and the governments-in-exile were inevitably in conflict with the relations which British military leaders in the Middle East and SOE established with local resistance movements.

The friction generated over Jugoslavia and Greece between the Foreign Office and SOE in London and – somewhat paradoxically, because their interests should have largely coincided – between Middle East Command and SOE Cairo had far wider effects than should have been the case. One of the prime reasons was the initial failure of government departments to recognise – and the corresponding failure of SOE to convince them of the essential truth – that the cause of the conflict was not left-wing tendencies or disloyal policies within SOE's own staff, but a highly disciplined and aggressive Communist underground on the spot. The Minister, Lord Selborne, and Sir Charles Hambro in the upper echelons of SOE at this time, it is worth pointing out, were staunch conservatives and monarchists; Lord Glenconner in charge of SOE Cairo came of a famous Liberal family, the Tennants, and his predecessor Colonel A. T. Maxwell from a well-known banking family, both well to the right of centre. Granted there were a few staff members of SOE and other organisations in Cairo with left-wing or even Marxist tendencies, but they were a minor and secondary factor. The prime cause was the successful underground work of the Comintern. The extent of this Communist control, concealed behind the flag of national liberation, was not appreciated by the governments of Greece, Jugoslavia or Britain until 1943.

Greece

Politics and democracy both originated in the fifth century in Greece, and both have always been of passionate interest to all Greeks. King George II had before the war provoked strong opposition by permitting General John Metaxas, a great Greek patriot and a first-class general, to establish a dictatorship. When the Italians came through Albania to invade Greece in October 1940, they met with resolute resistance from forces trained by Metaxas; but he died early in 1941. The Wehrmacht joined the invasion in April 1941, throwing out the small British, Australian and New Zealand expeditionary force, first from the mainland, in Operation Marita, and then in May, in Operation Mercury, from Crete. The King and his new Prime Minister, Tsouderos, a banker well known personally to Hambro, head of SOE, escaped via Crete to Cairo.

SOE had little time in 1940–1 to make post-occupational preparations, but had a few officers with the expeditionary forces. The number of Allied army personnel stranded in Greece, Crete or the Aegean islands was considerable. Helped heroically by the Greek population, many of them got away, often through neutral Turkey, and MI9 was active in helping these evaders. SIS seems to have left behind in Athens two or three agents with radio sets, and Cairo was fairly well informed about conditions in some urban areas. SOE's chief agent in Athens, Colonel Bakirdzis, known as Prometheus, was a valuable source of action possibilities and organised some shipping sabotage in the Piraeus. Another SOE agent was Peltekis, known as Apollo, who was brilliant both as an intelligence source on resistance matters and as an organiser of sabotage.

Soon after the occupation the Nazis appointed a puppet Greek government. By the irony of fate and before the Nazi–Soviet pact was dissolved in June, the Nazis released from Greek prisons several important Communists, including George Siantos, who on 27 September 1941 established Ethnikon Apeleftherotikon Metopon, EAM, the Greek National Liberation Front, which by 1942 controlled an army, Ellenikos Laikos Apeleftherotikos Stratos or ELAS. Of the nine leaders of EAM known to Colonel C. M. Woodhouse, in 1943 only one was a non-Communist and he was a Socialist who never uttered an independent opinion. EAM was indisputably founded by the Greek Communist Party and its first year was spent in organising a network of cells on the usual Communist pattern for underground propaganda and strikes and subversion. EAM's military arm, ELAS, first appeared in the mountains in the summer of 1942, and consisted of well-disciplined guerrillas right from the start under their leading military organiser, Aris Veloukhiotis, whose real name was Athanasius Klaras. Although EAM and ELAS were two separate organisations, one political and the other military, they were often referred to by themselves as one, even in official documents, where they would be designated EAM/ELAS. The growth of EAM/ELAS and the Greek Communist Party, Kommunistikon Komma Ellenikon, KKE, which controlled them, was already established before the first British contact was made with the Greek armed resistance in October 1942.

There were other resistance groups or *andartes*, usually formed and led by ex-officers, of whom the most important was Ethnikos Dimokraticos Ellenikos Sundesmos or EDES, the national republican Greek league which was right-wing, led by Colonel Napoleon Zervas, and looked politically to its well-known titular head in exile, General Plastiras. Another group in Athens known as the Six Colonels had radio contact with the royal government-in-exile, but they refrained from any operations which would provoke reprisals.

In October 1942 Lord Glenconner, the new head of SOE in Cairo, wrote a paper on general policy guidelines for his senior staff and sent copies to the British Ambassador to the royal government-in-exile of Greece, Sir Rex Leeper, previously the head of PWE or SO 1 in London; to the British Ambassador to the royal government-in-exile of Jugoslavia, Sir Ralph Stevenson; to Middle East Command and to SOE London. In it he outlined some general sociological reasons why the poorer classes in any country, having less to lose and more to gain than the rich, were generally more prone to play active roles in the resistance movements, and he concluded: 'For these reasons SOE finds itself for the most part drawn to collaborate with parties of the left.' At the Foreign Office, the Deputy Permanent Under Secretary, Sir Orme Sargent, minuted: 'This is a dangerous doctrine and should be applied sparingly.'

On instruction from the head of SOE, Charles Hambro, I visited Orme Sargent to talk over this doctrinal issue, which was destined to bedevil SOE's relations with His Majesty's Government. Orme Sargent in a genial mood said that, although it was an obvious issue, he hoped it did not matter in the case of Greece, because, he said, 'Glenconner and Leeper have clicked and are getting on well together.' This was a tribute to Glenconner's personality and diplomacy, since Leeper, as a result of months of friction in London between SO1 and SO2, detested SO2, later SOE. But the genial mood was not to last.

Now occurred the most important and successful operation in the history of Greek resistance, leading *inter alia* to direct British relations with the rival forces of both left and right, ELAS and EDES. The Gorgopotamos bridge and viaduct, not far from the pass of Thermopylae, was one of the three vulnerable points on the railway connecting Athens and the port of Piraeus with Salonika and ultimately with Germany. In preparation for the Allied landings in North Africa – Operation Torch on 8 November 1942 – the Eighth Army under General Montgomery in the Egyptian Western Desert opened on 23 October an offensive designed to catch Rommel's Afrika Korps in a pincer movement and eliminate it. Germany–Salonika–Piraeus–Tobruk was one of the most valuable supply routes to Rommel. The destruction of the Gorgopotamus bridge could, and did, cut his supply lines at a crucial moment after the Eighth Army's offensive at El Alamein. The project was carried out by SOE Cairo expressly to meet the strategic objectives of Middle East Command.

On 1 October 1942 a team of nine SOE officers and three sergeants under Brigadier Myers, who was posted to SOE for the purpose, and his second-in-command Colonel Woodhouse, an SOE officer with good Greek experience and a classical scholar, were parachuted into the Delphi area by three Liberator (B24) aircraft – Operation Harling. They succeeded – for the first and last time – in persuading EDES and ELAS to co-operate, and the attack on the bridge was planned jointly. The bridge was heavily guarded and the republican Colonel Zervas, head of EDES, with Aris Veloukhiotis, the

Communist leader of ELAS, on 25 November led a combined force to attack the Italian sentries. The SOE team laid and detonated the explosives with complete success (Hamson, 1946; Myers, 1955; Woodhouse, 1975). Myers's team, of whom Woodhouse was one of the only two officers who knew the country and spoke Greek, had been briefed in Cairo to carry out this important demolition and then (except for Woodhouse and one other officer) to move north-west to the coast of Epirus where they were to be picked up by submarine and withdrawn. Unfortunately, the submarine sortie was cancelled by the Navy owing to other operational needs, so the SOE Harling mission had to stay in Greece indefinitely, without having been briefed for a long-term liaison mission to the rival resistance groups. They were able to send radio reports of a highly complex and confused situation, but except for Woodhouse they had been selected and trained for a demolition project, not for military-political liaison. Woodhouse proved to be well qualified for both. Early in January 1943 Myers was sent new instructions from SOE Cairo to co-ordinate and develop the activities of the *andartes*. By July, after long negotiations, he and Woodhouse got first EDES and then ELAS to sign a 'national bands' agreement, to operate against the enemy under orders from Middle East Command.

The next major event arose from the Allied strategic deception plan before Operation Husky, the invasion of Sicily in July 1943. The Allied commanders decided on the need for a cover plan to divert two German divisions or more away from Italy, including Sicily, into the Balkans. For this purpose Greek resistance was encouraged by SOE to attack enemy communications in Greece so as to create the impression that the Allied landings would be in Greece not in Italy. Post-war evidence shows that the German forces in Greece, and indeed the German high command itself, were convinced that an Allied landing was imminent on the west coast of Greece with guerrilla support (Auty and Clogg, 1975, p. 125). This cover plan, Operation Animals, included another successful bridge demolition on the Salonika–Athens railway at the crossing of the River Asopos, somewhat south of the Gorgopotamos. It was timed after a German armoured division had crossed on its way south to the Peloponnese and the demolition effectively closed the line for four months. The SOE British team handled the Asopos project without any direct participation by ELAS, who ignored a request to co-operate.

Early in 1943, when reports from Myers disclosed a complex political scene, Leeper, the British Ambassador to the King of the Hellenes, demanded that an officer chosen by him, Leeper, for his knowledge of Greece and sound political sense should be attached to the SOE mission to ELAS under Myers and Woodhouse. This was Major David Wallace, an admirable choice, whom I saw in London in 1943 and again in Cairo in January 1944, shortly before he was for the second time dropped into Greece. He was unfortunately later killed in action, a tragic loss.

On 10 August 1943, Myers and Wallace were brought out of Greece by an air pick-up operation at Neraida in Thessaly organised by the Royal Air Force in conjunction with SOE. The same flight brought out six resistance leaders, headed by Tzimas of ELAS but including two non-ELAS men, for discussion on future resistance plans. At the last moment the ELAS representation was increased from one to four on their insistence. There was some failure of communication about the composition of the party (though pick-up operations usually involve some degree of improvisation depending on who is physically available at the landing strip at the right time). Leeper and King George II of the Hellenes and his ministers complained that they had not been consulted. At that time SOE signals were seriously overloaded and in arrears and there was an unquestioned failure in communication. Tzimas and his colleagues at the first meeting in Cairo demanded representation in the exiled government and an undertaking by the King not to return to Greece unless specifically invited by a post-war government after the taking of a plebiscite. The King refused and appealed for support to Churchill and Roosevelt, who were heavily engaged in Quebec on other important matters and were embarrassed and incensed against SOE for its part in this imbroglio. SOE were blamed for bringing delegates to Cairo with drastic proposals without proper preparations. No doubt Tzimas and his colleagues (or at least his three ELAS colleagues, since two others were non-ELAS) had intended to cause confusion in Cairo, or to exert pressure on the royal government to strengthen their own position and achieve left-wing dominance. No doubt Myers had failed to anticipate the political mischief which was intended. But equally there can be no doubt whatever that, if this demonstration of Communist-inspired anti-monarchism had not taken place in September 1943, it would have occurred on some other occasion before the final outbreak of armed hostility by ELAS against British liberating forces in Athens in December 1944. Wood-house in 1973 said: 'I do not think it can be disputed that the episode of the resistance delegation made civil war certain' (Auty and Clogg, 1975, p. 144).

So the Greek delegation flew back empty-handed and resentful to occupied Greece in mid-September 1943. By that time the crucial Italian armistice had been announced. ELAS succeeded in capturing most of the arms, equipment and supplies from the Italian forces in Greece surrendering under the terms of the armistice. They then turned to overt civil war and attacked republican EDES, with every intention of imposing Communist control on Greece. EDES sur-vived by withdrawing into north-west Greece, where General Zervas had strong connections; but, although they survived and lived to see the day of liberation, they were outside the main stream of events until January 1945, when British forces under General Scobie stood firm against ELAS. General Plastiras, to whom in exile EDES had looked as their political head, then became Prime Minister.

The consequences of the Cairo delegation affair in August 1943 on the top echelon of SOE were severe. In Cairo Lord Glenconner was forced to resign; Brigadier Keble, a controversial but dynamic figure, was re-posted to regular army duties. Brigadier Myers was, at the insistence of King George and Leeper, forbidden to return to Greece but Woodhouse was confirmed as his successor as head of the military mission. In London Sir Charles Hambro resigned and was succeeded by General Gubbins with H. N. Sporborg as his deputy. This was the third successive annual August reorganisation of SOE Cairo (now called Force 133).

As late as 23 January 1944 Sir Orme Sargent at the Foreign Office minuted: 'The truth of course is that the whole guerrilla movement in Greece has been largely fiction created by SOE to justify a vast expenditure of money and raw material in that country.' Foreign Secretary Anthony Eden himself, who was normally no defender of SOE, wrote against this passage: 'I really think that this is an exag-geration' (Myers, *Greek Entanglement*, 1955, p. 73). The Foreign Office in March 1943 had been arguing for 'a suspension of SOE activities in Greece and making a constructive effort to build up our official policy'. But the Middle East Defence Committee in reply said that they regarded 'the sabotage which Myers has organised and continues to direct in Greece as an important element in our plans. We believe that it is effectively disrupting the flow of enemy reinforcements and supplies and materially facilitating the eventual reoccupation of Greece' (Auty and Clogg, 1975).

A picturesque and unusual project was carried out in Crete in April 1944. The German divisional commander General Kreipe was captured by two SOE British liaison officers with the Cretan guerrillas, Leigh Fermor and Moss. Wearing German uniforms they ambushed his car and drove it successfully through several German control posts into the mountains. Thence by forced marches they took him to the south coast, where they had a rendezvous with a submarine which took them to Alexandria. The operation should have had a depressing effect on German military morale in Crete. But Sweet-Escott (1965, p. 98) heard long after the war from a friend in Hamburg who had been on the General's staff in Crete that the General was not popular, and that when the news of his kidnapping was announced in the officers' mess, a shocked pause was broken by one of his brother officers saying, 'Well, gentlemen, I think this calls for champagne all round.'

In September 1944 the Germans withdrew from mainland Greece and suffered some harassment from ELAS and EDES, though without any major results. A small British occupation force under General Scobie landed at the Piraeus in December 1944. They found that ELAS were for the second time trying to seize control of the entire country, in spite of a Soviet mission's advice in July that Greece was regarded as a British sphere of influence and that Russia would not support ELAS in anti-British military action. ELAS's threat was serious, because it might mean a demand for Allied reinforcements from Italy at the expense of the build-up for the final campaign to liberate north Italy in the spring of 1945; Churchill with Field-Marshal Alexander and his British political adviser, Harold Macmillan, flew to Athens to arrange and enforce a solution. General Plastiras was in their mind as a middle-of-the-road candidate who should be acceptable both to the monarchists and ELAS, as well as EDES, for whom he was virtually patron saint. It was agreed in January 1945 that Plastiras would become Prime Minister and that the King would not return without a plebiscite in his favour. Instead Archbishop Damaskinos would be regent in his absence. It was also agreed that the guerrilla forces would surrender their arms, but needless to say ELAS did not scrupulously observe this condition, and, as a result, spasmodic civil war lasted at least until 1947.

The military contribution of the *andartes* was marred by the overweening political ambitions of the Communist Party, the KKE, working through EAM. KKE did not shrink from civil war in enemy-occupied Greece or from hostile action against the British liberating forces in December 1944. Colonel Woodhouse, with unique personal knowledge of the subject, said, 'My conclusion would be that [Greek] resistance had no very great importance in the history of military operations in the Second World War; but in the political history of the war years, resistance is and should be an integral element, not only in the history of Greece but in a much wider context too' (ERM, 1960). Certainly the military contribution of Greek resistance was not in the same order of magnitude as resistance in France or Jugoslavia, but it did tie down a number of enemy divisions; and the substantial nature of its military contribution is assured by two operations alone, the Gorgopotamos bridge, Operation Harling, and the diversionary programme 'Animals' in support of Husky. It is worth noting that the military value of both these operations was realised not in Greece itself but elsewhere, namely in North Africa and in Sicily, one of many illustrations of the proposition that the military value of resistance must be appraised on a global basis.

The tragic climax of December 1944 had its roots in at least five causes. First was the King's insistence that he would return to Greece after the end of hostilities without waiting for a plebiscite, a posture that he abandoned only at the end of 1944, when it had already contributed to the outbreak of civil war. Secondly, the intensity of the Foreign Office commitment, shared up to a late stage by Churchill, to support the royalist cause, almost without regard to the hostile reaction from most of the population in occupied Greece. Thirdly, the confusion and conflict between the two elements in British policy; the military need for supporting Greek resistance so as to divert enemy divisions and to create strategic deception; and the political objectives first of supporting the King and later of at least preventing a Communist take-over by EAM/ELAS against the wishes of the overwhelming majority of the population. These two elements, which might well be called two policies, separate and almost incompatible, really implied a conflict between the Foreign Office and the military, meaning the Middle East Command and the chiefs of staff. But these two, who ought to have fought the issue out between them, somehow combined to belabour SOE as the scapegoat (Sweet-Escott, 1965, p. 175). One may observe without irreverence that the confusion was increased by the fact that Churchill, with all his power and prestige, was from understandable motives supporting the two conflicting policies at the same time (Sweet-Escott, 1965, p. 160). Fourth was the general failure to understand that the organisation of resistance in an occupied country produces political problems as an unavoidable by-product. It is useless and meaningless to instruct an external organiser to abstain from all political activity, because political aspirations, especially freedom and independence, are the main driving forces which turn the wheels of resistance. Fifth was the failure of SOE, notwithstanding the intelligence and experience of Lord Glenconner and the drive and forcefulness of his chief of staff, Brigadier Keble, to secure the support of the military against the hostility and invective of the diplomats.

Albania

Albania, with a largely Muslim population of a little over one million in the nineteen thirties, was the most backward country in the Balkans. There were two main racial groups, Ghegs in the north and Tosks in the south. In 1940 the only appreciable natural resources were copper and chrome, both of which were important to the German wartime economy. In 1924 Ahmed Zog, with support from Jugoslavia, had become king and thereafter he had made some modest economic progress in developing the country. He went into exile when the Italians invaded in April 1939, and Italian forces used Albania in the following November as a base for the invasion of north-west Greece, where they met a sturdy resistance. Hitler came to the help of Mussolini, and the Greek army's stubborn defence delayed Nazi plans for a month, which probably prevented the capture of Moscow in the winter of 1941. No resistance movement in Albania played any part in this vital strategic delay. Hitler no doubt only switched his divisions into Greece and Crete because of the British attempt, courageous but ineffective, to get another foothold in Europe in support of Greece, Britain's only remaining European ally at that time.

SOE inherited through Section D a small organisation based on Belgrade for studying Albania and preparing for action, if Italy, the occupying power, should become an enemy, as she did in June 1940. The Balkans being assigned to Middle East Command, an officer with Albanian experience was established in Cairo, Major Cripps, a former instructor of the Albanian *gendarmerie*. Colonel F. Stirling, with similar Albanian experience, was located in Istanbul to keep contact with Albanian exiles and sources of information. Belgrade ceased to be a base for SOE activities in Albania after the Nazi invasion in April 1941, and it was only in early 1943 that SOE missions in north-west Greece were available to receive and forward an SOE mission moving overland into southern Albania.

At the end of 1941, an Albanian Communist Party was formed in the south, in the Tosk area, under the leadership of Enver Hoxha, a tough young Comintern trainee from Moscow, who in 1981 is still President of Albania. He followed the standard Communist pattern of establishing an essentially Communist-dominated national liberation movement, disguised as a popular front, controlling an armed resistance movement or guerrilla organisation. Following on a large and well organised meeting at Peza in September 1942, Hoxha founded Levisiya Nacional Clirimtare, or LNC, the Albanian national liberation movement, and in due course a partisan movement was built up under its political direction. At about the same time the more conservative leaders in the country, seeing the revolutionary danger of the LNC as a long-term influence, set up a rival national front, the Balli Kombetar (BK).

In July 1943, Abas Kupi, a Gheg chieftain from the north who had resisted the Italian invasion of 1939, promoted an agreement for co-operation between the two rival movements. This development was short-lived, partly no doubt because the Italian armistice in September resulted in the LNC capturing large quantities of Italian arms, ammunition and supplies.

The first SOE mission, headed by Lt-Colonel W. MacLean (not to be confused with Brigadier Fitzroy Maclean, who headed the British military mission to Tito) and Major Smiley, had already entered Albania from northern Greece in April 1943. They established contact with LNC in the Tosk areas of the south, and later with BK and Abas Kupi in the north, and followed the usual policy of supporting and arming any party which proved to be engaged in active hostilities against the enemy. Some arms, ammunition and gold coin were parachuted in both to LNC and to BK. At this date, however, and up to the end of 1943, no air supply bases in south Italy were available, and supplies from North African bases were on a limited scale. Lt-Colonel W. MacLean was withdrawn in November 1943 for consultation in Cairo, and a senior SOE mission was dropped into Albania late in 1943, headed by Brigadier E. F. Davies with Colonel

A. Nicholls as second-in-command. They were soon overtaken by disaster in January 1944; Davies was captured by Albanian collaborators and spent the rest of the war in a German prisoner-of-war camp. Nicholls escaped but suffered frostbite and died from exposure. Previously one of General Gubbins's personal staff officers, he was posthumously awarded the George Cross for valour.

MacLean and Smiley, with Julian Amery, returned to Albania in April 1944, this time to Abas Kupi's area. Their SOE mission directives were to reorganise and give guidance to the various British liaison officers operating in the north and to try to bring LNC and BK to resume co-operation against the enemy. The latter task proved impossible, since LNC was obviously encouraged by the success in Jugoslavia of Communist-controlled Partisans to go all out for taking over the country when the Germans withdrew, as they did in September 1944.

The fall of Mussolini in July 1943 and the Italian armistice of September 1943 led to the surrender and disarmament of at least five Italian divisions in Albania, most of whose arms and equipment fell into the hands of the Communist-led LNC. The Germans reacted swiftly to the Italian defection. They took over the key areas, Tirana the capital, the coastal belt of Valona, Durazzo, Scutari, the chrome mines and the main lines of communication. Pursuing the guerrillas to the mountains, they took the usual reprisal measures, burning villages and killing civilians.

Albania cannot be regarded as a success for SOE, though several British liaison officers distinguished themselves in conditions of great difficulty and hardship. There is an obvious difference between the success (or failure) of SOE as a British organisation and of a resistance movement as such. The failure or relative failure of SOE was due to the impact of a rival subversive organisation, the Comintern, which in the person of one well-trained national organiser, Enver Hoxha, got into the act sooner and succeeded in capturing the major share of Italian arms and equipment at the Italian armistice in 1943. The Communist partisan aggression against the BK, who became penned into shrinking areas in the north, forced SOE and its missions, in the absence of any prospect of Allied regular forces landing in Albania, to withdraw progressively. It involved abandoning some good friends and allies, many of whom were executed by the LNC. The sad process is well described in Amery's *Sons of the Eagle* (1948).

The German withdrawal from Albania in 1944 was of course the result of the Red Army advance through the Balkans and not due to the resistance activities of either LNC or BK. On the political side it is interesting to note with hindsight that the post-war Communist government under Enver Hoxha, always hostile to Western democracy, has likewise been hostile first to its Communist neighbour in Jugoslavia and then to the USSR. Abas Kupi, who tried in vain to promote national unity in 1943, escaped in 1944 to Italy and died many years later in the USA.

Jugoslavia

Jugoslavia, land of the South Slavs, had been created in 1919, an important outcome of the First World War, which had started at Sarajevo in July 1914, following the Serbian assassination on 28 June of the Austrian Archduke Franz Ferdinand. The former kingdom of Serbia with the principality of Montenegro was one of the 'Allied and Associated Powers' in the First World War; but the rest of Jugoslavia was made up of fragments of the defeated Austro-Hungarian Empire. It was an uneasy multi-racial and multi-religious state, including Catholic Croats and Slovenes, Muslim Bosnians and Orthodox Serbs, dominated by Serbs under a Serb monarchy. At the outbreak of the Second World War in September 1939, the ruler was Prince Paul, regent for the young King Peter II, whose father, Alexander, had been assassinated by Croatian terrorists while on a visit to France. Paul, once described by Churchill as 'an amiable and artistic personage', was Anglophile but overawed by the Nazi Reich, and by the annexation of Austria in 1938 the Reich became an immediate neighbour to the north.

Unknown to the royal government and to the British (Deakin, 1971, p. 20), the Comintern in Moscow had built up secretly in Jugoslavia a strong underground Communist network, which could be, and in fact became, the nucleus of a well-organised resistance movement. It was headed by an experienced Croatian Communist, who had been in Russia at the time of the Bolshevik revolution in 1917, named Josip Broz, alias Tito, known in the Comintern in Moscow as Walter, and an active international organiser of support for the Republicans in the Spanish Civil War. Jugoslavia had had no diplomatic relations with the USSR until after the German–Soviet pact of August 1939, but after this a Soviet legation was established in Belgrade with, no doubt, an NKVD section in contact with the underground Communist party. But Broz/Tito/Walter received no orders to organise resistance in Jugoslavia until after the German invasion of the Soviet Union in June 1941.

Jugoslavia had some importance for Hitler's plans for expansion to the east because the Danube flowed through her territory on the way to Rumania, Bulgaria and the Black Sea. Moreover, control of Jugoslavia would open the road to Greece, though this only became an important factor after token British forces had moved into Greece in March 1941. A passive role as a subservient neutral was probably all that Hitler really needed, but on 25 March 1941 he intimidated the royal government headed by Cvetković, the Prime Minister, and Marković, the Foreign Minister, into adhering to the Tripartite Anti-Comintern Pact. This provoked an army *coup d'état* supported by the Serb patriotic clubs and acclaimed by the Serb population. A new government was set up under King Peter and General Simović (previously the Air Minister) as Prime Minister. This brave collective act of defiance was regarded by Hitler as a threat to the southern flank of Operation Barbarossa, then in an advanced planning stage. Within three weeks Jugoslavia was overrun and Belgrade was occupied after heavy bombing which caused over 10,000 casualties. The King and General Simović escaped by air into exile in London.

SOE had been subsidising the Agrarian Party, headed by Gavrilović who strongly supported General Simović and, along with the service attachés, had been encouraging patriotic elements in the armed forces. Apart from that element SOE had no claim to have had a direct hand in the *coup*. It was a spontaneous explosion of Jugoslav independence, reckless of the consequences, led by air force officers under Simović's deputy Mirković. Simović personally took no part in the *coup* but alerted the British Air Attaché, who was enabled to telegraph the Air Ministry in London a few hours before it occurred. Hinsley (1979, p. 370) summarises the position, 'that they [army and air force officers] had joined forces with the dissident political parties owed something to encouragement from the British Attachés and the SOE'. Section D, one of SOE's precursors, had built up a small organisation, based partly on the British legation in Belgrade and partly on British commercial enterprises. The leading British-owned company was Trepča Mines, controlled by the Selection Trust Group, whose chairman Alfred Chester Beatty was a staunch supporter of SOE. Two Trepča mining engineers, D.T. Hudson and S.W. Bailey, later played prominent roles during the enemy occupation. The head of the SOE Belgrade office was Tom Masterton, an experienced old Balkan operator since the First World War. He was supported in March–April 1941 by George Taylor, then Chief of Staff to the head of SOE, but seconded to strengthen the team in Jugoslavia at the crucial moment, a well-timed decision.

The SOE team in Belgrade had been planning sabotage on Danube shipping and enemy shipping in Adriatic ports. Their staff were fortunate to escape with the British diplomatic staff towards the Adriatic, where they were all captured by the Italian invading forces, moving up from Italian-occupied Albania. After a period of enforced residence in Italy, the diplomats were all released as a gesture of goodwill by the Italian Foreign Minister, Ciano. SOE staff members found their way back to London or to new assignments in the Iberian Peninsula or North Africa.

Colonel Draža Mihailović, Chief of the General Operations Division of the General Staff, had been personally known before the invasion to the British Military Attaché and had an excellent professional reputation (Auty and Clogg, 1975, p. 285). He took to the Serbian mountains in April 1941, where he soon gathered together small bands of soldiers and Serb patriots, who called themselves Chetniks after the nineteenth-century Serb resisters to the Turks. Numerous right-wing or anti-Communist units in various parts of the country took to the hills and also called themselves Chetniks. Some of them but not all owed allegiance of some kind to his central headquarters, but there is little evidence that he ever exercised effective control over many of them, either militarily or politically. His policy was to get from Britain (or any other source, even including the Italians) as much support, finance and arms as possible; to conserve them until the end of the war was in sight and to husband his resources on behalf of the Serb people to fight the Communist Partisans; and to refrain from active guerrilla warfare or acts of sabotage against the Germans, so as to avoid massive reprisals against the Serbs. In 1941 an early massacre of some 2000 Serbs at Leskovac as reprisal for some Communist Partisan activity confirmed him in his conviction that it was his duty to protect his fellow Serbs from extermination. The policy of conserving resources until liberation was in sight was at times favoured by groups in other countries, for example Milorg in Norway, but it was not, however, a policy which suited Allied strategy since it was passive and contributed nothing to tying up enemy occupation forces. Major Rootham, British liaison officer with the Chetniks in eastern Serbia from May 1943 to May 1944, says (Rootham, 1946, p. 103) that the ultimate causes of failure of the Chetnik resistance movement were the Chetniks' pretended willingness to carry out acts of resistance which they would actually only do if massive support was foreseen. He considered that the British criticism of the Chetniks for following a policy of lying doggo until the decisive moment came was inconsistent with the policy considered right for France, Poland and Norway. This view is somewhat over-simplified since in those three last named countries substantial programmes of sabotage and other forms of resistance were carried out as well as the long term build-up of secret armies.

SOE staff dealing with Jugoslav affairs tended to be on the Serbians' side because those in charge had had business connections with the Serbs in the inter-war period and knew them best, and also because 'there was a scarcity of British specialists informed on Croatian affairs especially in SOE ...' (Auty and Clogg, 1975, p. 286). Moreover, the royalist government-in-exile encouraged support of Mihailović and his Chetniks, who were Serbs and right-wing orientated.

After the occupation in April 1941 the Nazis divided Jugoslavia into three categories: the annexed territories – Slovenia divided and annexed in parts to Germany, Italy and Hungary; some Adriatic and Serb areas annexed to Italy or Italian-occupied Albania; south-east Serbia occupied by Bulgaria – the independent state of Croatia governed by Ante Pavelić and his right-wing USTASA forces and a truncated Serb State which included Belgrade. The Nazis appointed as head of the Serb State administration General Milovan Nedić. He had begun to organise a State Guard, a *gendarmerie* or a defence force for security purposes, sometimes also called Chetniks, and had secret contacts with Mihailović, to whom of course he was well known. There was also another Chetnik organisation, existing from pre-war days, headed by Kosta Pecanać, who soon after April 1941 had collaborated openly with the occupying powers.

In August 1941 there were growing rumours in the Balkans and Istanbul that guerrilla warfare had broken out in Serbia, the first such rumours in the Second World War. This was exciting news and it seemed inherently probable, given the historic independence and courage of the Serbs and the wild mountainous country.

SOE Cairo persuaded the British admiral in Alexandria in command of the eastern Mediterranean to provide a submarine from Malta to land in the Gulf of Kotor in Montenegro two royal Jugoslav officers, Ostojić and Lalatović, briefed by royal government officials, not by SOE, with a Jugoslav radio operator. At the last moment a British SOE officer, Captain Hudson, was added. He was a tough South African mining engineer from Trepča Mines, fluent in Serbo-Croat, who had worked for SOE before the German invasion, sabotaging enemy ships in Dalmatian ports. His orders were to contact all groups resisting the enemy, regardless of race, creed and political outlook. He had little briefing but there was virtually nothing known in Cairo or even in neutral Istanbul, apart from the rumours of guerrilla warfare coupled with mentions of Colonel Mihailović. For Hudson, this was to be the beginning of a long mission, from which he finally emerged in March 1944 in southern Italy where I saw him on arrival; and he was destined to be at different times attached to both sides in a bloody civil war. For eighteen months the only British officer in Jugoslavia, he commanded the respect of both sides, though naturally each suspected him of taking too sympathetic a view of the other. Although adventurous and astute, he found himself in deep waters, as indeed anybody would have done under such circumstances.

The joint mission, codenamed Bullseye, of the royal government and SOE landed safely and had an interesting journey on the way to Mihailović's headquarters. They radioed to SOE Malta that they had been picked up by an unknown guerrilla group on the coast, led by Colonel Arso Jovanović and Professor Djilas. On 6 October Hudson received orders by signal from Cairo to 'move as fast as possible to Serbia, as Mihailović was signalling messages *en clair* and urgently needed safe cyphers'. On 16 October, Hudson reported that the Communists were well organised and leading an action in Montenegro, and wanted everyone to unite in the resistance fight, but 'national elements were standing on one side and waiting'.

Hudson then left Montenegro for Serbia, accompanied by Ostojić and three Communist Partisan leaders, Jovanović, Djilas and Bačić, whilst Lalatović and the operator stayed behind with the radio sets. They reached Užice, the Communist Partisan headquarters, on 25 October 1941. Hudson there met the Partisan leader known as Tito and discussed a radio link to Cairo. He did not conceal from Tito that his orders were to proceed to Mihailović's headquarters at Ravna Gora. Soon after Tito and some of his senior advisers came over for a talk with Mihailović, but the latter refused to invite Hudson to be present at their meeting, which was obviously unproductive. Tito later said to Hudson he had 'nothing against the Old Man [meaning Mihailović] personally, but the Jugoslav officer corps as a whole was compromised'.

The internal position was complex and fluid. Mihailović's Chetniks, predominantly Serbs, though looking to the exiled royal government, were willing to collaborate with the Italians to obtain arms and supplies or with the puppet Nedić and his *gendarmerie* for joint action against the Communist Partisans, possibly even with the Croatian USTASA.

But after the end of 1941 there was no serious prospect of Mihailović's Chetniks co-operating with Tito's Partisans, although sometimes it suited Mihailović to maintain – in communications to London or Cairo or to Hudson – that he was trying to do so. It later became clear from Ultra and other decrypt sources that the Nazis continued as late as 1943 to look on the Chetniks as enemies and London-orientated although at times they also seemed willing to collaborate. One should remember that in any resistance movement there are secret contacts with the occupying power, often through the medium of double agents, and that Tito's Partisans themselves certainly used such methods.

Mihailović resisted or ignored Hudson's pleas for united action with the Communist Partisans against the German and Italian invaders. He felt fortified by the presence of Ostojić and Lalatović on behalf of the exiled royal government, confirming his hope that he was their legal representative in occupied territory. The hope was officially fulfilled when in 1942 he was appointed Minister of War in the exiled government, a position which he held until 1944 when he was dismissed by the royal government under British pressure. In spite of Hudson's efforts, fighting between the guerrilla groups broke out in November 1941, at first only in western Serbia, but inevitably destined to spread and widen throughout guerrilla areas. Hudson had supplied Mihailović with a code for communication with Simović via Malta. Hudson had his own code but he enjoyed neither the use of a radio set – the original operator had deserted to Tito – nor the facility of seeing or controlling Mihailović's communications.

In November 1941 the Chetniks received one air sortie from Malta, dropping one token supply of money in gold coins. Hudson had recommended that no arms or other supplies be sent to the Chetniks until they had accepted the principle of united resistance and a joint command. Under pressure from Simović on the Foreign Office in London there were some exchanges between London and Moscow designed to get Moscow to influence the Partisans to co-operate with the Chetniks. At the same time in London Churchill had ordered that 'everything in human power should be done to help the guerrilla fighters'; and Eden had written to Simović urging a united front of all patriots and congratulating Mihailović on the understanding which he had (wrongly) claimed to have reached. But, even if a united front had been formed, external aid on any scale was virtually impracticable at that stage of the war. Air bases were remote in Tripoli or Malta, the latter under heavy German air attack. Supply-dropping aircraft with trained crews were few; landing of stores by sea was impossible from Alexandria or Malta without major naval escort, and moreover Italian land forces held the coast.

The name of Tito, though early known to Mihailović and from October 1941 to Hudson, does not seem to have been heard in Cairo or London until late 1942, not even under any of his many aliases: Engineer Slavko Babic, Engineer Kostanjic, Tomanek or Walter. By late 1941, however, Tito now appears to have been the undisputed leader of his Communist guerrilla fighters, who, in all wartime literature on Jugoslavia, are known as Partisans with a capital 'P' in contradiction to the Chetniks, who were never even referred to as partisans with a small 'p'. Tito's Partisans proceeded to concentrate in Užice in western Serbia, a town which contained a rifle factory and a printing press, two rare and invaluable assets. Tito was in radio contact with the Comintern in Moscow and protested against the favourable build-up which Moscow radio, like the BBC, was giving to the Chetniks. Hudson, in one of his signals to Cairo, reported that he had attended a Chetnik–Tito Partisan conference and that the latter insisted on keeping their identity in any joint arrangements. The Chetniks had stressed serious shortage of ammunition. Tito's Partisans were at present stronger than the Chetniks, and considered that the people had lost all confidence in their former army officers as they thought that they had been responsible for the national collapse. Hudson also thought that Tito's Partisans would continue to fight the Chetniks unless they combined on Partisan terms.

At the end of November 1941 the Germans launched an attack against both Chetniks and Partisans in west Serbia. The Communist

Partisans were driven out of Užice west into the Sandjak. Hudson found himself with Tito and his staff, but later decided to rejoin the Chetniks. The Germans, however, encircled the Chetnik head-quarters on Ravna Gora, inflicted casualties and captured equip-ment and stores. Mihailović vanished with a few followers into East Bosnia, later into Montenegro and the Sandjak. Hudson became a solitary figure in peasant costume, who wandered for several months in western Serbia, cut off from the outside world.

In April 1942 Hudson, having survived a winter of intense hard-ship, succeeded in rejoining Mihailović at his new headquarters in Montenegro, where a strong Chetnik organisation had been built up by local leaders. During that summer there was some restoration of radio contact with Cairo or Malta, and twenty-five air sorties were made to the Chetniks from North Africa. Hudson still had no set or operator of his own. Communications were uncertain until the end of August when a British officer with two radio operators and improved sets were parachuted into the borders of Montenegro to handle signals traffic on a secure basis both for Hudson to SOE Cairo and for Mihailović to London.

Hudson had reported in July 1942 that the Chetniks were not undertaking any military activities and were increasingly set on obtaining political control through their Pan-Serb supporters. But Hudson was constantly exploring ideas for a revival of a true national resistance movement and planning acts of sabotage in areas where reprisals could not be taken. SOE Cairo, having as yet no direct contact with Tito and his Partisans, were still concentrating on ways to build up the Chetnik movement as the main force, and BBC broadcasts continued to give it propaganda support. The Chetniks already believed, rightly as events were to prove, that Italy would soon collapse and that they could then secure large quantities of Italian arms and equipment which could be used to defend at least Montenegro from the Germans.

As a result of loss of radio contact with Hudson for several months, SOE Cairo mounted three missions early in 1942 to trace Hudson and Mihailović and to make contact with any remaining resistance groups. One of these missions was headed by Major Atherton, a former journalist with a good Jugoslav background; he established radio contact with Cairo and was escorted to the head-quarters of the Communist Montenegrin staff, whose senior per-sonality, Milutinović, was later suspected of having him murdered.

Atherton was then taken to see Tito and Velebit and tried to discover evidence of Chetnik collaboration; he then disappeared and was never seen again. Tito was for many months thereafter fearful that the British authorities had refrained from sending him a liaison mission because of suspicion that Atherton had been killed by his Partisans. Tito was hoping for the arrival of a Soviet military mission in response to his repeated requests to Moscow, and he failed to realise that the Soviets could not provide air sorties because the Red Army had by now retreated almost to the Volga and great distances were involved. Tito did not get a Soviet mission until 1944, when Anglo-American forces had liberated southern Italy and its air bases and had provided the USSR with a suitable aircraft, the C47, which operated from Bari.

Whilst the Atherton scenario was being enacted, Tito was under heavy German attack and had to move his headquarters several times, ending up in Montenegro, where he was confronted by a dangerous combination of Italians in the town and valleys and Chetniks in the hills. He then decided to break out to the north-west where discontent had created a climate favourable to the growing local guerrillas. It is now known (Deakin, 1971, pp. 169–71) from Tito's own published archives that by April 1942 Tito had come to believe that British plans and policies were to intensify differences between his Partisans, the Chetniks and others to the point of civil war. He thought that after the collapse of Italy, the British would land forces on the Dalmatian coast and pose as liberators, and that to achieve these ends the British would land missions all over the country, ten having already arrived.

SOE Cairo, conscious of their failure to understand what was happening, sent in December 1942 to Mihailović a senior SOE mission under Colonel S. W. Bailey, a Trepča mining engineer with long Jugoslav experience. Bailey was a high-powered executive with good background on Jugoslav politics and a keen sense of policy issues. The mission's directive was to report on the military value of the Chetnik movement, to persuade their leader to undertake active sabotage operations, and to advise on how to implement the policy of creating a united resistance front. On arrival by parachute, Bailey spent several days in talks with Mihailović and Hudson. He then visited the immediate areas under Chetnik control and prepared a summary of his own impressions and of Hudson's past experiences. These were radioed to Cairo in a series of reports, leading to a

proposal for a territorial division of the warring resistance movements. His proposal was in effect to create two independent re-
publics, Western Croatia for Tito's Partisans and Serbia for the
Chetniks. He thought that Hudson ought to be the British emissary
to Tito 'who both likes and respects him'.

The Bailey territorial proposal was disliked by the Foreign Office
and the War Office, where opinion as to the best policy was not
unnaturally divided. In the first half of 1943, nine British missions
were dropped to Chetnik areas in Serbia. Their reports direct to
Cairo were mainly unfavourable. One mission organised an attack
on Danube shipping but was unable to persuade the local Chetniks
to attack the important BOR copper mines. Several members of
these nine missions were captured and shot by Bulgarian troops or
captured by Serb collaborationists and handed over to the Nazi
forces.

Whilst London remained pro-Chetnik, pro-Mihailović and pro-
Serb, despite these groups' consistent inactivity and refusal to co-
operate, information reaching SOE Cairo suggested that some of the
other Jugoslav underground movements might be much more enter-
prising.

The chief of staff of SOE Cairo in 1942 and 1943 was Brigadier
C. M. Keble. He had been recommended to SOE by Middle East
Command as a regular officer of great energy and ability, with a
recent background in the intelligence branch in Cairo. He was not
personally known to SOE London, who however recognised the
need to accept as their chief operational officer in Cairo, under the
general direction of Lord Glenconner, Head of Mission since September 1942, a man who enjoyed the confidence of army headquarters. Keble had held a senior position in the intelligence branch and
so was on the restricted circulation list of the top secret intercepts or
decrypts of enemy signals traffic, now known under the code name
Ultra. Whether by accident or intentionally, he continued on that
circulation list when he joined SOE, who previously had not had
access to that important source. During January 1943 he was struck
by certain enemy signals traffic relating to German battles in Jugoslavia, mainly in Slovenia, Croatia and Bosnia, with left-wing Partisan
forces. Hearing that Churchill was coming to Cairo at the end of
January, he prepared a paper (FO 371/37579 at the Public Records
Office, Kew) summarising this intercept evidence and urging that
SOE be authorised to send missions to make contact with these

Partisan groups with a view to sending supplies and supporting them, regardless of their Communist affiliations, in their fight against the enemy. Captain F. W. D. Deakin, then a junior staff officer in SOE's Jugoslav Section, was an historian who had worked with Churchill before the war; he had a personal meeting with Churchill in Cairo and handed him this paper which, along with Basil Davidson, then head of the SOE Jugoslav Section in Cairo, he had helped to prepare. As a result, Churchill sent for Keble, approved the proposals in his paper and on his return to London circulated it to the chiefs of staff who in due course decided to allot additional Halifax bombers to SOE Cairo for the support of Jugoslav resistance (Davidson, 1980, p. 119).

This change in British policy involved abandoning exclusive support to Mihailović as representing the royal Jugoslav government and was naturally opposed by the Foreign Office and also by SOE London. SOE Cairo was divided between supporters of Chetniks and Tito's Partisans, but Keble, who had of course by-passed both the army staff and the Foreign Office representatives in Cairo by obtaining direct access to the Prime Minister, proceeded with plans for SOE missions to the Partisans. Keble was thus the moving spirit in a major change of policy which not only caused upheavals in Cairo and London, but affected the future of Jugoslavia for many years to come.

At the end of May 1943 Keble instructed Bailey, without consulting London, to inform Mihailović forcefully that he should move east into Serbia around Kopaonik and his area of command, to which alone air supplies would be sent, would be to the east of the River Ibar; but he must stop all collaboration with the occupying forces and instead he must attack enemy lines of communications. Keble then planned an official SOE mission to be sent to Tito, whose location was now known for the first time. As a preliminary to this mission, three Canadian Croats, recruited in Canada by SOE, were dropped close to Partisan regional headquarters in Croatia – Operation Fungus. Jovanović and Ribar from Tito's central headquarters happened to be visiting Croatia at the time and reported back to Tito the arrival of a 'British American' mission. Fungus established radio contact with SOE Cairo, who then dropped two British officers, Jones and Hunter, to the same area in Croatia and another mission to eastern Bosnia. Meanwhile the main Partisan forces were advancing through west Bosnia and liberating substantial though fluctuating areas. By now the Communist Partisans claimed to have an army of 150,000, with systems of communication and supply, and to represent a popular front against Fascism. The Middle East Defence Committee in a telegram of 8 June 1943 stated: 'The Partisans are now the most formidable anti-Axis element in Jugoslavia and our support for them is therefore logical and necessary' (Howard, 1972, p. 482). The Foreign Office strongly objected to this view; so did SOE London, Lord Selborne included. The Foreign Office recommended on 16 June no change in policy and the rescinding of Keble's orders for the Chetniks to abandon all territory west of the Ibar. The chiefs of staff disagreed and considered, 'He should supply Croatian guerrillas and Communist Partisans with war material, as these groups represent the most formidable anti-Axis elements existing outside Serbia.' After further exchanges of views in London, the chiefs of staff on 27 June informed Cairo that support for the Chetniks should be continued so long as they accepted the British directive, and the instructions to withdraw east of the Ibar should be suspended. They also said that the Partisans should be supplied with war material, but those operating close to the Chetnik areas should be required to give assurances that no operations would be carried out against the Chetniks except in self-defence.

In mid-May 1943, the Germans launched against Tito's Partisans 50,000 troops, including the First Alpine and specially trained Brandenburg and SS Divisions, with 40,000 Italians plus Croats and Bulgarians, a total of over 100,000 men. They had heavy air support and made good use of air supply for their outlying detachments in wild and often inaccessible country. Tito's plan was to move southeast away from the enemy but this move was blocked, and the prospect of encirclement in a barren mountainous zone with no supplies appeared imminent. He had, however, an alternative plan for break-out to the west and north, aided by diversionary attacks from Jovanović's fifth division in central Bosnia, which succeeded despite heavy losses.

Whilst the Germans' massive onslaught was being stemmed, the first British officers were dropped to Tito's headquarters, Captain Deakin of SOE and Captain Stuart. Stuart was killed by a bomb, which also wounded both Tito and Deakin but Deakin managed to push Tito into a foxhole and fall on top of him, thus saving Tito's life. Later Deakin, though wounded, sent to Cairo a series of illuminating messages which left no doubt of the military value of Tito's movement. This confirmed the knowledge already in the hands of Keble from Ultra sources from January 1943, but not known to SOE in London until later.

By the following winter the Mediterranean Allied air forces and SOE/OSS had set up their special operational bases with signals and packing stations in southern Italy, and now aircraft were able to operate into Jugoslavia from Bari. Bomber and fighter bases were also set up in other parts of Apulia from Foggia down to Brindisi. The Luftwaffe was soon swept out of the Jugoslav skies, and ceased to threaten south Italy. There was one bomber raid in December 1943 on Bari harbour, destroying an ammunition ship and seventeen other vessels; but this was the last enemy air raid. Naval bases were also set up in Apulia, and the island of Vis, two-thirds of the way across the Adriatic, was occupied by the Royal Navy. Now for the first time special operations by air and sea could begin to be carried into Jugoslavia on a massive scale.

Tito's Communist Partisans' prestige was greatly enhanced by their success in surviving the German offensive. The fall of Mussolini and the subsequent Italian armistice enabled both Partisans and Chetniks to capture large quantities of Italian rifles and ammunition and they were now able to liberate considerable tracts of mountain area. Tito established his headquarters at Jajce, fifty miles inland from Split, where he anxiously awaited Soviet military aid and supplies which had long been promised but never appeared.

In September 1943 SOE sent Brigadier Armstrong to Mihailović. Armstrong's mission was inevitably a total disappointment and before long in 1944 on his own recommendation his mission and other SOE officers with the Chetniks were withdrawn. The Americans continued to maintain with Mihailović their intelligence mission under Colonel McDowell (OSS) and a number of liaison officers with other Chetnik units to help rescue and return to Italian bases USAAF fliers who had been shot down after bombing missions against targets in the Reich. The Allied (mainly British) decision to discontinue support to the Chetniks aroused strong feeling in certain American circles. During the post-war trial of Mihailović in Belgrade in 1946, a commission of enquiry was set up in New York, and several of the five hundred US airmen saved through Chetnik efforts gave evidence in New York on his behalf.

Brigadier Fitzroy Maclean was dropped near Jajce in Bosnia in September 1943 as head of the British military mission to Tito. A former Foreign Office official who had served in Moscow before the war, he was a friend of Randolph Churchill and had the status of personal representative of the British Prime Minister. He detested SOE, with whom he had clashed violently in Cairo following his appointment in London by the Prime Minister. His account of this episode given to a conference in London in 1973 shows SOE Cairo, especially Brigadier Keble, in a bad light, but as the top echelon of SOE Cairo was drastically reorganised soon after, it is a noteworthy prolongation of a feud for over thirty years (Auty and Clogg, 1975). His achievements in Jugoslavia were impressive and his combination of diplomatic experience with a knowledge of the USSR and Russian made him well suited for the post. One SOE officer (Hamilton-Hill, 1973) wrote that 'his astonishing personal drive and amazing ability to deal with the most stratospheric levels of command have already been described in *Eastern Approaches*, his own fascinating account of the campaign'. He insisted that his mission was no part of SOE but that he was directly responsible to Middle East Command in Cairo, later to AFHQ, Caserta, with a personal direct line to Churchill in London. His mission, which included British liaison officers (selected by him, not SOE) attached to Tito's headquarters and to Partisan regional and local units, continued to have the benefit of the SOE supply and signals organisation (now beginning to operate on a large scale, both in Western Europe and the Far East as well as the Mediterranean) and the SOE air operation section and the packing and despatch stations developing at Bari. He had as chief of staff a first-class officer in Colonel Vivian Street, and to Street must go much of the credit for good military relations with the Partisans.

The winter of 1943 saw the progressive eclipse of the Chetniks and an increase in the activities and influence of Tito's Partisans. They were now being supplied by sea and air by the Allies, mainly the British, for the Allies dominated the air space over Jugoslavia, the Adriatic and southern Italy.

Early in 1944, with General Stawell, I studied the relative advantages of locating our new SOE Mediterranean headquarters at Caserta or at Bari. We were advised on good authority that the great *palazzo* of Caserta already held a combination of British and American War Office, navy and air ministries, plus Foreign Office and American State Department officials, so that there was no space left except on the fifth floor, and that on the fifth floor we should be just as remote from the first floor as if we were on the other side of the Apennines. This proved to be sound advice. So we set up Special Operations Mediterranean headquarters at Mola di Bari on the coast between Bari, where the air base was for the Balkans and Italy, and Brindisi, which had the principal air-supply base for Greece and Poland and later also for Italy. By the summer of 1944 our headquarters were running a non-stop airborne operation into the Balkans, north Italy, and, up to August, Poland. The greatest tonnage of stores and number of 'bodies' in and out was for Jugoslavia.

Because of the scale of special operations by the middle of June 1944, a new air headquarters was established at Bari called Balkan Air Force, under Air Marshal Sir William Elliot. Balkan Air Force co-ordinated all special operations with SOE, including supply-dropping sorties to Italy, the Balkans, Poland and Czechoslovakia. It also co-ordinated bombing operations – tactical as opposed to strategic – over the Balkans, including Jugoslavia, plus fighter sup-port for resistance movements, of which the largest and nearest was Tito's Partisans, and co-ordinated the coastal raiding actions of Land Forces Adriatic and naval units. The extent of these and other operations in terms of tons and stores, numbers of personnel infil-trated and exfiltrated by air and sea in the Mediterranean theatre (not merely the Jugoslav figures after the formation of BAF) will be found in Appendix E1, which were prepared at SOM head-quarters by Q.Ops Department at my request shortly before I left the Mediterranean in August 1945.

The establishment of Balkan Air Force at Bari was a great success, partly because it was conceptually sound, partly because of two outstanding RAF officers in Air Marshal Elliot and his second-in-command, Air Commodore Sinclair. They had to be tactfully discouraged from trying to take over the SOE operational machine, which always presented irresistible temptations to intelligent and ambitious officers of the regular armed forces. That done, relations were good. But the most spectacular – and least publicised – opera-tion of all was accomplished with remarkable speed, daring and success shortly before Balkan Air Force came into existence. At the end of May 1944 the Germans launched their offensive in a final bid to capture Tito, his headquarters staff and the liaison missions – British, American and (since February 1944 under General Korneyev) Soviet.

One evening a German Fieseler Storch light reconnaissance aircraft was circling round Tito's headquarters' site near Drvar; Vivian Street, who in the absence of MacLean was in command of the British mission, had the instinct and intelligence to recognise the prelude to an early attack. He persuaded Tito to move the whole of his headquarters a mile or two. At dawn a day or two later, German paratroopers were dropped on and round the site which had been vacated. With this brief start Tito, Street and the US mission and Soviet General Korneyev and their respective staffs were just able to get away a few jumps ahead of the enemy. They were hotly pursued for three days, at the end of which they found themselves at a possible but untried air landing strip. Shortly after noon Street signalled *in extremis* to the SOE/RAF base in Bari, giving their map co-ordinates and requesting a pick-up operation for about one hundred men. Before midnight on 3 June 1944 they had all been successfully brought back to Bari airfield by C47 aircraft of a USAAF squadron, operating from Bari under RAF command.

General Stawell and I, warned that this operation was in progress, drove into Bari half an hour before the estimated time of arrival, mainly in order to meet Tito for the first time. Arriving at the airfield we found that the one Soviet aircraft, a US C47 made available under the Lend-Lease programme and based at Bari under RAF command, had had an independent signal from General Korneyev's mission, had taken off without orders and without waiting for the US squadron to be lined up ready to go, and on landing in Jugoslavia a few minutes ahead of the squadron had picked up Tito as well as the Russians, on the pretext that the Anglo-Saxons would never arrive in time before the Germans captured the landing strip. On arrival at Bari, the Soviet C47 taxied to a far corner of the airfield, where a staff car provided for the Soviet mission was waiting to take them to the Soviet mission's villa. 'Walter' had come home to his masters; or so it seemed, but history from 1948 onwards shows that this would have been a premature judgement.

The vast number and scope of the airlifts from southern Italy into the Balkans was only possible because General Ira C. Eaker USAAF and Air Chief Marshal Sir John Slessor RAF, the air commanders-in-chief, arranged for US C47 Dakota transport and troop carriers to be used for the first time for special operations. Though slow and unarmed, they could operate over the Balkans now that the Luftwaffe was seldom seen. By using Dakotas for special operations, whenever feasible, the air forces were left free to carry on with their normal bombing functions with bomber aircraft. Dakotas were well able to land and take off on airstrips only roughly levelled; this made it easier to transport heavier and bulkier equipment, such as vehicles or guns, and meant that on return journeys many thousands of wounded and sick Partisans could be brought back to Italy for hospital treatment.

Tito, having been brought out to Italy by Anglo-American efforts, wished to get back to Jugoslav territory as soon as possible, concealing that he had ever had to leave his country. So the Royal Navy took him by night to the island of Vis, which was Jugoslav territory and also an advance base for air and naval operations, as well as an artillery school for Partisan gunners. Enemy radio services would obviously soon detect from the growing volume of signals traffic that there was a new Partisan headquarters on Vis, so I asked our signals people to devise a signal deception plan by despatching a radio operator by air to one of the Partisan brigade headquarters with instructions to operate his set heavily on regular schedules. This would give the enemy signals service the impression that Tito, whose whereabouts they were most eager to establish, was still in Jugoslavia and had joined up with one of his subordinate headquarters. Before long, enemy aircraft started to overfly the area and the local Partisan commander soon interpreted the situation correctly. So our radio operator was forbidden to operate his set and had to return to base. But the deception worked for a time.

The final stages of enemy withdrawal from Jugoslavia were now in sight. A concerted attack on enemy communications, Operation Ratweek, was planned and carried out by the Balkan Air Force and the British military mission with the Partisan high command. An important new move was the Partisan drive into Serbia under Koca Popović, the Chetnik movement having dwindled as a result of inactivity; some of the senior Chetnik commanders were actually deserting to the Partisans, starting with Djuric in May 1944. Mihailović himself was captured in 1945 and tried and executed in June 1946. A tragic figure, he pronounced his own much quoted epitaph in giving evidence at his trial: 'I wanted much, I began much, but the gale of the world swept me and my work away.'

In October 1944 Belgrade was captured from the Nazis by combined efforts of the Red Army and the Partisans. This event marked both the triumph of Tito and the end of guerrilla warfare in Jugoslavia. During 1944 Tito had visited Italy for talks with Churchill and Field-Marshal Alexander about relations with the royal government and co-operation between Allied forces and his Partisans. He had also visited Moscow for talks with Stalin about the Red Army's role which, on Tito's insistence, was defined in an agreement as 'temporary for the purpose of defeating Hitlerite Germany'.

At the Churchill–Tito talks in Caserta, proposals had been made for Dr Ivan Subašic, Governor of Croatia, to join King Peter's government in London to try to negotiate a coalition or compromise government with Tito pending elections after the final liberation of Jugoslavia. Predictably this last effort by the British Government to help its courageous ally of April 1941 was destined to end in frustration. But, following a mention in the communiqué of the Yalta Conference between Churchill, Roosevelt and Stalin in February 1945, Tito announced in Belgrade that he had formed a new united government with Subašic as Minister of Foreign Affairs. There were six other members of the former royal government in various posts, but naturally with the key positions in Communist control.

In the history of resistance movements, in their organisation and direction, their methods of equipment and operation, Jugoslavia was unique. Historically it lay on the frontier between Teuton and Slav. In the 1940s it became the westernmost outpost of Soviet Communism. The dominating feature of the Partisan movement was obviously Tito, a many-sided figure, with practical army experience in the First World War, revolutionary experience in Russia, clandestine training by the Comintern in the USSR, underground activity in Jugoslavia in the Thirties, leader, controller and organiser with rare independence of mind and a fantastic endurance and survival capacity.

Tito's Partisan resistance movement was also unique in Europe, because it was based on a pre-war clandestine organisation whose members were professionally trained in security measures and methods of secret communication. The para-military detachments and brigades in the mountains knew little or nothing of the clandestine cells or networks in the towns and cities, including the cellar in Zagreb where Kardelj and his men maintained radio contact with Moscow. The Chetniks, picturesque amateurs by comparison, had nothing like this background and no hope of becoming a successful nationwide resistance movement. Tito's headquarters clearly had a good working radio network for communication with subordinate headquarters who reported progress over the air and received orders in a way which worked, even though their codes and cyphers were broken and read by the Germans.

The most striking feature of Tito's Partisan movement was its ability to secure arms, ammunition and supplies in the country, before it became possible to deliver large tonnages by air and sea from external Anglo-American sources, and before the Italian surrender. The Communists were conscious of the necessity of secure domestic arms sources as early as 1941 when their occupation of Užice included the benefit of its rifle factory. Since Užice had not only a rifle factory but a printing press, the Partisan occupation for some time after September 1941 would seem to have been the result of intelligent planning and no accident.

The Communist Partisan movement was highly developed and efficient before Deakin was first dropped to Tito's headquarters in May 1943, hence neither SOE nor Brigadier MacLean's mission took part in creating or organising that movement. But, because of its maturity and efficiency and the scale on which it operated and other geographical and military features which were present from September 1943 onwards, the British contribution to air supply and air support and improved communications was on a scale unequalled in any other country. The apportionment of credit between the British, the Americans, special operations, military missions and the air forces would provide an interesting study but it is a secondary matter. Not surprisingly, however, many British liaison officers returning in 1944–5 from Balkan countries 'liberated' by the Red Army were depressed to see their wartime efforts to free the local people from Nazi oppression go awry as the Communists took over. To those many officers who came to SOE headquarters at Mola di Bari, or later to Siena, for debriefing we could only give consolation and hope that their achievements would not be without influence on the course of future events. In the case of Jugoslavia, Tito's 1948 break with Moscow was at least a partial fulfilment of those hopes.

In three decades since 1945 controversy has continued on both sides of the Atlantic about right-wing Chetniks and Communist Partisans and the British change of policy in switching support in 1943. When did SOE and the British service departments first become aware that serious resistance to the occupying power was coming from Communist guerrillas called Partisans and only nominally after 1941 from Chetniks? When did they realise Tito's identity and his location? In a discussion in 1973 (Auty and Clogg, 1975) George Taylor (ex-SOE) said that by July 1942:

'Everybody in London, SOE, the Foreign Office and Chiefs of Staff all knew that practically all the fighting in Jugoslavia was being done by Partisans. But SOE were still working under a clear directive, that the policy of HMG was to support the Royal Jugoslav Government and Mihailović its Minister of War . . . It was Glenconner [head of SOE] who began to get the idea in about October/November [1942] that we ought to make contact with the Partisans. Thus the idea developed in Cairo of backing both horses, continuing to support Mihailović in his limited area but making contact with the Partisans. This, though discouraged from London at the beginning, was finally approved . . . Keble decided this was going to be an important development and he was going to hang on to it for SOE. Later when you [MacLean] came on the scene I am quite sure, knowing Keble as I did, that he simply made up his mind to stop your entry.'

Fitzroy Maclean in the same 1973 conference (Auty and Clogg, 1975) put the question thus:

'Through Hudson SOE first made contact with Tito and the Partisans in September 1941; the enemy certainly knew all about the Partisans, whom they were fighting; how then did the most effective resistance movement of World War II remain practically unheard of and certainly unhelped for about two years? It is disturbing that for almost two years a number of people should have been able . . . to suppress vital information and so prevent action being taken.'

Earlier, Maclean quotes Churchill as saying to him in London in the summer of 1943:

'He had begun to have doubts about Mihailović's contribution to the war effort and wanted to know more about a shadowy figure called Tito whose Communist Partisans seemed from enemy intercepts to be operating on a considerable scale in Bosnia, Montenegro and elsewhere.'

It appears from Davidson's, Deakin's and Seton-Watson's recol-

[125]

lections that intercepts or decrypts of enemy communications first became available to SOE Cairo in about January 1943 when Keble received them, probably because he had been on the limited circulation list when in military intelligence in Cairo. The first SOE mission to the Partisans in Croatia was Fungus, dropped in April 1943, and Deakin himself was dropped to Tito in May. The two-year delay which Maclean alleged was in theory only from the end of October 1941 to the end of May 1943, namely less then twenty months, and in fact much less because Hudson was out of communication with Cairo from November 1941 till summer 1942. It should be remembered that, in spite of SOE's prolonged support of Mihailović under British Government direction, it was SOE Cairo (Glenconner in November 1942, then Keble in January 1943) who first had the idea of contacting and supporting the Partisans, obtained Churchill's approval and sent Deakin in on his mission to Tito.

British supporters of the Chetniks ask similar suspicious questions about the reason for British abandonment of the royal Jugoslav government in favour of the Communist Partisans. How did it come about that Mihailović's rational pro-Serb policy of conserving his resources, making use of easy-going Italians, when he could, and fighting the Partisans, who threatened to overwhelm him and ultimately did, was misrepresented as a policy of collaboration with the enemy and refusal to co-operate with the British in Cairo? What other policies or practices could he be expected to follow when he received only token supplies of arms and equipment from British sources, and was forced to get what he could from the Italians? One answer, which I have had from more than one former colleague with strong pro-Serb and anti-Communist feelings, is that from 1942 there was a growing left-wing element in SOE Cairo's Jugoslav Section (including the able Klugman, a well-known British Communist in post-war days) supported by like-minded elements in other organisations, who suppressed from reports to Middle East Command or to London the favourable news about Chetnik activities and on the contrary built up the case for support to Tito to a point which led to a major change of British policy. But, even if this theory were well founded, it must be outweighed by the massive success of Tito's Partisans which, later if not sooner, was bound to justify Allied support.

A similar line was taken in the USA in post-war years, largely because of the good work by the Chetniks in rescuing and evacuating to Italy some five hundred US airmen shot down over Jugoslavia. A volume, *Patriot or Traitor?* (Martin, 1978), records proceedings of a private commission of enquiry set up by a New York based 'Committee for a Fair Trial for General Mihailovich', after the court in Belgrade had refused to hear the US evidence at the General's trial for treason in 1946. The evidence submitted to the commission in New York included depositions by well-known British liaison officers attached to Chetnik missions about Chetnik attacks on German and Bulgarian forces in 1943, and claims that, although Chetniks certainly arranged accommodations with certain Axis forces in their own interests, the Partisans did likewise, and that any Chetniks who collaborated with the Germans were quisling guerrillas not under Mihailović's command. Statements were also collected saying that there were no Allied witnesses of the Chetnik attacks on the occupying forces in the summer of 1941 and that Hudson's reports on them had been destroyed in Cairo when Rommel reached El Alamein and many other documents were destroyed. There was also testimony by US officers attached to General Mihailović that he had a great hatred for the Germans and never indicated any sympathy with them. Many Americans continue to believe in the thesis of an ally betrayed, and are critical of their own government as well as the British authorities.

The tangled history of 1941–4 will be the subject of passionate disputes long after all the participants are dead. British policy from the Nazi bombing of Belgrade in April 1941 until Deakin's drop to Tito's headquarters in May 1943 was based largely on loyalty and gratitude to the royal government. Was its loyalty misplaced because of Mihailović's insistence on saving Serb lives rather than sacrificing them on the altar of Allied strategy? Many will continue to say that loyalty to friends is never misplaced and should override all arguments of mere self-interest. Some may theorise that, if Tito and his Partisans had never existed, the Chetniks could have become a respected name in the list of European resistance movements, even if they bided their time until Allied liberation forces were in sight. If so, could Belgrade in 1944 have been another Warsaw when liberated by the Red Army? Few, I hope, will endorse the Maclean innuendo that SOE deliberately suppressed vital information and for almost two years prevented action being taken to help the Partisans. All will agree that the Partisans were a ruthlessly efficient movement which (jointly with Allied deception planners under Brigadier Dudley

Clarke) made a great contribution to Allied strategy by tying down twenty or more enemy divisions. Tito himself had good reason to be grateful to the British and to the Americans for his personal survival, first when Deakin of SOE pushed him into a foxhole in May 1943 and both were wounded; secondly when Street of the British military mission forecast the German airborne attack on the Drvar headquarters in June 1944, and thirdly when the Allied air forces saved Tito and his staff from capture.

8

North Africa and Italy

North Africa

In 1942, the first year after America had become a belligerent, the Allies were under pressure from Moscow to open a 'second front' in the west and thus take some of the Nazi pressure off the Russians on the eastern front. It was soon seen to be impossible to make an opposed amphibious landing on the continent of Europe at such an early date, when American forces had not yet begun to be mobilised, trained and equipped on any scale. Throughout the summer of 1942, intense study was given in London and Washington to all possibilities, including an Allied landing in North Africa. To some extent such a landing could be deemed to constitute a 'second front' in the west and it might open the way to a subsequent Mediterranean offensive against Italy, with possibilities for subsidiary landings in the south of France or the Balkans. There were also two further important advantages to be gained from an Allied landing in North Africa: first, it would bring French overseas territory and many Frenchmen back into the war on the side of the Allies, and it would also clear enemy forces, especially air forces, out of the Mediterranean, which could thus be fully reopened to Allied shipping.

Since 1940, after the Italian entry into the war, and especially after January 1941, when German bombers reinforced the Italians in their Sicilian bases, Malta, then the key British naval base in the central Mediterranean, had been under constant air attack. By 1942, it was no longer possible for convoys from Britain to the Middle East to pass through the Mediterranean, even with strong naval escort. They had to be routed round southern Africa and the Red Sea to Alexandria, an immense drain on scarce shipping resources. Thus the elimination of enemy air bases in Sicily, whether by bombing or invasion from North Africa, would have a high priority and was alone a sufficiently powerful strategic argument for invasion.

After the fall of France in June 1940, French North Africa, comprising Morocco, Algeria and Tunisia, came under the control of the Vichy government. The British, fearing that the French fleet, a large part of which was then at the port of Mers-el-Kebir near Oran, Algeria, might fall under German control, demanded of the French Admiral Gensoul certain measures with several alternatives. They included sailing to Alexandria in Egypt to be immobilised, or to French ports on the west of the Atlantic, such as Martinique. Failing this, the Royal Navy would be bound to immobilise the French fleet by bombardment. After consulting Vichy but without mentioning the alternative of sailing to Martinique, Admiral Gensoul, refused all the alternatives. The British, after final warning notice, bombarded the French fleet, inflicting heavy damage and over 1400 casualties (Marder, 1974, pp. 233–52). This action was ordered and directed by Churchill personally. It caused bitter resentment in French naval circles and in French North Africa generally and was exploited by Vichy for propaganda purposes. British consular representatives were withdrawn from French North Africa and so the nearest British official posts were the legation in Tangier, the fortress of Gibraltar and the embassy in Lisbon. My London directive in December 1940 for SOE activities in Lisbon specifically mentioned collection of information from French North Africa, including contacts with an SOE representative then being sent to Tangier (under cover of the expert tea dealer whom I have mentioned before); and contacts with Gibraltar, where another SOE mission would always be based.

In April 1941 I had a visit in Lisbon from a Greek, Nicholas Souliotis, who was living in Rabat, which was the headquarters of the Resident-General, then General Weygand, responsible to Vichy for the government of Morocco, Algeria and Tunisia. Souliotis, obviously experienced in military intelligence, was security minded to an impressive degree. Although I had a series of talks with him he never went further than admit that he came with the authorisation of somebody '*au prés de la Résidence*'. He wished to explore the possibility of Anglo-French staff talks: British officers should come by submarine to a rendezvous near Rabat, but in American uniforms; complete secrecy must be maintained. I pointed out the impossibility of Britain undertaking a major landing in North Africa while fighting alone, but of course reported it all to London with special care for cypher security. I tested his integrity and his influence in Rabat by asking him to rescue and despatch to the United States Vagliani, Tarchiani and Cianca, three important anti-Fascist Italians of the Giustizia e Libertá movement, then living under false names in Casablanca. Eventually I heard from Washington through London that the three had arrived, all of whom were helpful in wartime and most important politically in post-war Italy. It was a security risk to disclose their names and addresses to Souliotis but it was worth taking. Later he went back to Rabat and I did not see him again until I met him by chance in Paris in 1946 as Greek Military Attaché. Nothing came of our talks in 1941, but I was told that they were a useful confirmation both to SOE London and to the War Office that in spite of general anti-British sentiment in French North Africa, there were still persons in high places who were looking forward to better days.

Two of my adroit SOE colleagues in Tangier, well known socially and often to be found in the local casino, were later given the task and necessary funds to lose heavily to El Glaoui whenever he came to the tables. El Glaoui was the most important character in Morocco; he was the Pasha of Marrakesh and virtual sovereign of the Berber tribes, who inhabit the Atlas range from the Atlantic to Tunisia. He lived a full life and was one of those whose income was never sufficient for his tastes. My colleagues' ploy was, of course, transparent after a time, but the Pasha's lifelong devotion to Britain was fortified with useful results.

In the Second World War Tangier was an international zone surrounded by a belt belonging to Spain, called Spanish Morocco. Because of its international status, Tangier was a great currency centre and British services made use of it for essential but secret purposes. SOE, doubtless not exclusively, was responsible for purchasing out of secret government funds currencies for other departments, including the War Office, MI9 and the Air Ministry, to help escaping prisoners of war and shot-down pilots. The Spanish Zone, being part of Spain, was subject to the virtual veto on special operations imposed by the British Ambassador in Madrid, Sir Samuel Hoare. Tangier was different, though usual standards of discretion and security applied, perhaps even more strictly, since the secret services of all the belligerents spied on each other in the courtyard of the El Minzah Hotel and elsewhere.

Late in 1941 it was discovered that in a house in Tangier belonging to the German Consulate on the cliff facing out to sea there was an infra-red station set up to guide U-boats through the Straits into the Mediterranean. Reconnaissance showed that this house was guarded to prevent any outsider discovering this unneutral and unconsular activity. Personnel of the SOE mission recruited and trained a suitable local operator and provided him with two plastic explosive bombs with four-minute time fuses. Operation Falaise was successfully carried out in January 1942, and the house and signalling equipment were blown up. Rumours were circulated, apparently with some success, that the Germans had blown themselves up in error. The Tangier police immediately suspected the local head of SIS, who was, of course, entirely innocent. But the German services, rightly suspecting that the explosives had been smuggled into Tangier from Gibraltar, retaliated by placing a bomb of their own alongside the next British diplomatic bag on the quay, resulting in an explosion with numerous casualties. Operation Falaise must have saved incalculable tons of Allied shipping in the Mediterranean and must have protected from submarine observation and reporting major troop movements such as the Allied landings in November 1942 and the invasions of Sicily and southern Italy in 1943.

Although Britain had no diplomatic relations with the Vichy government either in France or in North Africa, the Americans had an embassy in Vichy and a team of twelve United States vice-consuls under Robert Murphy in North Africa. Officially they were there to supervise the distribution of cotton, sugar, tea and petroleum from the United States and to see that these did not fall into enemy hands. The Americans also had an Arab expert, Colonel William Eddy of the United States Marines, in Tangier. All these people helped to supply information through a clandestine radio network which was established by or with help from SOE and which linked Casablanca, Algiers, Tunis and Oran with Tangier and Gibraltar. They were also able to advise on the chances of the French co-operating, if the Allies should decide to land. Robert Murphy visited Washington in August 1942, after the landings had been given the go-ahead by President Roosevelt, and said that he thought the French would co-operate with the landing forces if there were no Gaullist or British participation. But British participation had already been planned. It was among other things to be the first combined action by OSS and SOE.

The first OSS officer to be based on the mainland of Europe was Colonel Robert A. Solborg, who was posted to the US Embassy in Lisbon under the cover of Assistant Military Attaché in February 1942. I was in the British Embassy under the same cover till June 1942, and much of our time was taken up with ideas and contacts

useful or necessary for a North African operation. Other preparatory work was initiated by my colleague Hugh Quennell in
Gibraltar, Colonel William Eddy and my colleague Edward Whar-
ton-Tigar in Tangier. On one occasion, Quennell and Eddy came to
Lisbon for a joint conference with Solborg and me on North Africa.
Solborg, a brilliant man of Russo-Polish origin, had previously been
in North Africa in 1941, officially on business but primarily to
enable the US War Department to contact elements who might be
willing to resist German penetration or even domination of North
Africa.

At one stage Murphy, supported by Eddy, put to Washington a
project by the Lemaigre–Dubreuil group to organise a rebellion in
the French colonial army and set up a pro-Allied government in
French North Africa. But the US joint chiefs of staff and State
Department did not favour it, nor did Donovan.

Murphy developed in the summer of 1942 a lead to General
Giraud, who had recently escaped from Koenigstein, a German
prison camp; in Murphy's opinion he was the one Frenchman who
might get France back into the war. At about the same time – and
I believe independently – Solborg developed the same idea. He told
me in June 1942 (my last week in Lisbon) that he planned to go to
Casablanca to contact another general, whom he later disclosed to
be General Bethouard, who had close links with Giraud. I said
to Solborg that I knew he was forbidden by his chief, Donovan, to
visit North Africa while Assistant Military Attaché in Lisbon,
because he had been in North Africa the previous year in a civilian
capacity and his visit would arouse comment and speculation. He
replied that he had cleared it with Intelligence at the War Department and that he was sure he could fix it with Donovan. He went
there, contacted Bethouard and established a line to Giraud, but was
later dismissed by Donovan for disobeying orders. This was an
exception to the general rule (Harris Smith, 1972, p. 6) that 'insubor-
dination became a way of life for OSS officers, but Donovan was
unconcerned'. After the war, Donovan and I were then co-operating
on some legal matters in Eastern Europe and I told him that I always
regretted he had sacked Solborg, one of his ablest officers, for having
played, even though against orders, a key role in a vital link in
Operation Torch, a crucial turning point in the war. His predictable
reply was that you lose confidence in an officer who knowingly
disobeys orders. Solborg continued in Lisbon as Assistant Military

Attaché on behalf of the American War Department till the end of the war; but after the expulsion of enemy forces from North Africa in May 1943, Lisbon lost much of its importance as an intelligence centre.

The SOE signals unit in Gibraltar played an invaluable role both in the preparatory work for the North African landings and the actual landings themselves. Regular schedules were maintained from Gibraltar with Tangier and Lisbon, as well as with the American vice-consuls in the main North African centres, and also with boats based on Gibraltar doing landing and pick-up operations on the south coast of France. The most important pick-up in that area was General Giraud, whose participation in the top command structure for Torch was considered all-important for securing the co-operation – or at least the passive non-resistance – of French forces in North Africa. The General's pick-up was organised not by SOE but by SIS under the personal direction of Colonel Sir Claude Dansey, in co-operation with the Admiralty and the US Navy. In November 1942, the US Navy had no submarine with any operational experience in the Mediterranean, so a British submarine had to handle the task. In order to maintain – for the sake of relations with the French in North Africa – the appearance of an American operation, a US naval officer, Captain Jerauld Wright, hoisted his flag, the first time in history that anyone but a British officer had been put in command of a ship of the Royal Navy. General Giraud was safely landed in Gibraltar and delivered to General Dwight D. Eisenhower's headquarters shortly before 8 November. He assumed that he was to be supreme commander and that Eisenhower would serve under him, and some time was taken up before he was persuaded to accept a less supreme title. Events were to prove that although he was a gallant and distinguished officer who had never collaborated with the enemy or the Vichy government, he had no political sense at all. He was a disappointment to his American supporters, who were critical of General de Gaulle and hoped that Giraud would create and lead a rival French movement both in North Africa and in metropolitan France. But Giraud soon faded into obscurity, outmanoeuvred by de Gaulle's superior skill.

Eisenhower's tactical headquarters staff arrived in Gibraltar less than two days before the Allied landings in North Africa. Murphy in Algiers was in touch with Gibraltar by clandestine radio, mainly

SOE, but his programme was upset by the change in plan over Giraud. Instead of coming direct from France to Algiers, Giraud was taken in his submarine to Gibraltar for two days' talks with Eisenhower on the command structure and his place in it. Murphy complained that OSS/SOE had assured Colonel Eddy in Tangier that deliveries of arms to French 'underground fighters would be made on isolated beaches in good time but he was convinced that the British SOE let us down because they had no confidence in our judgement or our French underground' (Murphy, 1964, p. 126). But Brooks Richards, then a member of SOE's naval section based on Gibraltar, tells me that he was conducting officer responsible for the landing of arms from a 400-ton naval auxiliary, *Minna*, commanded by a Royal Naval Reserve officer; that the rendezvous was some twenty miles west of Algiers, near Sidi Ferruch; that the ship went on each of the three appointed nights to a position seaward of the rendezvous, which was easily identifiable, but the light signals were never exhibited and *Minna* had to return to Gibraltar with her cargo. So SOE did genuinely attempt to deliver arms to at least one pro-Allied group in Algeria.

In Operation Torch, US forces crossed the Atlantic in convoy to land at Casablanca and Rabat on the Atlantic coast, and British forces, passing through the Straits of Gibraltar, landed on the North African coast at Algiers and Oran. During the early planning stages of Torch there had been some concern, especially in Washington, that enemy reaction might be violent and might even include invasion of the Iberian Peninsula and Morocco, which would threaten the supply lines of Allied forces landed inside the Mediterranean. It was therefore decided not to land forces further east than Oran, which in the event was ultra-prudent. Although Torch was a great naval operation, eight hundred ships converging from the United States and Britain on some twenty landing beaches on over a thousand miles of coast, the military resources available – little over 100,000 men – were so small as to make the whole operation risky and vulnerable. The ultimate geographical coverage was smaller than originally planned, as a result of the cancellation of a landing of 5000 men in Tunisia, but the speed and scale of the subsequent German reaction in invading Tunisia showed that the cancellation was prudent.

To sum up: North Africa, the scene of the first combined Anglo-American military operation of the war, was an area which had not been under enemy occupation. Therefore, unlike the later patterns in other countries, there was no resistance movement to be organised or supplied by SOE or OSS. There was only a small secret minority of French officers and civilians who were in favour of joining forces with the Anglo-Americans and were prepared to join a secret conspiracy with the Allied representatives. Consequently, the role of SOE and OSS in the preparatory work leading up to the Allied landings was limited to doing by secret undercover means those things which the regular forces obviously could not do for themselves. This meant making use of the only available British posts, the fortress of Gibraltar and the legation in Tangier, and making use of the invaluable local American asset, Murphy's network of vice-consuls. Thus SOE and OSS were responsible for setting up this network with the Allied headquarters, which for a brief but critical period was situated in Gibraltar, and for smuggling arms, equipment and supplies into Algeria and Morocco, mostly overland from Tangier, sometimes by sea from Gibraltar. After Operation Torch proved a success and the French in North Africa decided to co-operate, there was little for SOE and OSS to do there except to create and equip bases for operations into Italy and the south of France. However, SOE's role in the preparatory stage before the landings and in the provision of an established and efficient signals system during the landings was well recognised by the Supreme Allied Commander, General Eisenhower, and his staff. This experience of the value of special operations was to prove important in 1944 when Eisenhower became Supreme Commander for the much bigger cross-Channel operations into France and Belgium.

Italy

The Italians can be said to have had a resistance movement from 1922, when many reacted against Mussolini's march on Rome, and the murder of the anti-Fascist deputy Matteotti in 1924. Another anti-Fascist leader from those early days was Emilio Lussu, the Sardinian who made a spectacular escape from the prison camp on the Lipari islands in 1939. Lussu was a brave and brilliant operator, whom I was told to rescue from France where he was living under a false name. Without any action on my part he turned up in Lisbon with his wife in 1941. There we contacted him and after several talks we sent him to London where numerous plans for his role in resistance and the timing of his return to Italy were discussed, and his wife was trained as a radio operator. In 1945 I called on him in Rome, where he was a rather unsuccessful Minister of War Damage, and reminded him of our earlier meetings. 'Those,' he said, 'were happy days, those days of *clandestinitá*, when I could sleep at nights. Now as a Minister I am overwhelmed with insoluble problems, and sleep little.'

Of several anti-Fascist movements the Partito d'Azione, or Action Party, was the most prominent, including its offshoot the Giustizia e Libertá. In addition to the three leaders of the latter, whom I had asked Souliotis to rescue in 1941 from Casablanca and send to the United States p. 130, I had orders in Lisbon to find Pacciardi who had been head of the Garibaldi Brigade in the Spanish Civil War and was believed to be in Oran. I could not trace him, but he managed to get away from North Africa and proved to be an important political figure after the war when he became Minister of Defence.

One man, whom I came to know well in the last year of the war and afterwards, was Alfredo Pizzoni, who was also known as Pietro Longhi. When Italy entered the war in June 1940 he said to a close friend, 'This war will end with a revolution and I shall lead it' – an unexpected ambition for a banker. He became the Chairman of the central Committee of National Liberation of Northern Italy, the CLNAI, in 1944 and was disappointed not to be the first post-war Prime Minister, an honour and burden which fell to his friend and colleague Ferruccio Parri, but he was probably better suited as chairman of the Credito Italiano. Pizzoni was an outstanding man of exceptional strength, candour and good humour, trusted by everyone.

The Communist leader was Palmiro Togliatti, who had been for seventeen years a senior member of the Comintern in Moscow; he returned openly from Moscow to Italy in January 1944. Through the Communist network a number of left-wing partisan movements were built up in 1943, mainly in the industrial north. They were known as the Garibaldini; they had smartly appropriated the name of the nineteenth-century national liberation hero who, needless to say, would never have supported the cause of Communism. While some of the Garibaldini brigades certainly fought the occupying forces when opportunity offered, their major effort was to conserve their energies and ammunition for political post-war purposes. An officer of the OSS (which usually tended to support Garibaldini groups with more enthusiasm than would have been expected) reported, when dropped into north-west Italy, that the 'Garibaldini leaders were 20% for liberation and 80% for Russia' (Harris Smith, 1972, p. 115).

In the closing months of the war the Communist-controlled Greek resistance movements attacked the British liberating forces in Athens. After that lesson had been digested, the Allies took precautions to prevent the Italian Communist partisans from engaging in civil war or unseating the new democratic government of Italy. Nevertheless, after the war the Italian Communist Party became for many years the largest and strongest in Western Europe.

Unique in the Italian anti-Fascist movement was Count Carlo Sforza, who had been Minister of Foreign Affairs and ambassador to France before the Fascists seized power in 1922. He was usually derided by the Foreign Office in London, and Churchill's view of him as 'a foolish and played-out old man, incapable of facing let alone riding the storm' was perhaps affected by the Foreign Office attitude. On this judgement, Murphy's comment was, 'The description is harsh. The difficulty is that both of them wished to do all the talking' (Murphy, 1964, p. 201).

Fascist Italy had been oppressive and dictatorial, but had never touched the depths of brutality, mass murder and genocide achieved by the Nazis. So, in spite of a broad opposition to Fascism, mostly expressed in ribaldry rather than physical resistance, Italy did not have the same crusading spirit or moral outrage which in Nazi Germany seethed below the surface in substantial sections of the aristocracy and the officer class, among Catholic and Protestant, not to mention Socialists and Communists. Naturally, in both Germany and (up to the armistice of September 1943) Italy, there was a conventional moral deterrent to any loyal citizen joining a resistance movement, namely that he was being a traitor to his country in time of war. In Italy the armistice removed this deterrent, and from September 1943 onwards many fine Italians of all classes and backgrounds joined the various resistance groups. Although the groups varied from the right-wing Badogliani and Fiamme Verde to the left-wing Garibaldini, it was fortunate that the co-ordinating Committee for the National Liberation of Northern Italy, known as the CLNAI, was under the firm non-political guidance of its chairman Alfredo Pizzoni.

From June 1940 to the North African landings in November 1942, SOE's activities in Italy were mainly handled from Switzerland, the only adjacent neutral country. A highly competent SOE officer, Jock McCaffery, destined to operate from Berne for four subsequent years, passed through Lisbon in February 1941. I was able to arrange certain supply lines for him through a friendly diplomatic bag, until the south of France was occupied in November 1942. He established contact and good relations with most of the leading figures in the Italian resistance and was the main source of Italian information to SOE London.

The signing of the Italian armistice on 9 September 1943 transformed the background for resistance activities. SOE had played a modest but unusual role in the preliminaries, which started on 15 August 1943 when General Castellano, secret emissary of Marshal Badoglio, called at the British Embassy in Madrid. He was then sent to the Embassy in Lisbon to meet Eisenhower's Chief of Staff, General Bedell Smith, and Director of Intelligence, General Strong, who had flown up from Algiers, and Major Rosebery, the head of SOE Italian Section from London. At the end of the Lisbon meeting, the communications problems were discussed; and the SOE special radio set which I had installed in 1941 in the Embassy was handed to Castellano with the information that on returning to Milan he would find an SOE radio operator, Lieutenant Mallaby, in a certain prison, having been captured the previous week after being parachuted into Lake Maggiore. Two days later Mallaby, who had been roughly treated in gaol, was surprised to be taken to the Central Station, put into a first-class carriage with an armed guard and taken to Rome to Marshal Badoglio's office. There he was shown the radio set from Lisbon and told to code and transmit a signal to General Eisenhower. Thereafter he continued to handle all the armistice traffic between Rome and Algiers (Castellano, 1945, p. 123; Strong, 1968, p. 111). Strong records that this was only one of the many occasions that he received help from SOE and OSS in intelligence matters during the course of the war.

Before the armistice, SOE had made little progress in Italy beyond establishing contacts with anti-Fascist figures, such as Lussu, outside Italy and one or two self-styled resistance groups in northern Italy by lines of communication with Switzerland. At least one of these groups proved to be double agents run by Servizio Informazioni Militari, the Italian military intelligence network controlled by the general staff. The armistice made a great difference to SOE for it gave an impetus to resistance, which became a national cause and every Italian patriot felt that Italy had taken the first step towards national redemption. The main terms which affected SOE were an immediate cease fire by the Italian armed forces, the release of Allied prisoners of war, surrender of the Italian fleet, the delivery of Italian-occupied Corsica to the Allies as a base for operations and the recall to Italy of all armed forces abroad.

In September 1943, the Allies landed from North Africa at Salerno, south of Naples, and Montgomery's Eighth Army crossed the Straits of Messina from Sicily into Calabria. The armistice and the liberation of southern Italy up to and north of the line Naples–Foggia made it possible, starting from October 1943, to establish SOE bases, including packing stations and airfields, from Brindisi to Bari. At the same time a new SOE unit was created as No. 1 Special Force with headquarters at Monopoli to organise special operations in Italy and to bring help to the partisans who were beginning to emerge in the German-occupied territory in the north and centre. SOE is criticised, especially in Italy, for having been slow to make effective use of these bases for the development of resistance, but it takes months to bring supply bases into effective use, to establish contacts with resistance groups and arrange approved dropping zones and procedures for communication and reception. The Germans, who had naturally suspected that the Badoglio government was secretly negotiating with the Allies, reacted with their usual speed and efficiency. Several divisions, which had been earmarked in readiness, moved through the Alpine passes to take control of northern Italy and Rome and to reinforce the troops already prepared from Rome down through southern Italy to resist the anticipated Allied landings.

The infant resistance groups in northern Italy, composed of dispersed Italian soldiers, escaped prisoners of war and refugees from urban areas, were first identified and contacted by SOE, the American OSS and other Allied agencies, mainly through Switzerland. Then, before SOE could organise air transport from its new southern bases, small missions consisting of an Italian liaison officer with a radio operator were infiltrated overland from the south through the German lines. Their first objective was to appraise the quality and potential of various groups and report back, and the second to identify suitable dropping grounds for reception of arms and demolition material.

The first such liaison mission, 'Rudder', reached Rome, contacted resistance leaders and maintained radio contact with SOE Monopoli for over six months, providing valuable military and political intelligence. By November 1943, six liaison missions were operating with various emerging resistance groups, and over one hundred Italians were being trained as organisers and demolition specialists. SOE at Monopoli set up a radio station and training schools, on the lines of those in Britain, for training Italian organisers, radio operators, parachutists, guerrillas and saboteurs. By June 1944 some resistance movements in mountainous areas of north Italy were sufficiently advanced to permit the despatch of British and later American liaison officers in uniform to guide and train and organise. They would be needed for the final co-ordination of resistance activities with military plans, under directives to be issued through SOE and OSS/SO.

Two particularly effective and outstanding early Italian resistance groups with whom SOE had already established close relations in late 1943 were, first, the Otto organisation, which was based in Genoa, headed by Dr Balduzi, and operated in Piedmont and southern Liguria, being supplied by sea transport from Corsica as well as by air; and, secondly, the Franchi group headed by E. Sogno, a brilliant and fast-moving leader who operated in the north with four regional headquarters and a well-conceived organisation based in Milan.

Up to August 1944 SOE's No. 1 Special Force at Monopoli had trained and dropped some 150 Italian volunteers into the area between Rome and Bologna to act as instructors to the various partisan bands. Considerable success was achieved in harassing enemy communications, and enemy forces were diverted into defensive measures. But autumn 1944 found the Italian resistance movements in the north with a series of problems. Air supply was inhibited by bad weather and by lack of aircraft. At the same time pressure upon the partisans increased because the US 7th Army, under General Patch, had been removed from the Italian campaign to help with the invasion of southern France. The Overlord landings in Normandy and the Rastenburg attempt in July to assassinate Hitler and overthrow the Nazi regime, coupled with the Anvil–Dragoon landings in Provence, made it legitimate to think that by the end of the year the war might be over in Europe, or at least that the German forces might have withdrawn from Italy, except for the pre-Alpine region. Many contingency plans were made on those assumptions, and many of the Italian partisans tended to be over-optimistic and to neglect preparations for another winter in the hills. At the same time the special duty air squadrons had to be diverted to supply arms to the Poles fighting in the Warsaw rising: flying into an urban area mainly controlled by enemy anti-aircraft defences led to heavy losses of aircraft, pilots and specialist crews.

In November 1944 an unfortunate broadcast, made in the name of the Supreme Allied Commander in Italy, Field-Marshal Alexander, but not cleared with his staff or SOE or OSS, said that the Allied advance had been held up by winter conditions and the partisans were directed to abstain from any large-scale actions, to conserve their ammunition and to concentrate on providing military intelligence to prepare for the final offensive in the coming spring (Davidson, 1980, pp. 239, 240). This broadcast had an unduly depressing effect on partisan morale. During the winter, directives were issued to the partisans stressing the importance of 'counter-scorch' plans to prevent the enemy destroying power plants, factories and communications in the vital industrial areas of northern Italy as they withdrew. The Allies particularly urged the partisans to protect the port installations of Venice and Genoa, either by disconnecting or destroying any enemy explosive charges at the right time, or by firing on the German demolition units before they could detonate the charges.

These directives were passed to the para-military groups who assembled in the hills through the committees of national liberation which had been formed in the cities under the aegis of the main political parties, the Christian Democrats, the Action Party, the Socialists, Communists and liberals, all of whom worked together under the chairmanship of Alfredo Pizzoni, alias Pietro Longhi. After the liberation of Rome in June 1944, an Italian government had been set up with Ivanoe Bonomi as Prime Minister. The central committee of national liberation, CLNAI, wished to be recognised as the representatives of the new Italian government in the enemy-held territory of the north, for they felt that they had the best chance of controlling the various activities of the politically diversified resistance groups. This move was encouraged by General Raffaelle Cadorna who was parachuted into Lombardy in August. In November a CLNAI delegation came secretly via Switzerland to Rome and Naples for discussions with the new Italian government and at Allied Headquarters. The delegation consisted of Alfredo

Pizzoni, Professor Parri of the Action Party, Pajetta from the Communist Party and Sogno of the Franchi group from Milan. This delegation successfully negotiated agreements by which the CLNAI became the channel for political and military directions and the allocation of funds and equipment.

SOE Mediterranean's next task was Operation Herring, the parachute training of some five hundred Italian army volunteers, who were to be dropped behind the enemy lines in the Bologna area to attack enemy lines of communication. This operation was synchronised with the Allied offensive in mid-April. Properly trained and equipped, these volunteers were reported by 15th Army Group as a thoroughly successful unit, which materially assisted the ground offensive. By the beginning of 1945, numerous British liaison officers with previous SOE experience were dropped into strategic areas in north Italy to work with and direct the partisans. Two of them in particular, Colonel Peter McMullen and Colonel John Stevens, accepted the surrender of German divisions in Genoa and Turin in May 1945. This was a fine climax for Stevens, who had had five previous operational spells in occupied territory, two in Greece, two in France and one in Italy, and for McMullen, who had previously been in Greece.

Early in 1945, General Karl Wolff, acting commander-in-chief of the German forces in Italy, was seeking to negotiate a surrender to Allied Force Headquarters, independently of developments on the western front and the eastern front. By strange chance the same SOE signals officer, Mallaby, who had been involved in the Italian armistice traffic in September 1943, was parachuted into north Italy in March 1945 and again captured. With infinite panache he claimed to have a special message from Field-Marshal Alexander for General Wolff, to whom he asked to be taken. As a result of the interview Wolff was encouraged to get in touch with Allen Dulles of OSS in Berne, and this was the first step of the negotiations leading to the surrender of the German armies in Italy (Dulles, 1963). In April 1945 SOE's No. 1 Special Force estimated that the partisans took over 40,000 German and Fascist prisoners and liberated over a hundred towns.

In Italy the history of resistance therefore fell into three phases: up to the liberation of Rome in June 1944, which consisted of small-scale harassing and occasional diversion of enemy troops, plus help to escaping prisoners of war; then a second phase up to the liberation of Florence in September 1944, when direct attacks on specified road and rail targets took place and enemy troop movements were hampered by over one hundred and fifty trained Italian volunteers parachuted, between February and August, into central Italy between Rome and Bologna. The third phase was the winter of 1944, when communication was established with the CLNAI in Milan as the controlling authority of all partisans; CLNAI had a military organisation and chain of command, as well as a civilian organisation for handling finance and supply. This enabled a network to be created for distributing instructions coming through SOE and OSS channels based on directives emanating from the Supreme Allied Commander and including the important instructions on the 'counter scorch' programme to preserve power stations, railway bridges and other priority installations from enemy demolition.

Authoritative tributes to the military achievements of the Italian partisans are contained in two telegrams reproduced in Appendix C from the commanders-in-chief of German Army Group South-West in February and April 1945. For these I am indebted to Colonel Threlfall of Force 139, who obtained them in May 1945 from the files at German headquarters in Bolzano. They show through enemy eyes the recognition of the value of unified 'organisation' as ordered by the Allied High Command, the growth of 'commanding leadership of the partisans', the growing threat to vital lines of communication in February, which by April had become 'a large number of supply routes only usable in convoy' and to some extent completely in partisan hands. They also stress the continuous process of armament and supply by air and the increasing leadership of Anglo-American officers.

At the end of April, the Italian Instrument of Surrender was signed at Allied Force Headquarters at Caserta and came into effect on 2 May 1945, several days before the Instrument of Surrender in Northern Europe. General Gubbins, who was then in Italy, issued on 8 May 1945 an order of the day to all ranks at the headquarters of SOE (Mediterranean) and No. 1 Special Force as follows:

'The magnificent results achieved during April by the Allied armies in Italy have already taken their place in history. The Prime Minister in his message of congratulations to Field-Marshal Alexander described it as the greatest German surrender of this war, and this great victory has been won in spite of the repeated diversion of troops and equipment from the Italian to the western front.

'You will wish to know what part you have played by your work of organising, supplying and directing the Italian patriots behind the enemy lines. I cannot do better than repeat the words of Field-Marshal Alexander in his message (passed through your signals channels) to the Chairman of the National Liberation Committee in Milan:

' "Now that the campaign in northern Italy has ended victoriously, I would be pleased if you would convey to General Cadorna and all subordinate patriot commanders and units my admiration and gratitude for the successful part which they have played both in the destruction of the enemy and the preservation of installations and plants vital to the future life of Italy.

"I have noted also with particular pleasure the efficiency and speed with which the CLNAI has been able to turn from these military achievements to the equally important task of restoring in conjunction with my Allied Military Government officers civil administrations in liberated Italy."

'Field-Marshal Alexander personally told me yesterday of the important contribution that the Italian patriots had made to the success of his operations by their capture of many towns behind the enemy line and by the number of prisoners they had taken.'

This contemporary tribute from Alexander, one of the outstanding supreme commanders of the war, is conclusive and authoritative evidence of the value of the Italian resistance movement and its 'military achievements'. It received little publicity at the time, and his fourth and final report on the Italian campaign, published in 1951 and prepared, no doubt, by staff officers and historians with little if any first-hand knowledge, allotted to the resistance movement only a few lines out of sixty-six pages. Alexander's message, though not expressly limited to the final months of the Italian campaign, was naturally composed with that period in 1945 in mind, when all conditions were favourable to partisan action; adequate air support, numerous experienced Anglo-American liaison officers in the field, and the general conviction that victory was in sight. The earlier period from 1943 through 1944 had seen partisan action on a smaller scale but preparatory to the final build-up in 1945.

It is the essential nature of an organisation such as SOE that it operates by creating or encouraging the formation of other groups or movements, which it then seeks to supply and guide and influence in desired directions. It works through other groups or movements, which may be receptive or independent or even hostile. But it cannot in the nature of things work in its own name or proclaim its own achievements. The achievements of the Italian resistance movement in 1945 were the result not only of the work of organisation, training, planning and supply carried out in Italy after the armistice of September 1943; they were also the result of SOE and OSS experience, trial and error, in other countries over a long period. Much of the credit to British and American liaison officers in northern Italy in 1945 is due to experience they, or some of them, had gained in Balkan countries or France from 1942 to 1944.

9

France

Resistance movements in France during four years of enemy occupation were inhibited and encumbered by three overriding problems, two of which were constitutional: the signature of the 1940 armistice by a French government whose claim to be legally constituted was open to question; the doctrine of *légalité*; and the third a personality problem, the giant but forbidding presence of Charles de Gaulle.

The two constitutional problems impeded many patriotic, conscientious but confused Frenchmen from joining the Gaullist movement. For example, General Giraud, a gallant, patriotic, non-collaborationist, non-political officer escaped from a German prison camp, returned to unoccupied France in 1942 and immediately signed a declaration of loyalty to Marshal Pétain. 'Like many senior officers of the French army, he distrusted the resistance as revolutionary and the Gaullists as mutineers' (Howard, 1972, p. 148). The problem of *légalité* overshadowed the whole genesis and growth of French resistance. How different it would have been if the French Government had refused the armistice terms and withdrawn to French North Africa. There would have been a true government in a department of its own territory with its own armed services, at least in part, above all its own navy, able with British naval and air forces to keep open the Mediterranean sea lanes, and able to organise its own special operations to encourage and support a growing French resistance movement in metropolitan France. The population of metropolitan France (excluding Algeria, then legally a French department) would indeed have suffered total enemy occupation from July 1940, as they suffered in fact from November 1942, but even though the Nazi forces would have reached the Riviera in July 1940, two years and four months earlier than they actually did, France would have been spared the conflict of allegiance and the confusion caused by the doctrine of *légalité*. The problems created by Vichy,

Pétain and Darlan would not have occurred and there would have been no conflict of loyalty between the legalistic and timid supporters of a puppet regime and the courageous but rebellious supporters of a true France, which was a concept for idealists but juridically a non-event. But fate decreed otherwise.

The personality problem prevented de Gaulle himself from working constructively with Churchill and from having any relations at all with Washington until a very late stage. De Gaulle also suffered severely from the alleged indiscretion of some member of his entourage who was said to have leaked to Vichy the news of the planned assault on Dakar in September 1940. Although this leak is now denied or even disproved, neither Churchill nor the British chiefs of staff would trust him from then on with any operational secret. Roosevelt even rejected Churchill's proposal that he should be informed of Operation Torch a few hours beforehand. The US State Department were antipathetic until 1943; likewise the OSS, though one or two senior OSS officers were favourably impressed by leading Gaullists such as Passy and d'Astier de la Vigerie.

Eden took a more favourable view than Churchill or Roosevelt. As early as June 1942 Eden wrote in a Cabinet paper, 'I have been impressed by recent testimony to the large amount of support which General de Gaulle enjoys in occupied France.' This testimony included a recent May Day message from trade unionists and statements from the left-wing Christian Syndicalists and the militant section of the Socialists (Barker, 1978). This was an authentic broadly-based tribute to de Gaulle as the symbol of French resistance. Eden himself is entitled to high praise for his steadfastness in supporting de Gaulle even through 1943, when at times both Churchill and Roosevelt wanted to break with him. Correspondence now published between Churchill and Selborne, as Minister of SOE, shows Churchill in June and July 1943 urging that 'the direction of French resistance be taken out of the hands of de Gaulle and his satellites', and Selborne replying that 'organised resistance is almost solid in favour of de Gaulle' (PRO, Kew File PREM 3–184(6)).

Since there was no French government-in-exile, the British Government, having no relations with Vichy, was free to take responsibility for clandestine operations in France, which de Gaulle resented. He had arrived in London shortly before SOE was created, and it was naturally some time before he knew of its existence, but when he learned that it was engaged in sabotage and subversion, projecting himself – as always – into the future as the only free true representative of France, he reacted violently and continuously against SOE carrying out special operations in French territory without his consent. He had no grounds for objection to SIS operating in France in the collection of secret intelligence, obviously necessary for the war effort, and his chief of secret operations, Colonel Passy, soon established good relations with SIS. Nor could he object to the activities of MI9 (largely controlled by SIS) in organising the escapes of prisoners of war and evaders, such as pilots of aircraft shot down over France. But SOE was perhaps inevitably an object of intense dislike and suspicion to him, because it was seeking to build up a will to resistance with a long-range objective of creating secret armies, contrary to his own ambition to do those very things in his own exclusive way. At the end of 1941 he proposed to the Foreign Secretary, Anthony Eden, and ambitious plan that the British organisations (not only SOE) 'should conduct their activities in France exclusively through Free French channels', provoking a strongly negative reply in January 1942 (Foot, 1966, p. 230).

Early in 1941, de Gaulle had set up in London his Bureau Central de Renseignements et d'Action, or BCRA, which had originally been called Service de Renseignement. Colonel Passy, a young army engineer-instructor from St Cyr of high intelligence and great courage, was in command. As its name indicates, it was responsible both for intelligence (secret and open) and for action (special operations, including the support and direction of the resistance). In March 1943 de Gaulle moved BCRA to Algiers, leaving a rear echelon in London called BRAL. These two fields were for de Gaulle the two most vital areas in the absence of diplomatic relations to which he naturally aspired. He was never able, until after liberation in September 1944, to achieve recognition even as a *de facto* government of France. So, although his personal contacts with the British Government, and after 1942 occasionally with the American Government, were of great importance to him, BCRA was the only organisation through which the Free French movement could effectively operate into France.

For the purposes of special operations France had some important physical and geographical advantages: the size of the country, relatively not highly populated; the possibility of organising operations by air and sea both from England and after 1942 from North Africa; and the possibility of bringing persons in or out of France either by air pick-ups at night or by land routes across the long frontiers with neutral Spain and neutral Switzerland. Finding dropping zones and landing grounds was not therefore too difficult; air sorties were possible all year round, even in the shortest summer nights, and important people, whether agents or political figures, could be brought back to London when needed.

By the second half of 1940 SOE had already set up an independent French F Section soon after the fall of France. Staffed by British officers, F Section was headed successively by H. R. Marriott and from late 1941 to 1945 by Maurice Buckmaster. It recruited and trained French-speaking British personnel, officers or others, and Frenchmen who did not wish to work for de Gaulle. F Section was kept out of contact with the Free French, who refused to acknowledge its right to operate in France without their consent. Over four years F Section set up a series of circuits or *réseaux*: fourteen in August 1942, twenty-four in August 1943, fifty-two in August 1944. Inevitably active circuits suffered reprisals or penetration and had to be closed down and replaced or built up anew. But the first principle of F Section was that each circuit should be independent with no contact with the others and no subordination except to F in London. This was beyond question a sound security system, much less vulnerable to disaster than the BCRA organisation of a national resistance council in France, with a chairman and a military commander. The tragic consequences of the arrest and death under torture of the Council's chairman, Jean Moulin, could not have happened under the F Section system. By September 1944, when France was liberated, forty-three F Section circuits had been closed down – thirty-one by enemy action, ten on London's orders and two from other causes. F Section sent 480 agents to France in four years, of whom over fifty were women, and over 100 did not survive. F and RF sections together sent over a thousand agents in all.

After a series of complaints from de Gaulle, it was decided to set up within SOE (but in a separate office at 1 Dorset Square) a new RF Section to work with BCRA on special operations in France. RF Section was headed successively by E. Piquet-Wicks, B. Sweet-Escott, SOE's most versatile and ubiquitous officer, J. R. H. Hutchison and L. R. Dismore. Its primary role, although it carried out a certain number of *coups de main* in the sabotage field, was to build up a secret army with units in every part of France.

SOE's French operations at various times were conducted

through six different SOE sections: the already-mentioned F and RF, DF which specialised in secret movements and escape lines for SOE agents in France, Belgium and Holland, and AMF which was created after the North African landings in November 1942 and established a base near Algiers for operating into France, including Corsica, in 1943. Then there were 'Jedburghs', the code name for operational teams devised in 1944 to support Overlord in co-operation with the American OSS. Each team consisted of three men, one British, one American and one French, for directing resistance groups in assisting the invasion forces under General Eisenhower. There was also EU/P which dealt solely with the large Polish population in the north of France round St Etienne and also those near Clermont-Ferrand who were valuable regional elements in the French resistance.

All these six SOE sections, together with the two country sections for the Netherlands and Belgium, were from 1943 co-ordinated by a senior director, Colonel Robin Brook, under the overall command of Brigadier Mockler-Ferryman, in charge of all operations in Western Europe.

The Nazi *blitzkrieg* in May 1940 swept through France with such speed that the German–French armistice was signed within six weeks and all contact between British and French secret services was severed for seven months. An SOE air sortie had been attempted in November 1940 but failed because the agent refused to jump, the only time a refusal ever occurred (Foot, 1966, p. 150). In January 1941, soon after my arrival in Lisbon, Leslie Humphreys of SOE arrived to make contact with Commandant Brochu of the Deuxième Bureau with whom he had worked closely in Paris up to June 1940. Their rendezvous in the cathedral at Belem took many days to achieve, but fortunately my colleague was a good Catholic, and, after many days of praying, they met. This was the first direct renewal of regular effective contact between the Deuxième Bureau and a British secret service man since the fall of France.

The earliest F Section operation in 1940 was untypical. In Operation Shamrock a submarine landed a naval lieutenant (not SOE) and five French seamen in the Gironde estuary to collect specified intelligence, returning to the Falmouth base in a captured French fishing smack. Operation Savanna in March 1941 dropped five Free French parachutists into Brittany to attack certain specialised Luftwaffe pilots in transit between their lodgings and the airfield; the main objective proved impossible, but much valuable information was brought back and much essential information on living conditions and travel controls. Both were operations organised by SOE but using non-SOE personnel, Free French or naval. After a number of exploratory operations in different areas, resulting in contact with some vigorous and capable organisers, such as the Vômecourt brothers, a major drop of six agents was made near Châteauroux in September 1941, with a range of different objectives. One was a reconnaissance of oil targets, for future attack, since the RAF had now discovered that most oil plants were too small for effective bomber operations.

The first SOE agent to be put into France from a Lysander aircraft was Major Gerard Morel, in September 1941. He accomplished his mission and then made his way through Spain and Portugal to Lisbon, where he contacted my colleague Mortimore in the British Embassy, who sped him on his return journey to London. Landings on the Channel and Atlantic coast became harder and fewer as the Germans became more efficient. A certain amount of traffic in and out was possible on the Mediterranean coast, which was still under French control, until November 1942 when the Allied landings in North Africa caused the armistice conditions of June 1940 to be annulled.

Desperate shortage of special duty aircraft was the biggest limiting factor to the growth of special operations in France until 1943, when American aircraft production started to make itself felt. SOE did however succeed by 1942 in getting two special duty squadrons allocated to it in Britain; 138 Squadron at Tempsford, Bedfordshire, for air-dropping operations of men and supplies, and 161 Squadron, also at Tempsford but with an advance base at Tangmere, Sussex, for Lysander pick-up operations.

By the end of 1941 F Section had achieved little in terms of sabotage and had suffered the loss of several valuable agents. But it had learned many lessons and was beginning to establish the nucleus of an organisation in several areas. Already in July 1941 Dr Dalton had claimed in a paper to the Prime Minister that SOE could now get in motion large-scale schemes for revolution in Europe, and in France could assemble 3000 men in sabotage groups by the autumn of 1942 and organise and arm 24,000 in a secret army, always provided that sufficient air sorties, estimated at 1200, would be available. These claims, though cautiously worded, may have been over-optimistic but they show a well-founded confidence that the organisation was beginning to function.

By the end of 1941 (Sweet-Escott, 1965, p. 110) Passy had accepted with good grace the necessity for Buckmaster's F Section's existence. Passy paid in his memoirs (Passy, 1947, Vol 1, p. 206) a striking tribute to F Section which he said in the strictly military sense was 'undeniably effective, even more effective than the action we were able to undertake on our side', though he felt that what Buckmaster's people had failed to do was to further the object of creating resistance movements. 'It began to look,' wrote Sweet-Escott, 'as if it would probably be on the Buckmaster parties that we must rely for sabotage and *coups de main* rather than on the Free French who were more concerned with creating country-wide organisations for action on or shortly before D-Day.' Expectation of invasion caused acute conflict between short-term needs for maintaining active organisations with vigorous plans for sabotage, and long-term needs for building up secret armies to assist the Allies on D-Day.

In May 1941, just before the Nazi invasion of the Soviet Union in June, the strong French Communist Party set up the Front National, which soon developed an effective resistance movement, FTP, Franc Tireurs et Partisans. As in the early stages of other Communist-controlled movements, such as ELAS in Greece and Tito's Partisans in Jugoslavia, many of its personnel did not at first know where the control resided, though the facts of life became evident before long. The FTP relied on SOE for arms and equipment. In the course of the next three years FTP certainly contributed to the achievements of French resistance in the main industrial areas and certain country areas by sabotage and assassination. But post-war Communist claims that French resistance was largely Communist-inspired should not be taken seriously. SOE, the RAF and the Gaullist movement, together with the American OSS and USAAF in the last year of enemy occupation, were beyond question and with the support of overwhelming evidence, the main external forces which made resistance possible, resistance by all classes of the French nation.

Throughout the period 1941 to 1944 invaluable work of the highest quality was quietly and continuously carried out by DF Section's clandestine transport and communication network, which came to cover Belgium and the Netherlands as well as France. One of the most useful services I was able to render SOE during my time in Lisbon was the recruitment of L. H. Mortimore, a British businessman who had spent most of his life in Paris and was really more French than British. I was impressed by his powers of observation and his precise and inventive mind. I cabled London that here was the key man for F or DF Section in Lisbon. Leslie Humphreys, head of DF, interviewed Mortimore during a visit to Lisbon in the spring of 1941 and immediately recognised his merits, immense attention to detail, wide business contacts, judgement of men and knowledge of the world. For over three years he operated as DF's representative in Lisbon without, so far as I know, ever making a mistake. Couriers came and went without a slip; specimen ration cards were secured from the Food Ministry in Vichy weeks in advance of the month for which they were valid, so as to allow time for land transport to Lisbon, air transport to London and reproduction in London and for parachuting into France before the first of the month in question. This was a record of continued perfection for which I know no parallel. Mortimore was originally recommended to me in advance of his arrival in Lisbon by the Jewish Agency, who in many ways and several countries were a source of great help to SOE.

It was only recently that I discovered from M. R. D. Foot's *Six Faces of Courage* (1978) that the great Jean Moulin on his first visit to London spent some weeks in Lisbon in Mortimore's care, unfortunately at a time in September 1941 when I was away in London seeking a revision to my Lisbon directive. The Free French movement at the end of 1941 welcomed the arrival in London of Jean Moulin, the heroic ex-Prefect of Chartres and the strongest, most intelligent, most impressive figure in the whole French resistance, until his death under torture on the way to Germany in July 1943. Using two or more *noms de guerre* he represented three movements – Combat, led by Frenay, the Libération National and Libération under d'Astier de la Vigerie. He reported that French resistance had now developed to a stage which justified and demanded arms and supplies. He impressed everyone he met in Lisbon and in London, including de Gaulle, who appointed him official delegate in France of the Free French forces. On his return to France his orders – microfilmed into a matchbox – included the organisation of cells on classical lines designed to maintain security and to minimise the risks of capture or penetration: no cell to know another; only the leader to know the identity of his superior; propaganda services to be separated from para-military groups. He was dropped back 'blind' with other agents into the unoccupied zone on 1 January 1942. Under the cover names of Max or Rex he organised the essential services and sections; the main units were to collect tactical intelligence but not national strategic intelligence; they were to plan sabotage and to organise couriers, reception committees for parachute and pick-up operations, radio and press information (under Georges Bidault) for use in London broadcasts. By the summer of 1942 he found in General Delestraint the man he thought qualified to head the secret army. This was soon to become urgent, when the enemy occupied the south of France after the North African landings, because early in 1943 young men started to escape to the woods and hills to create a *maquis* and avoid being sent to forced labour in Germany.

In March 1943 Jean Moulin and General Delestraint were picked up by a Lysander in the Jura Mountains and brought back to London. BCRA was still under the direction of Colonel Passy but André Philip had now been appointed de Gaulle's Commissaire Nationale à l'Interieur. RF Section was now headed by Colonel James Hutchison with Wing Commander Yeo-Thomas (who had made a long visit to France with Passy in 1942), later famous as the 'White Rabbit' and recipient of the George Cross, as Number Two. Since November 1942, the two zones were now both 'occupied' and known as north and south. There was a case, apart from security aspects, for creating a Conseil National de la Résistance (CNR) to co-ordinate activities in both zones. Moulin welcomed it; de Gaulle decided to create it and to make Moulin the president. Moulin and Delestraint returned to the Mâcon area at the end of March and established the CNR in May. Delestraint, lamentably unsuited to clandestine life and deficient in security sense, was arrested in Paris in June. Sharp detective work by Barbié, the Lyon Gestapo chief, led to the arrest of senior members of the CNR, including Moulin at Caluire, a suburb of Lyon. Moulin died under torture at the hands of the Sicherheitsdienst in a train on the way to Germany (Piquet-Wicks, 1957, p. 81 and Foot 1978, p. 43).

The disaster of Caluire and its tragic consequences led to intense controversy and recrimination in London between SOE and BCRA. SOE, always unhappy on security grounds at the centralisation of resistance in enemy-occupied territory, insisted that the mistake should not be repeated. It was then discovered that BCRA proposed to appoint two heads for the two zones, north and south, a proposal slightly less dangerous than a single CNR but still subject to similar security risks. Yeo-Thomas of RF and Pierre Brossolette of BCRA went over to Paris to appraise the damage. Arrests of the Gaullist high command continued day after day. There were no more than five radio operators left in France for the action section of BCRA (Sweet-Escott, 1965, p. 184). Brossolette himself, a brilliant Socialist intellectual and one of the most vivid figures in BCRA, was captured in Brittany (Piquet-Wicks, 1957, p. 70). At the Paris headquarters of the German security forces in the Avenue Foch he jumped out of a fifth-floor window to ensure that he could give nothing away. Yeo-Thomas was also caught and after surviving more than one concentration camp he succeeded in the almost incredible feat of escaping from Buchenwald and survived the war.

By contrast, the Communist FTP with its strong security sense suffered less disastrous casualties in spite of constant resistance activities. Nevertheless the Gaullists continued to follow their dangerous path, and the CNR was reconstituted under Parodi and Georges Bidault, later Prime Minister of France. Fortunately it only had one full meeting before liberation in September 1944. Moreover, during the final planning period of French resistance support for Overlord, the BCRA were persuaded to accept in some degree the security arguments against centralisation by adopting a system of regional military commanders who were to be in direct touch with London and Algiers.

On the counter-intelligence side the German SD and the Abwehr (which lost its independence in February 1944) were formidable adversaries. With the help of a small and dwindling minority of French collaborators, they built up a good picture of the various resistance groups in France and of the set-up and the principal figures in London. Numerous units or circuits were broken up or penetrated and dissolved in 1942, 1943 and 1944; one, Prosper, where hundreds of arrests were involved, was reported to Hitler, who believed it was a major set-back to Allied invasion plans.

The German SD was well equipped with mobile direction-finding vans; they cruised around the streets in urban areas day and night, and caught many radio operators in the act of transmission or immediately after. Brevity of signal and speed of transmission were thus two of the secrets of survival. Another secret, valid not only for radio operators but all clandestines, was to use a house or apartment with at least two entrances and exits. In spite of all precautions instilled into them at SOE's Beaulieu training school for a *sortie de secours* and other security techniques, some agents and some radio operators continued under pressure to make mistakes and forget precautions, often with disastrous results. Several sets were at various times being played back under enemy control. The year 1943 was known in France as *l'année terrible*. André Malraux said in 1943, '*La vraie résistance a perdu les deux tiers des siens*' (Fourcade, 1968, Tome II).

In February 1944 SOE mounted Operation Ratweek throughout Western Europe, designed to kill as many senior German SD officers as possible. It succeeded well in south-eastern France, where the Jockey circuit, organised by F. Cammaerts, a British officer of Belgian descent, was strong both offensively in action and defensively in security.

In Lorraine in early 1944, the German SD had another major success. They captured a radio set, codebook and security checks, and deceived F Section in London for several months by competent playbacks, resulting in stores and agents being dropped to German reception committees. There were numerous other operators captured at various times and places, usually the result of the mobile direction-finding vans, especially in the neighbourhood of Paris. Foot (1966, p. 345) has a table of nine circuits in northern France under enemy control in 1943–4 to which substantial sums in *francs* were dropped, indicating that F Section (or the SOE signals section) was unaware of the enemy control. Buckmaster in a post-war public statement said: 'Of the 480 service members of F Section 130 were caught in five years.' Of the 130 caught it is known that 117 died.

During *all* the years the Germans occupied France, the principal acts of sabotage were the destruction of an air screw factory at Toulouse; the destruction of power supply arrangements at the biggest armament works in France at Le Creusot; demolition of the Gigny barrage on the River Saône thus holding up German E-boat traffic to the Mediterranean in two successive years; demolition of Radio Paris installations, used for jamming and propaganda, and continuous rail attacks, particularly against supply trains carrying oil to submarine bases (Gubbins, 1948).

In the summer of 1943, the combined chiefs of staff in Washington decided to appoint a 'chief of staff to the Supreme Allied Commander', COSSAC, so that when the Supreme Allied Commander was appointed, he would find planning for the cross-Channel operation in 1944 as far advanced as possible. So the strategic planning for the role of French resistance in the invasions of 1944 started in the summer of 1943 in discussions between the COSSAC staff, SOE, the American OSS and others. At a much later stage, after the appointment of General Eisenhower as the Supreme Allied Commander in January 1944, Gaullist pressure and the obvious need for co-ordinating the seven or eight resistance groups led to the recognition of the Forces Françaises de l'Interieur, FFI, as a para-military organisation and part of the Allied forces with its main headquarters or Etat Major based in London. This Etat Major of the FFI or EMFFI was headed by the French General Koenig, who operated under Eisenhower's orders. Two joint Anglo-American-French units were responsible to General Koenig; in London Special Force Headquarters, combining the special operations in France of BRAL, OSS and SOE; and in Algiers the Special Projects Operation Centre, combining the special operation in the south of France of BCRA, the OSS unit and the SOE unit ISSU 6 under Colonel John Anstey.

Two main Allied operations were involved: Overlord, the cross-Channel assault on northern France from British bases, and Anvil (later renamed Dragoon) into southern France from North African, Italian and Corsican bases. An important preliminary operation was Neptune, the seaborne and airborne landings from Le Havre to the Cotentin Peninsula, south of Cherbourg. Finally there was a vital strategic deception plan, Bodyguard (later renamed Fortitude), designed to persuade the enemy that the main assault would come in the Pas de Calais, even if an initial diversionary attack was launched further west. Resistance, however, could do little in the Pas de Calais, which was densely occupied by German troops guarding the sites for V1 secret weapons aimed at London, or otherwise preparing to resist an invasion.

Elsewhere in the north plans were made for organising and equipping resistance groups in a wide arc from Brittany to Belgium. In the south the growing numbers of the *maquis* of the Drôme, Isère and Savoie (especially the Vercors plateau south-west of Grenoble) were capable of disrupting enemy communications then retreating into woods or mountains before reinforcements arrived.

Fortunately no serious division or conflict occurred between forces controlled by F and RF Sections, partly because of the unification of command of resistance groups under EMFFI, partly because by D-Day most Frenchmen and certainly most of the leading F

Section organisers in the field were united in favour of de Gaulle. The main exception was the Communist FTP, whose leaders distrusted de Gaulle and anyway were playing their own game by their own rules – to build up men, resources, money and organisations in war and to use them for political purposes in peace. It must be admitted that the Gaullists too had been building up organisations and re-cruiting men and women in war with a view to a post-war political *prise de pouvoir*, but the Gaullists were acting and thinking in nationalistic terms born of Frenchmen's devotion to France.

The original Allied plan was that Operation Anvil (Dragoon) should be launched some time before Overlord. The intention was to retain enemy forces in the south and draw in reinforcements from the west and north, thus reducing the forces available to oppose the major landings in Normandy. Dragoon, however, was delayed to 15 August, by which date not only had Overlord been launched, but after hard and heavy slogging by BEF 21st Army Group the breakout under General Patton from the Normandy bridgehead had begun. It has thus been doubted by many whether Dragoon, having lost its original function of facilitating the Neptune landings in Normandy and diverting major enemy forces in the early and most risky phase of Overlord, had enough military justification. It had little military value for the liberation of France, except that it obviously took much weight off the resistance groups in the south and saved many French lives. But it diverted Allied resources from the Italian front which might have resulted in the liberation of north Italy by the end of 1944. Dragoon was launched because of French political pressures, since a large part of General Patch's army in Algeria were reconsti-tuted French divisions and it was essential for French prestige that French forces should play a conspicuous part in the liberation of France from the south.

On the night of 5–6 June 1944, Operation Neptune, airborne and seaborne landings in the north of France, at last took place in spite of stormy weather. The BBC French news broadcast hundreds of action messages that evening. This and other events did not escape the notice of the German SD, who warned their high command that invasion was imminent: but fortunately there had been too many false warnings in previous weeks and miraculously no notice was taken. Inside France the best organised circuits, all of whom had their pre-arranged targets for D-Day and after, attacked that very night, including nearly one thousand railway targets. Immediate action was taken not only in the rear of the invasion area in the north from Brittany to Belgium but also in the Rhône valley and the south-west.

Twelve Jedburgh teams (each with three men, one British, one American and one French, all in uniform) were dropped into France in June and the remaining seventy in July and August. Most of them dropped to reception committees in the SOE network, a sound scheme which assured – so far as anything in the resistance world can be assured – immediate contact with the local resistance groups and prompt radio communications with London. Their achievements were substantial (Foot, 1966), but it was generally agreed in postoperational reviews that they could have achieved far more if they had been dropped in some weeks earlier. The delay was due to doubts about the survival capacity of small groups in uniform if dropped in some weeks before the anticipated date of enemy withdrawal from France.

American OSS operational groups, each some thirty strong, were dropped into southern France from Algiers, to strengthen major resistance areas, including the Vercors *maquis*. The British SAS (airborne commando units of the Army, no part of SOE and not under the command of EMFFI) had over 2000 men operating behind the main combat areas, some dropping to reception committees, some operating in heavily armed jeeps far behind the enemy lines; they suffered heavy casualties but they supplied the trained military direction which FFI inevitably needed. SAS, which included some French parachute units, had outstanding success in Brittany, often in liaison with SOE. Commandant Bourgoin, commanding officer of a 400-strong French SAS parachute battalion, soon had a force of 30,000 Bretons behind him and had good grounds for regarding his men in the SAS as largely responsible for liberating Brittany. When the US Army broke out from the Normandy bridgehead at the end of July, General Patton drove south and then swung east, with the aim of surrounding the retreating German forces in the Falaise Gap. Brest was captured by the Americans at a heavy cost in September 1944. The German forces occupying St Nazaire, Lorient and the Channel Islands were not overpowered but surrendered after VE day in May 1945.

The main contribution of the French resistance was in delaying the moves of German reinforcements to the Normandy bridgehead, by sabotage of railroads and rolling-stock, derailment of trains, and by ambushes and bridge demolitions in the case of road transport. Two vivid examples of delay have been frequently quoted: 2 SS Panzer Division stationed at Toulouse on D + 1 day did not reach the Normandy bridgehead until D + 17, on a move which normally should have taken only three or four days; and 11 Panzer Division, which had taken only a week from the eastern front to reach the Rhine, took another three weeks to reach the bridgehead. Naturally the destruction of major bridges, road and rail, such as those across the Loire, was assigned to the Allied air forces rather than to the resistance (Foot, 1966, pp. 397–9).

SOE did not play any major role in the liberation of Paris. The general assumption in Anglo-American military circles had been that some Allied military government would be set up pending a general election, but the Gaullist triumph was complete: none questioned de Gaulle's appointment of a provisional government, with his supporters taking over every ministry. He refused, rightly, to recognise the existence of the Vichy government or to have dealings with Pétain or Laval. The Communist threat of a *prise de pouvoir* evaporated in the heat of the overwhelming welcome to de Gaulle. The Communist FTP had liberated many banks, had laid the foundations of a well-heeled post-war political party and paid off many old scores against collaborators and others in the periods before and after liberation when law and order were conspicuous by their absence. They had also assassinated and harassed enemy forces of occupation long before D-Day and provoked reprisals, which fanned the flame of resistance. But there is no foundation for extravagant claims by left-wing writers that FTP were the core and heart of French resistance (Tillon, 1962). Their contribution to Overlord was limited. Their propaganda that de Gaulle was the tool of English bankers was ludicrous. Fortunately for France the Red Army, which would have put them in the seats of power if it had been present, was a thousand kilometres away.

In September de Gaulle visited the south-west. In Toulouse he met George Starr of SOE's F Section, a local hero, denounced him as a mercenary, threatened him with arrest and said, 'Your place is not here.' A similar episode, equally resented by the local population, occurred in Bordeaux. However, SOE avoided, whether by accident or design, involvement in post-war French politics. F Section representatives in France were soon withdrawn without any other regrettable incidents. There seems to be no doubt that the unification of command of all resistance groups, except the Communist FTP, under EMFFI in the final stages had brought SOE and SO and BCRA closer together and the common pride in victory dispelled the suspicions and friction of earlier years. Even de Gaulle himself after August 1944 could no longer complain that SOE was working against him and his movement or that the Anglo-Saxons were seeking to impose a post-war government on France. It seems clear that he feared and disliked the Americans more than the British. In Britain there was always a strong popular sentiment for de Gaulle, as the sole French leader to continue the fight after the fall of France, and deep down in that icy and arrogant soul there was an occasional spark of warmth for Britain's long and solitary stand from 1940 onwards. The Americans, however, had no such background reason to respect him; they had, moreover, an historical distrust of generals in politics, with a few conspicuous exceptions from the distant past such as George Washington and Andrew Jackson. They probably felt almost unconsciously that he was undemocratic at heart. Another source of de Gaulle's antipathy for America was the maintenance of US diplomatic relations with Vichy, which had condemned him as a rebel and an outlaw.

Resistance casualties, hard to verify in any country, have been the subject of varying estimates. It seems probable that well over 20,000 men and women were executed in France, including the victims of Oradour-sur-Glane, who in August 1944 were apparently executed in error (Foot, 1966, p. 399), and that over 110,000 were deported to concentration camps, from which less than half survived and returned home. In addition, there were the battle casualties sustained by the *maquis*, impossible to compute with any accuracy but probably running into tens of thousands.

Available statistics on air supply (Foot, 1966, p. 473) show some remarkable features: from 1941 to September 1944 the total number of successful sorties flown to France by the RAF and (from January 1944 only) USAAF from Britain and the Mediterranean bases combined was nearly 7500, including both parachute drops and pickups. Of this total over 6750 successful sorties, or 90%, were flown in the nine months from January to September 1944 when the USAAF began to operate in support of French resistance. Conversely, only 750 successful sorties, or 10%, were flown in the three years 1941, 1942 and 1943. Nearly 10,500 tons of stores were delivered by air from 1941 to September 1944. Of this total over 9850, over 94%, were delivered in the last nine months – January to September 1944. Conversely only 650 tons, or 6% of the total, were delivered in the three full years 1941, 1942 and 1943. The total number of agents put into France by air (both parachute and pick-up operations) was 1784, including the American OSS operational groups. Of this total 1369, or 77%, were put in in the nine months of 1944. Conversely only 415, or 23%, were put in during the three full years 1941, 1942 and 1943. It is interesting to note that over 150 agents were put in during 1942 as the result of 93 successful RAF sorties.

These statistics show with striking clarity the minuscule scale of air sorties with which first SOE and then SOE and OSS including the Free French BCRA had to operate in the first three years of activity. They further show by massive contrast the large scale attained when a Supreme Allied Commander was appointed to plan the Neptune phase of Overlord and the regular Allied land forces needed help from the resistance, and when the USAAF added its vast resources to those of the RAF.

F Section sent thirty-nine women agents to France, while RF and DF Sections sent eleven (Foot, 1966, pp. 465–9). Of these fifty, at least eleven were executed or died on active service. Many of them were recruited into the First Aid Nursing Yeomanry, some were Women's Auxiliary Air Force, while others belonged to the Corps Auxiliaire Feminin, the French equivalent of the British Auxiliary Territorial Service. Some were parachuted in, some landed by Lysander or Hudson aircraft, some by *felucca*, and two by normal civil channels overland with passport and visa, including the American journalist Virginia Hall.

F Section agents, mostly British subjects, received three George Crosses (all women), twenty-seven DSOs, thirty-two Military Crosses, two George Medals and numerous MBEs. In RF Section most of the agents were of French or other foreign nationality and naturally received French decorations and relatively few British; but the decorations awarded to two British subjects, formerly head and deputy head of RF Section in London, should be mentioned, Hutchison's DSO and Yeo-Thomas's GC and MC.

10

Norway, Denmark, Belgium
and the Netherlands

Norway

When the Nazis invaded Norway without declaring war on 9 April 1940, King Haakon and his government were rescued and brought to England by sea. From the start there was a government-in-exile in London and an outraged and resentful population at home; few in numbers but strong in spirit, hardy, athletic and resolute. A Nazi puppet, Quisling, whose name has passed into history as a synonym for traitor and collaborator, proclaimed himself Prime Minister, but was soon overshadowed by a *Reichskommissar* from Germany named Terboven. Norway never surrendered and was at war with Germany till the end.

Anglo-French forces were being organised to occupy Norway after Nazi violation of her neutral territorial waters; but the Nazi invaders got there first. The Anglo-French attempts to help the small Norwegian forces were unprepared, improvised and, except for some naval exploits and some commando-type operations, ineffective. Colonel Gubbins was in charge of five independent companies who were forerunners of the Commandos and did some useful work, with local help, in attacking enemy communications. Four other MIR officers (later SOE officers) were sent to Narvik, Trondheim, Bergen and Stavanger to act as liaison officers with local commands and later played important parts in organising resistance.

Norwegian maritime traditions were a source of great strength throughout the five years of Nazi occupation and the large merchant navy was a source of funds for the government-in-exile. Sea landings of agents and stores and escapes by sea were priceless assets of the Norwegian resistance groups; they did much to compensate for the limitations of air supply, which during the short nights of the Arctic summer was at first impracticable. Air-supply operations increased substantially from 1943 to 1945 and eventually landed over two hundred agents and three hundred tons of stores.

The long land frontier with neutral Sweden enabled Norwegian agents to escape to neutral territory. In October 1940, Sir Charles Hambro, then head of the SOE Scandinavian Section, visited Stockholm and set up an office that later functioned as a combined SOE/SIS office for handling resistance affairs, including intelligence, in Norway and Denmark. By the end of 1940 Norwegians were becoming united in a will to resist, though their long history of peace and their traditions of open government and individual freedom made them – unlike the Poles and Czechoslovaks – unaccustomed to clandestine ways and to security practices.

During 1941 a military organisation or Milorg was set up by former military officers and others, aiming at seizing control of the country, if Allied support justified it, but Milorg was averse to sabotage and *coups de main* which would provoke reprisals, an attitude somewhat similar to Mihailović's right-wing Serbian group after 1941. At first the government-in-exile was loath to recognise or support Milorg. But during 1941 and 1942, after one of the leaders, Captain Rognes, arrived in London and Colonel John Wilson, an outstanding personality, became head of SOE's Scandinavian Section, the problems of principle and objectives were progressively solved. Two Commando operations suggested by SOE against the islands of Lofoten in 1941 brought back to England a valuable group of Norwegian volunteers, but predictably brought down severe enemy reprisals on the local population. This confirmed the fears of Milorg leaders, who remained more than ever attached to the concept of long-term preparations for a secret army, to go into action only when liberation was in sight. SOE, following British strategic needs, could not accept this concept. SOE's sabotage programme included four conspicuous items: demolitions at Orkla pyrites mines; demolition of torpedo and submarine oil stocks at Horten; destruction of the Skefco ball-bearing works at Oslo and selective destruction of key equipment in the Norsk Hydro heavy water factory and stocks at Rjukan. These four acts of sabotage were eventually accomplished.

Odd Starheim, an outstanding agent trained by SOE, landed in Norway in December 1940 and returned in March 1942 with several resistance friends, who, disguised as passengers, had captured a coastal ship and escaped to Scotland. One of the team was Skinnarland, engineer to the Norsk Hydro heavy water plant at Rjukan, which was being used by the Germans to produce an element then thought to be essential for the atomic bomb. He was trained by SOE in less than two weeks in sabotage, security and parachuting and was dropped back within three weeks of leaving his post at Norsk Hydro. Four Norwegians, all taught at SOE centres and all natives of Rjukan, were given special extra training for the task. In October 1942, they were parachuted into an area some distance from Rjukan with orders to move to another area south of Rjukan and await further instructions.

Meanwhile Skinnarland reported to London by radio that orders had been received from Berlin to pack and ship to Germany the entire stock of heavy water. In London the War Cabinet, the chiefs of staff with their scientific advisers and Lord Louis Mountbatten as chief of the Commandos, decided that this news represented a risk of the utmost gravity and that, rather than leave it as a sabotage operation for four young Norwegians, however courageous and competent, the Commandos should be called on for an airborne operation on a bigger scale. In mid-November Commando Operation Freshman took place. Over thirty officers and men of the First Airborne Division took off from northern Scotland in gliders towed by two bomber aircraft. The gliders were to land in the area where SOE's four Norwegians would meet them and act as guides. Freshman was a tragic disaster. One tow rope broke over Norway and the glider disappeared into cloud; the other aircraft crashed on a mountainside; the bomber crew were killed on impact but some of the glider crews survived. All the survivors of both gliders were captured and, although in uniform, wounded or not, were executed by the Nazis. This was a major war crime which they attempted to disguise by claiming that both bombers and gliders had been shot down by fighters of the Luftwaffe. After the liberation in 1945 the British corpses were dug up and found to be in uniform with their hands tied by barbed wire.

SOE now initiated Operation Gunnerside. Latest information on the Norsk Hydro factory was provided by the former chief engineer, Professor Brun, who came out through Sweden. Large-scale models were built at an SOE training centre and all details of the approach routes, the demolition targets, especially the eighteen stainless steel cells producing the heavy water, and the withdrawal routes were studied and rehearsed. Six Norwegians under Joachim Ronneberg were specially trained for this task; its inherent difficulty was increased by the reinforced security measures, which the German

General von Falkenhorst had ordered after the disaster of the Commando airborne operation had clearly shown the Germans that Norsk Hydro was an important target. In mid-February Gunnerside was carried out with total success. The eighteen cells and other key installations were destroyed together with several months' production of heavy water in stock, and even after months of repair work the plant never again operated to capacity. Von Falkenhorst inspected the damage in person and pronounced it the most skilful sabotage operation he had ever seen. All the six Norwegians got safely away, some escaping to Sweden, others hiding in Norway. Two were awarded DSOs, the others MCs or MMs. Starheim was later killed during another hi-jacking operation, when his ship was dive-bombed in the North Sea. Himmler ordered reprisals for Gunnerside; hundreds of Norwegians were driven from their homes in the area and many put into concentration camps as hostages. Sweet-Escott (1965, p. 114) says: 'It was the classic proof of our contention that one aircraft which drops an intelligent and well-trained party can do more damage than a whole fleet of bombers.' Leverkuehn of the Abwehr wrote in 1954 that of all the acts of sabotage on either side in the Second World War, only the attack on Norsk Hydro could claim to have been really effective, in the sense that the extent of the damage done and the period needed for repair were both of decisive importance.

As an inspired afterthought a year later the Norwegians placed high explosive charges on a ferry carrying a further six months' stock of heavy water to Germany, which effectively ended Nazi hopes for an atomic bomb. It was only done after fruitless attempts by the USAAF to bomb the Rjukan area, resulting in the loss of several aircraft and over twenty Norwegian civilian casualties.

Winston Churchill had been First Sea Lord at the time of the German invasion of Norway and he had always had strong views on its strategic importance, especially in a naval war. So in 1942 he advocated an Allied invasion of Norway, against the advice of both his own chiefs of staff and the exiled government. He only gave way when the combined chiefs of staff in Washington objected most strongly, as it was utterly inconsistent with the plan to build up forces and equipment for Overlord. This episode, though it proved to be a non-event, caused friction with the exiled government, not for the first time. SOE had been required to produce a paper on Norwegian policy for the chiefs of staff before the end of 1940.

When the exiled government read this paper in 1941, they were extremely critical because of the aggressive role foreseen for Norwegian resistance and the extent of control envisaged for SOE. Although relations were much improved after 1942, there was always a potential area of friction between the adventurous nature of the resistance forces with the efficient and aggressive SOE Norwegian Section, and the exiled government's fear of reprisals and its concern to protect its people at home.

One of SOE's agreed functions was to co-operate with the chief of combined operations in London and to provide him with trained saboteurs and local assistance in landing operations on the Norwegian coast. SOE suggested two raids on the Lofoten Islands in 1941 and provided SOE officers who knew the area and a number of Norwegian officers and men to join the raiding party. Several small ships were sunk, factories destroyed and Germans and local quislings taken prisoner and brought back to Britain. German reprisals were severe but no doubt both the raid and the reprisals fortified the spirit of resistance. Still more savage reprisals, including burning houses and taking over two hundred hostages to German concentration camps, where many died, resulted from an attack on Luftwaffe installations near Stavanger. These raids and many acts of sabotage kept the Nazis in constant fear of armed uprisings. At the end of 1943 over 400,000 men in the Wehrmacht, plus naval and air personnel, were needed to repress three million Norwegians, though the Germans needed men to reinforce the Russian front and the Nazi defence forces in France. Norwegian resistance thus made a major contribution to Allied strategy.

A continuing joint Anglo-Norwegian project, of greatest value in promoting good relations, was the 'Shetland Bus'. In five years the SOE fleet of fishing boats and submarine-chasers sailed over 150 trips, landed in Norway over 220 agents and over 300 tons of stores and brought out over 60 agents and 350 refugees. The USAAF accomplished some daylight drops during 1944 and 1945, when the Luftwaffe was seriously weakened, but even so they lost five aircraft while the RAF lost over twenty aircraft in night sorties over five years. By 1945, when victory was in sight and resistance was widespread, air supply included arms for over 25,000 men and 22 tons of high explosives. A valuable element throughout the years of occupation was the admirable work of the Stockholm SOE/SIS office.

Denmark

The Nazi invasion of Denmark on 9 April 1940 encountered a brief but futile resistance from a few units. The King immediately but inevitably ordered a cease-fire and declared Danish neutrality, so there was no government-in-exile in London. In spite of the veneration in which the King was held by his compatriots, over a million tons of Danish shipping and some five thousand sailors, who were on the high seas at the time, adhered to the Allied cause and served in the Allied merchant navies. In October 1940 a small group of patriotic Danes set up a Free Danish Council in Washington and London. This was achieved in spite of discouragement from the British Government, which with short-sighted compassion was reluctant to encourage any measures which might lead to reprisals in occupied Denmark.

The intelligence field in Denmark was a rare and exhilarating example of close collaboration between SIS and SOE. A group of Danes known as the Princes, mainly staff officers and policemen, provided a stream of information especially valuable to naval intelligence in London. They also sent over photographs of the experimental V1 which crash-landed on the island of Bornholm. The Princes, like the Norwegian Milorg, favoured formation of a secret army to co-operate with the Allies in the closing stages of the war but were averse to sabotage. After the Danish Government resigned in August 1943, following a series of repressive acts by the occupying power, the Princes disbanded, many escaping to Sweden.

When SOE came into existence, Sir Charles Hambro was soon in contact with individual patriotic Danes, including Captain W. M. Iverson and Dr C. J. Bruhn. Early in 1941 the SOE Danish Section had a liaison unit in Stockholm and fifteen recruits in training in England. Bruhn, an outstanding man, was groomed by SOE to be the first organiser of the Danish resistance and was dropped 'blind' with a radio operator in December 1941. His parachute was of a new and faulty design; it landed him horizontal and so killed him. His operator survived and did noble work in the early days of resistance, but lacked specialist training. No replacement was found for Bruhn until the spring of 1943 when Muus, selected, trained and briefed by SOE over many months, parachuted in – this time safely.

Muus had all the qualities of a resistance leader, organisational ability, a strong security sense and a combination of courage, cunning and diplomacy. Even in a country mostly united (with a few conspicuous exceptions) in its detestation of the occupying power, there were diverse elements in need of co-ordination. He arrived just before the Danish Government resigned and so was soon able to encourage the Danes to accept sabotage as a necessary measure. The sabotage programme, starting in 1943, concentrated on railways, factories, shipyards, particularly the famous Burmeister and Wain, and sinking ships in harbour, including fourteen ships in the nine months preceding the invasion of Normandy in June 1944. In September 1943 a Freedom Council was set up which included Muus. The Danes adopted clandestinity with outstanding success; their sabotage projects were well conceived and executed with precision. Late in 1943 a public meeting in Copenhagen was being addressed by an SS Oberführer Best, who after uttering ferocious threats announced: 'From today acts of sabotage will cease.' Seconds later a ship blew up with a louder than usual explosion in the adjoining harbour: the meeting broke up in disorder.

Two valuable external projects were RAF precision bombing raids in 1944 and 1945 on two Gestapo offices in Aarhus and Copenhagen. In the first raid many Gestapo men were killed and files destroyed. In the second raid only a few Gestapo were killed but numerous captured resistance men imprisoned on the top floor were able to escape, and one on his way collected the Gestapo card-index of their Danish helpers. Tragically, some severe civilian casualties were caused by a bomber crashing on an adjoining school. In spite of these deaths, the resistance movement as a whole welcomed the raids.

Starting with a surrender to an overpowering invasion, never officially at war with the Nazi Reich, and being of the Nordic race, the Danes were treated initially with relative mildness as a model of an occupied state. After a slow build-up, partly due to the faulty parachute which killed Bruhn, the first organiser, in December 1941, resistance only took off in 1943 when the second organiser had arrived and found his feet, just in time for the repressive Nazi measures in August leading to the resignation of the Danish Government. From then onwards the flow of intelligence was supplemented by well-organised acts of sabotage.

Belgium

Overrun in less than three weeks' fighting in May 1940, Belgium was occupied by the Germans for the second time in twenty-five years. The clandestine press prominent in the 1914–18 war came to life again as well as various intelligence circuits. Pierlot formed a government-in-exile in London. However, King Leopold ordered the Belgian armed forces to surrender and he remained in the conquered country, taking no part in government. Belgium, with its historic linguistic divisions into French Wallonia and Flemish Flanders, with even a small German minority in the border province of Eupen, was further divided in wartime between supporters of the King, supporters of the exiled government and a small minority who collaborated with the Nazis.

As time passed and the prospect of an Allied victory brightened, the vast majority of the population became more and more pro-Allies and pro-resistance. Even in the black days of 1940, after the fall of France, there were many brave and patriotic Belgians who set off on the long route through Spain and Portugal to London and freedom. I saw something of this flow in Lisbon in 1941, when I was helping with SOE funds the representatives of the Deuxième Section of the Ministry of Defence to establish their own lines of communication and escape. These Belgian lines were separate, of course, from SOE's lines, which DF Section was building up through France, Belgium and the Netherlands.

The Congo Belge, now Zaire but then a colonial territory, was a great asset: a source of funds for the exiled government in London, a priceless source of uranium ore for the American development of the atomic bomb and an area to which at least in the early days of occupation Belgians could legitimately travel and then move on to Britain. But human resources have always been the most important asset for an exiled government. I found it remarkable to discover just how many leading Belgians in public life did at some time during the war work in London for the exiled government and its services: Spaak, Foreign Minister in wartime, later one of the founders of the European Economic Community; Hubert Ansiaux, Director and after the War Governor of the Central Bank and a leading figure in the Marshall Plan and in post-war international finance; Camille Gutt, leading banker and post-war the second Managing Director of the International Monetary Fund in Washington; Fernand Lepage, head of Sûreté intelligence and counter-intelligence; Ganshof van der Meersch and Frederic Dumon, both later leading legal figures rising successively to the top post of Procureur-Général;

Henri Bernard, head of the Deuxième Section of the Defence Ministry, charged with responsibility for the Belgian resistance movement, in touch with the occupied home country and after the war the outstanding historian of the Belgian resistance movement and, more remarkable, also of the German opposition movement, in an inspiring book entitled *L'Autre Allemagne* (Bernard, 1976). I had the good fortune in Lisbon in 1941 to work closely with Dumon, a man of exceptional clarity, intellect and integrity, who became a lifelong friend. Lepage, whom I did not meet till long after the war, was described (Foot, 1976, p.256) as 'a man of equal energy, capacity and tact', who handled relations with SIS, MI9 and SOE.

It was no doubt partly due to the wealth of able and ambitious Belgians working in exile in London and partly to their inherent divisions, linguistic, religious and constitutional, that Belgians tended to be considered by the Foreign Office and SIS as a nation of divided intriguers, and at least until 1942 somewhat unreliable. In late summer 1941, when I had established close relations with Dumon in Lisbon to our mutual advantage, I had a telegram from 'T', head of SOE's Belgian Section, saying that SIS had recently had some doubts about Lepage, head of Belgian intelligence, for reasons unspecified. I replied immediately, 'Is this a temporary whim of SIS or does it affect my relations with Dumon?' I later heard from 'T' by letter through the diplomatic bag: 'I hasten to reply somewhat less publicly to your telegram,' and he went on to say that unknown to me copies of all SOE telegrams in or out went to the deputy chief of SIS, with the sole exception of those marked 'personal' to (or from) the head of SOE; and that my telegram had produced a blast of indignation from the deputy chief of the Secret Service to Charles Hambro at the arrogance of his man in Lisbon daring to refer to the mental processes of SIS as a 'temporary whim'. I stored this incident in my memory as a warning for the future, but was amused to find that my sceptical and impertinent question was fully justified. 'T' informed me a few weeks later that SIS's doubts had been assuaged and that Lepage was restored to favour.

The Belgian Sûreté, headed by Lepage, had the usual difficulties of a wartime security service; torn from its own headquarters, bereft of those precious files which are the repository of all past knowledge, dependent on another government's services for facilities and information of all kinds. The fact that he survived for four years in a foreign country as head of his own security service and resumed that important post in Brussels after the war is a tribute to his strongly balanced perceptive qualities. The supervision and support of the Belgian resistance movement was entrusted to the Sureté and to the Deuxième Section of the Ministry of Defence directed at different times by Colonel J. Marissal and Henri Bernard.

A Belgian secret army had been formed in 1940 by those officers and men who, after King Leopold's surrender, had refused to lay down their arms and resolved to carry on the fight clandestinely. The first commander, Colonel Bastin, was arrested and died in captivity; he was succeeded by Colonel Gerard, who in turn was succeeded by General Jules Pire, who was in command at the crucial period in 1944, when the secret army made an outstanding contribution to Allied military operations. Two major figures in the secret army were Jean del Marmol, chief of staff to Pire and also charged with liaison with the various civilian resistance organisations, and Laurence Wolters, chief administration officer. SOE provided signals communications between the Ministry of Defence and the secret army units in Belgium. The signals network for several months preceding liberation in September 1944 linked not only the secret army but the civilian resistance groups with Eisenhower's headquarters. More than a dozen resistance organisations were officially recognised by the Belgian Government as active participants, with members totaling over 60,000. The leading organisations were: Group G, formed in 1940 by academics specialising in technical projects; Front de L'Independence, which included left-wing partisan militants, and Mouvement National Royaliste, mostly military personnel who were responsible for the brilliantly successful preservation of the port at Antwerp from destruction by the departing Germans.

SOE was responsible for training Belgian agents, for their briefing, equipment and despatch by air, and for providing, packing and parachuting in weapons and supplies of all kinds. The outstanding demolition project, planned and carried out by Group G with SOE's advice and help, was 'la grande coupure' or the great cut, which in January 1944 put out of action over thirty pylons and much electrical generating plant serving industrial areas; this project caused an immediate loss of 50,000 kilowatts of electrical power to Belgian industry which was then working under German orders.

The sabotage programme developed by the Ministry of Defence and SOE (Gubbins, 1948) included three main fields of activity; destruction of power stations and transformers; demolition of locks on main waterways between Belgium and France, which were the main channels of transportation for heavy or bulky materials; and the destruction of high-tension cables and pylons. But it was on the intelligence side that Belgians were most prominent, producing an enormous amount of information of all kinds which they took across France to Lisbon. On one main route, the express train from Lille to Lyon, the fireman was the courier and kept the reports under the coal, so in case of need they could be shovelled into the firebox of the engine and instantly destroyed.

Of many heroic and dedicated characters, special mention should be made of Dr Albert Guérisse (alias Pat O'Leary) who, being left behind by error in an SOE operation, set up an escape line for MI9, handling over five hundred people each year; captured and imprisoned, he later received thirty-two decorations, including the George Cross. Dédée de Jongh was also exceptional; for three years she ran an escape line which sent several hundred people from Belgium through to Spain (Foot and Langley, 1978).

Geographically, Belgium is not favourable country for secret armies except for the mountainous Ardennes. Lengthy preparations and plans were made for action to help the Allied forces as the enemy withdrew from France into Germany, but the speed of events was such that Belgium was freed in a few days. Though many gallant acts have been cited there was not time enough to test the adequacy of the plans. But a most valuable contribution was made in the field of 'counter-scorch', the frustration of enemy measures for demolition of ports, bridges and other installations as the Germans withdrew. In the great port of Antwerp elaborate enemy demolition programmes had been made but were almost totally prevented by the skill and courage of local resistance units working on well prepared plans (ERM, 1960, pp. 257–83). Overall, Belgian resistance casualties were heavy, over fifteen thousand having been executed, killed in action or died in concentration camps by the end of the war.

The Netherlands

The Nazi invasion of the Netherlands started at dawn on 10 May 1940 without ultimatum or declaration of war. The invading paratroopers tried, but failed, to capture Queen Wilhelmina, who with her family and her government were evacuated to Britain soon after, to constitute yet another exiled government. The Dutch forces were outnumbered and soon overwhelmed; the centre of Rotterdam was destroyed and fighting ceased after four days. Colonel Chidson (then of Section D but later of SOE) had the unusual task of taking away with him a quantity of industrial diamonds, whose value to the war effort in Britain was doubtless far in excess of their market value in 1940. They were used for grinding and shaping precision instruments and metal; there were never enough of them to meet demand but SOE managed to maintain a steady underground flow from Western Europe to Britain throughout most of the war, a considerable achievement.

With territorial possessions in the East and West Indies and substantial foreign assets, for which numerous protective measures had been taken, the government-in-exile was in a relatively strong position. The Dutch fleet, based on Java, suffered losses at the hands of the Japanese, but some scarce and precious vessels survived, especially submarines which, based on Ceylon (Sri Lanka), landed numerous SOE agents in South-East Asia from 1943 onwards. It was, however, in Europe that the first of many tragedies occurred in the operations of British secret services in Dutch territories.

Before the Nazis invaded, the SIS had already suffered two major disasters in the Netherlands. Since 1935, the Sicherheitsdienst had been photographing from a canal barge all visitors to the SIS Hague offices, whose accountant made disaster doubly sure by leaving behind in May 1940 records of all persons to whom he had paid out secret funds. And in November 1939 Captain Payne Best, head of SIS in The Hague, and Major Stevens, SIS visitor from London, had been decoyed – by the Sicherheitsdienst pretending to represent a dissident anti-Nazi group in Germany – to a rendezvous in Venlo, a frontier post, where they were kidnapped and taken to Berlin. From that episode several grave consequences followed. The identity of many of SIS's agents in the Netherlands became known to the Nazis, some were even listed in a paper in Stevens's pocket at the time (Cookridge, 1966) and the structure of SIS was compromised. Most serious of all, SIS became so cautious and so sensitive that subsequent approaches from genuine anti-Nazis were rebuffed or discouraged on the assumption that they too might represent another double-cross by the Sicherheitsdienst or the Abwehr. As a result, genuine anti-Nazi groups found a more constructive reception from the American OSS, especially Allen Dulles in Berne.

SOE had not developed any pre-war contacts or plans for the Netherlands in its pre-war capacity of either MIR or Section D for it was recognised that the country presented considerable difficulties for guerrilla warfare with its open terrain, few woods and no mountains. Movement by land meant long and arduous routes through Belgium, France and Spain or Switzerland to Gibraltar or Lisbon or, harder still, the northern route through Germany, Denmark and Sweden. The sea routes were hazardous in the extreme, because of the flat, straight, easy-to-guard beaches, so unlike the rocky fjords and bays of Norway, Brittany or Greece. Air supply was also hazardous, because from 1941 onwards a dense flak and fighter belt was built up from Denmark to Belgium to deter the RAF night bombers on their way to attack the Ruhr or Berlin, and this belt was especially dense in the Netherlands (Jones, 1978). However, by 1941 SOE had set up a Dutch section in London.

Resistance groups within the Netherlands itself came into existence spontaneously after the *Reichskommissar*, Seyss-Inquart, started arresting leading figures in religious, political and trade union circles. Several clandestine news sheets were produced and distributed and a general strike was organised in February 1941; twelve or more organisers were shot and many hostages were taken and imprisoned. Anti-Jewish measures were taken by the security forces, and a few thousand Dutchmen, usually with racialist beliefs, were willing to collaborate with the Nazis as Waffen SS, working as confidential agents to betray the resisters.

In London Colonel van t'Sant, a former police chief, became secretary to Queen Wilhelmina and was responsible for her personal security and that of the government-in-exile. He also established a Central Intelligence Bureau (CIB) in close contact with SIS. In August 1940 they parachuted the first Dutch agent into the Leyden area; he established radio contact with London, collected intelligence material, but he and his two or three local helpers were captured by the Germans a few weeks later and executed. He left behind him a radio set and operator to assist the Stijkel group, the first unit of the Dutch resistance, but they were also captured in April 1941, while attempting a getaway by sea, and were executed.

During 1941, the exiled government set up in London a resistance liaison unit known as MVT under Colonel de Bruyne, a Dutch Royal Marine. Both branches of the Dutch secret services, CIB and MVT, resented the inevitable SOE insistence on controlling radio traffic and the mounting of special operations, not, as it happened, without reason.

SOE, like the other secret organisations, was obsessed with secrecy and control; they were always afraid that one day an agent might be captured and used against them without that fact being recognised. This could mean not only penetration of a whole network of agents but loss of codes, the chances of further agents being dropped straight into the enemy's hands, probably capture and torture of helpful local inhabitants and a widening ripple of disaster. Various safeguards had been invented to stop agents being dropped into foreign countries knowing too much either about the SOE set-up and methods or about the missions of other agents. There were special technical checks to make sure that radio operators were not transmitting under duress. On the whole, SOE's system seemed to have been reasonably successful in most countries considering the large scale of operations and the efficiency of the Nazi security services, but the Netherlands proved an exception.

During the summer of 1941 the Abwehr sent a highly intelligent officer to The Hague to take charge of military counter-espionage in their section 111F. H. J. Giskes was a Catholic Rhinelander who had seen active service in the First World War and from 1938 had been 'in the Abwehr section under Admiral Canaris' (Giskes, 1953, p. vi). He was under orders to collaborate in the Netherlands with the Nazi security police, SIPO. Giskes's job was to discover the secret plans and communications system of the London intelligence service so as to mislead and thwart its projects. He gave high priority to capturing radio operators transmitting to London and then to forcing them to 'play back' their sets in such a way as to mislead. The first operator caught in the act of transmitting was arrested by SIPO, who handled the affair clumsily. Although they found the man's Dutch naval code and copies of recent reports, they failed to make him transmit to London under duress but had him executed instead. Giskes decided that next time he would take a more prominent role and he gave the programme for arresting operators and making them play back the Abwehr code name *Nordpol* (North Pole). SIPO had a separate code name for the programme or for their part in it, namely *Englandspiel*.

In March 1942 SIPO and Giskes's Abwehr jointly captured a radio operator, Ebenezer, in The Hague with his associates. After a week in prison, Ebenezer, whose real name was Lauwers, was persuaded by Giskes to send the three messages which he had been about to transmit on the night of his arrest. He agreed to do this but he carefully omitted at the end of each message to send the security check which every SOE-trained operator was taught to include (but did not always remember to do so) as evidence that he was transmitting freely and not under duress. It has been said that SOE signals unit failed to notice and failed to draw the attention of the SOE Dutch Section to the fact that the security check was missing. This was denied by SOE in the post-war enquiry and it seems that the absence of the check was noticed, but, as operators often forgot it, there was a decision in London to accept the signals as authentic.

Soon after, London signalled plans to drop another agent in Holland, to be known as Operation Watercress, and gave details about the need for another dropping zone for supplies. Ebenezer refused to be a party to the capture of another agent, though he was prepared to co-operate in frustrating plans to send over arms and explosives. Giskes eventually persuaded him by an assurance that neither he nor any other captured *Nordpol* agents would suffer the death penalty if he, Ebenezer, continued to co-operate. Operation Watercress took place and an SOE agent called Abor was dropped with some containers of stores straight into the hands of a German reception committee consisting of SIPO and the Abwehr, who radioed London to report the safe arrival of Abor. This was the first of a long series of calamities for the Dutch Section of SOE.

Then a dead parachutist, Martens, was found with a broken skull because he had landed on a concrete trough, and it became clear to Giskes that London must have other radio operators in the Netherlands besides Ebenezer who was now under German control. In fact three groups of agents had been dropped in the first few months of 1942 and Martens should have been their radio operator. Now that he was dead, London instructed two other agents to communicate with them through Ebenezer, so two more agents were added to the German bag due to a clear breach by SOE of sound security principles. Another agent named Pijl was the next to be arrested, then Jeffers in May, who was caught together with his transmitter. Giskes now had three transmitters under control and the number progressively increased up to eleven, and each one was sending phoney German-invented information back to SOE in London.

SOE agents continued to be parachuted to German reception committees, including in June 1942 Professor Jambroes, briefed to be chief organiser of a secret army and adviser to the leaders of the resistance movement. Jambroes brought with him detailed written instructions, all of which fell into the hands of the Abwehr or SIPO, including plans for co-operation by the Orde Dienst, the military network of resistance groups, with a possible future invasion force. Giskes produced a series of progress reports purporting to come from Jambroes through radio sets in different locations, as he presumably travelled around the country.

After some six months, London found progress unsatisfactory and pressed for Jambroes's return for consultation. Early in 1943 a special team was dropped to organise his escape route. They were all captured and Giskes produced another series of progress reports to London on their imaginary activities, including a recommendation that Jambroes should follow an escape route already controlled by the Abwehr through an agent called Richard Christman. This man, a former member of the French Foreign Legion and Deuxième Bureau, had specialised in penetrating resistance groups and escape lines in France, Belgium and finally the Netherlands, under various names. As Arnaud he was awarded a Military Cross for organising the escape of four SOE agents in Belgium who were in fact German Feld Polizei sergeants from the Abwehr, a feat reported to London by Giskes through one of his playback channels. The award of the MC was annulled in 1944. Finally Giskes disposed of 'Jambroes' by sending a Dutch-speaking Abwehr man through France as far as Toulouse, where under the name of Jambroes he was reported in the local press as having died as a result of a car accident. The news of the false Jambroes's death reached Baker Street through several French channels. The real Jambroes remained in prison until executed with other SOE agents in a concentration camp in Germany in 1944.

Early in 1943 a leading Dutch double agent or collaborationist with the enemy, Van der Waals, established contact with members of the national committee of the resistance. The Nazis soon had a full list of all the members and Van der Waals acted as a channel of communication from the committee to the exiled government in London. The committee members were left at large for some time but were all arrested in April.

At the end of August 1943 two genuine Dutch agents, who had been captured on arrival in April, escaped from prison and succeeded in reaching Switzerland; they reported the enemy penetration of Dutch resistance groups to the Netherlands Embassy, who promptly advised London. This was the beginning of the end of *Nordpol–Englandspiel*. Giskes made a desperate but ingenious attempt to rectify his situation by sending Baker Street a message that these two had been 'turned round' by the Gestapo and were now working as Gestapo agents. When they reached London they were put into Brixton Gaol to be on the safe side, and were only released after prolonged interrogation had shown their stories to be true. Later in 1943 three more SOE agents escaped from prison in the Netherlands; the first two of these escapers reached Switzerland and from there came through Spain to Gibraltar and London. Gradually the whole *Nordpol–Englandspiel* operation, an Anglo–Dutch tragedy and an Abwehr triumph, was exposed.

Between 1942 and 1943 over fifty SOE Dutch agents were captured and one MI9 woman agent, who had the misfortune to be sent to a reception committee under German control. An enquiry was held in the autumn of 1943 by the Joint Intelligence Committee in London; it was obvious that errors of judgement and disregard of security rules had occurred, but no evidence was produced either then in 1943 or to a post-war commission set up by the Dutch Government in 1949 to substantiate fears that there had been treachery in London or that there had been a German agent in Baker Street. It was even alleged that Major Bingham, head of SOE's Dutch Section, had been the German agent. The Abwehr representatives had consistently told agents immediately after capture that they knew everything that went on in London where they had a well-placed agent. This trick was sometimes successful in persuading captured agents to talk while in a state of shock at such a revelation; but it was a relief to know that it was unfounded. Lt-Colonel Giskes and SS Sturmbannführer Schreieder of SIPO were held in Dutch prisons for some years after the war and were questioned in depth by the Dutch commission, when both denied the allegations that there was a German agent in Baker Street.

The result of the Joint Intelligence Committee enquiry was an initial over-reaction; orders were given to SOE in December 1943 for all activities in the Netherlands, Belgium and Denmark to cease forthwith. Fortunately for the Danish resistance, their leader Muus was in London at the time and had no difficulty in proving that the Dutch disaster had not been or could not be repeated in Denmark; movements from Denmark to neutral Sweden were relatively easy and known members of the Danish resistance were frequently seen face to face by SOE officers in Stockholm or Gothenburg. The Belgian Section were able to prove that their resistance movement was intact and not penetrated by the enemy, so the order was soon rescinded. But the impact of the operation *Nordpol–Englandspiel* was disastrous to the Dutch resistance movement and for a long time to Anglo-Dutch relations. On 14 December 1949, when British witnesses made statements in London to the president of the Dutch commission of enquiry, the Foreign Office issued a statement intended to put the whole affair in perspective; in it they confirmed that there was no ground for suspecting treachery and no ground for allegations that Britain had objectives in the Netherlands which led to the deliberate sacrifice of the lives of Dutch patriots.

In spite of the casualties and the lack of equipment, because so much had been dropped to enemy-controlled reception committees, the Dutch resistance survived and managed to arm itself by raids on enemy magazines. A new organisation, the Army of the Interior, took over control and was just beginning to co-operate with units of 21st Army Group when the failure of the airborne operation Market Garden to capture Arnhem meant that the liberation of the Netherlands had to be postponed through the hard winter of 1944–5. British and US aircraft flew over two hundred successful sorties in the winter months, dropping arms and supplies and combat teams of three nationalities, similar to the Jedburghs in France. In the final advance of April 1945 the Dutch gallantly played their part in spite of starvation and reprisals. From the end of 1943 the two SOE sections dealing with the Low Countries had been co-ordinated under Commander P. L. Johns.

The wider question, which inevitably presented itself forcibly to the Joint Intelligence Committee in 1943 with the support of the critical SIS, was how many other resistance movements or individual resistance groups supported by SOE were also penetrated by the enemy? The historical answer seems to be remarkably few, which is a tribute to SOE's generally sound security principles. The question was answered in some detail by Lord Selborne in a paper circulated on 11 January 1944 to the Defence Committee of the War Cabinet as DO(44)2 (Public Records Office reference CAB 69/6 XP 326). However, *Nordpol* was a triumph for the Abwehr and a disaster for SOE's Dutch Section.

Germany and Austria:
The Anti-Nazi Opposition

On 5 November 1937 Adolf Hitler convened a secret meeting of five: General von Blomberg, Minister of War; General von Fritsch, Chief of Army Staff; Admiral Raeder, Commander of the Fleet; von Neurath, Minister of Foreign Affairs and Lt-Colonel von Hossbach of the General Staff to discuss possible courses of action for the future of the Third Reich. Germany could take economic measures to ensure supplies of key raw materials, acquire overseas colonies by conquest, or participate peacefully in the world economy, but Hitler dismissed all these approaches. His one solution was to obtain living space in Europe which could only be achieved by war. 1943 would be the most suitable time, for by then the army, navy and air force would have achieved their planned expansions and their arms and equipment would be up to date. But first Austria and Czechoslovakia must be conquered to make the Reich's frontiers shorter and easier to defend. Von Blomberg, von Fritsch and von Neurath objected and queried the Führer's proposals. The only three to do so, they were later dismissed. None of the three later played any known role in any wartime resistance group, but at least they had had the courage to dissent from their leader.

The number of military men from the highest ranks who were well-attested dissidents is remarkable, considering that as early as 1934, when the army was enthusiastically in favour of the secret rearmament programme which was the direct result of the Nazis coming to power, every officer had been forced to take a ceremonial oath of personal loyalty to the Führer as Supreme Commander of the Wehrmacht. This oath was obviously a serious obstacle to any action of disloyalty. General Ludwig Beck, Chief of Staff of the army in May 1938, showed clear opposition in August 1938 when Hitler first told his service chiefs of the decision to strike at Czechoslovakia by force. Beck resigned and hoped all the generals would resign with him, but General von Brauchitsch, although a sympathiser, took no action. Another sympathiser, but inactive, was General Franz Halder who succeeded Beck as Chief of the Army Staff. One of the staunchest opponents of the Nazis, General von Hammerstein-Equord, resigned as early as 1934. Oster of the Abwehr (secretly protected by his chief Admiral Canaris) and Hans Gisevius, then in the Ministry of the Interior and close associate of Goerdeler, ex-Mayor of Leipzig and an opposition leader, were a liaison link between military and civilian opposition groups.

On 24 August 1939, immediately after the signature of the Nazi–Soviet pact, Hitler told von Brauchitsch and Halder of the imminent attack on Poland: 'We can now mock at any British blockade, and anyway all Western politicians are little worms.' In September 1939, after Poland had been defeated, General von Hammerstein-Equord and Count Fabian von Schlabrendorf were planning to arrest Hitler, who was due to inspect the western defences. But Hitler, with his usual intuition for frustrating plots against him, changed his mind at the last moment. The bomb attempt against him at Munich in November 1939 resulted in such tightening up of security measures that he became virtually unapproachable. He never again left his fortress home at Berchtesgaden or one of the Wehrmacht headquarters except for ceremonial meetings with Mussolini, Franco or Pétain until his last days in the Berlin Chancellery in 1945. He never visited the front lines or reviewed the Wehrmacht.

In November 1939 Hitler was planning the autumn invasion of neutral Denmark, the Netherlands and Belgium. The headquarters of the German high command was then at Zossen, where von Brauchitsch and Halder with support from Stulpnagel were planning a *coup d'état* to thwart the invasion plans. Parties to the *coup* were Oster (Abwehr), Helldorf (Berlin Police), Gisevius (Ministry of the Interior), Beck and Goerdeler. The crucial moment was to be von Brauchitsch's meeting with Hitler on 5 November, when he was to burn his bridges and come out into open rebellion, if Hitler maintained his insistence on attacking the three small neutrals. But when Hitler exploded with rage and accused his generals of being afraid to fight, von Brauchitsch's nerve failed; and the crucial moment passed. Hitler was – rightly – convinced that a conspiracy had been hatched at Zossen; four years later in 1943 he expressed his admiration of Stalin, who by purging his generals in the 1930s had eliminated all opposition. Immediately afterwards, on 8 November 1939, Hitler attended the Bürgerbraükeller in Munich in memory of his *putsch* of

1923. By leaving early he narrowly missed a bomb explosion which killed several men. The author, a simple unattached individual named Elser, a convinced Christian, was imprisoned and ultimately executed. Goebbels's propaganda machine propounded the theory that this Munich bomb was an attempt by the British Secret Service to avenge the recent capture of Best and Stevens at Venlo in Holland.

In June 1940, after the conquest of the West, Field-Marshal Witzleben wrote to his wife that the recent great victories were no good augury for the future. In July 1940 Goerdeler in a clairvoyant mood produced a paper for certain officers foreseeing an explosion of European resistance, the same month when the Churchill government in London was resolving to create an organisation, SOE, for that very purpose. The defeat of Goering's Luftwaffe over Britain in 1940 was discouraging both for the morale of the Nazi armed services and the civilians. Some saw it rightly as the turning point of the war. In June 1941 the invasion of the USSR and in December the Japanese attack on the USA brought the world's two largest powers into the war as enemies of the Third Reich. For men such as Goerdeler and Beck, final defeat became a certainty. By the end of 1942 the crushing Nazi defeat at Stalingrad and the Anglo-American landings in North Africa were disasters from which the Nazi–Fascist Axis never recovered.

The Communist element in German opposition was mostly active in the fields of intelligence and clandestine presses. The best known group was the Rote Kapelle or Service Otto headed by Leo Trepper and covering France, Belgium and the Netherlands as well as Germany; it included sections headed by Schultz-Boyssen of the Luftwaffe and Harnack of the Economics Ministry; it suffered heavy casualties, some seventy-eight, at the hands of the Gestapo. In religious circles both Catholics and Protestants played their parts, but the priests and pastors were more impressive than the prelates. There were three outstanding Roman Catholic bishops, von Galen of Westphalia, Faulhaber of Munich and Preysing of Berlin. They had the courage in 1941 to attack publicly the barbarisms of the Gestapo in Germany and the murder of 'unproductive citizens in mental asylums'. A small Catholic group publishing a clandestine paper, the *White Rose*, led by Hans and Sophy Scholl, a young brother and sister who were idealistic students in Munich, showed a rare courage and devotion to Christian morality. Both were executed in February 1943 after distributing leaflets on the fall of Stalingrad, the last of which said,

'We refuse to be any longer the accomplices of the monsters who govern us.' Nearly one hundred fellow students were liquidated at about the same time.

Ideas for the future of Europe were prominent in opposition circles in Germany, as in other countries. In France the underground press had a wealth of good authors and thinkers, many of whom felt strongly that 'the aim after liberation must be to work together for the construction of a free and democratic Europe, even with those with whom we fight today'. These words were addressed by Henri Frenay to General de Gaulle in London, in the course of a complaint that he was scandalised by the spirit of narrow nationalism that he saw in many of the General's Free French entourage. In Germany in wartime there were three conceptions of post-war Europe: the Nazis' view of conquest and enslavement; Goerdeler's group, including Ulrich von Hassell, visualised a permanent economic council but with Austria and Sudetenland remaining part of Germany; the Kreisau circle (Adam von Trott zu Stolz, Helmuth von Moltke and other liberals) wanted a United States of Europe on the basis that the conflagration of the Second World War offered the first chance to reorganise Europe since the decline of the medieval Church. The *White Rose* (Scholl) group likewise believed in a future united Europe; 'Freedom of speech, freedom of belief, protection of citizens against criminal dictatorial states are the foundation of the New Europe.'

The Casablanca Conference in January 1943 resulted in Roosevelt and Churchill announcing a policy of unconditional surrender. It produced, predictably, intense disappointment and resentment in German opposition circles. Their main hope had been to negotiate terms for an armistice as a basis for a *coup d'état* to eliminate the Nazis.

Those who had made or maintained secret contacts with Britain included Goerdeler and von Schlabrendorf, both of whom had visited Churchill, then a backbencher, after the final take-over of Czechoslovakia in March 1939; von Trott and von Moltke had also visited London at that time. Their secret contacts with the Allies had led to nothing and continued to do so. Secret contacts continued from late 1942 with Allen Dulles of OSS in Switzerland. Dulles himself regretted the Casablanca formula and knew it had greatly complicated his task of helping Gisevius, Goerdeler and the opposition to overthrow Hitler.

[185]

The Rastenburg assassination attempt occurred on 20 July 1944. The barbaric reprisals on over 4000 Germans, believed by Himmler and his Gestapo to have been in some way linked with leading anti-Nazi figures, are evidence of the existence of potential action groups who, but for Rastenburg, might have been described as no more than anti-Nazi dissidents. Claus von Stauffenberg was not a lone operator, but was linked with and backed by a network of men in high places, not only in Germany but in Paris (von Stulpnagel), Brussels (von Falkenhausen), the Eastern Front (von Tresckow) and Zurich (Gisevius).

Claus von Stauffenberg was a brilliant young officer with a first-class brain, an artist, musician and man of affairs; he was gravely wounded in Tunisia where he lost an eye, his right arm and two fingers of his left hand. After discharge from hospital he became chief of staff to General Olbricht and then decided at the end of 1943 with a group of like-minded friends to kill Hitler.

A provisional government was planned, ready to take over after the *coup*, including Beck as President, Goerdeler as Chancellor, von der Schulenburg or von Hassell as Minister of Foreign Affairs, Gisevius as Secretary of State and Witzleben as commander of the army. A proclamation to the population was ready; peace negotiations would be opened at once. But after Stauffenberg left the conference room, leaving the bomb in his briefcase close to Hitler, it is said that another officer by sheer accident moved it slightly so that the blast was diverted. The Führer had nine more demoniac months to live, Europe had another winter of war and the Red Army advanced many hundreds of miles further west. The bomb incidentally contained SOE plastic explosive, captured by the Abwehr from an F Section circuit in 1942, but it was not an SOE bomb.

But for the accidental moving of the briefcase at Rastenburg a German anti-Nazi Cabinet might have taken power and negotiated an early surrender; and the German groups concerned would have received from their contemporaries, even from their enemies, the honours which they deserved. But the course of history has left it open only to those who decades later have studied the evidence of the past to pay tributes to thousands of courageous and civilised Germans, who faced not only torture and death, but the charge of treason, in the belief that one day they would be honoured everywhere, including their own country.

For several years after 1944, few outside West Germany believed that there had ever been in Nazi Germany any resistance groups worthy of the name, apart from groups of foreign workers in the last days of the collapse and chaos in 1945. Hans Gisevius, a key figure in liaison with Dulles of OSS in Berne, wrote the first book to disprove this, *To the Bitter End*, in 1948. Later several German authors assembled material to record the names and restore the reputations of many who had been condemned to death as traitors and been executed or died under torture. Some critics have called it part truth, part legend. Doubtless there must always be a measure of uncertainty – as in all underground movements – as to the true facts of clandestine meetings, attempts to recruit others to secure the backing of influential figures, plots to organise sabotage and assassinations, all inevitably without any contemporary record, because security made any record a potential death sentence. But there was no resistance movement in Nazi Germany in the sense of a movement to hamper the war effort. There were opposition groups aiming at a change of government, occasionally in clandestine contact with the Allies but never under Allied direction or control.

Nobody who reads it can fail to be impressed by Professor Henri Bernard's *L'Autre Allemagne* (1976). The historian of Belgian resistance, once wartime head of the Deuxième Section in London and twice on missions in occupied Belgium, has produced a review of the German opposition. He records the range and variety of the groups concerned, right wing, left wing, aristocratic, socialist, Communist, military, professional and religious. He reminds us that Dachau and Buchenwald were created in 1933 as the first Nazi concentration camps to receive not foreigners from occupied lands but dissident Germans, of whom 250,000 – without counting Jews – were condemned between 1933 and the outbreak of the war in 1939; that from 1932 over 570,000 Germans (including 30,000 Jews and 2000 writers) emigrated and settled abroad. He mentions the sad case of the writer Stefan Zweig and his wife, who in 1942 (the very year in which the tide began to turn against Hitler) committed suicide in Brazil in despair at seeing Europe enslaved by the Nazis.

Bernard gives a limited roll of honour of those who died as a result of the Rastenburg assassination attempt on 20 July 1944. Out of 4000 or possibly 6000 he cites the names and descriptions of over 150 of the best known, with the dates of their executions or suicides. They included sixty officers of military or naval rank, one field-marshal, Witzleben, one admiral, Canaris, and twelve generals, including Hans Oster of the Abwehr (a pivot of the military opposition group, who in 1940 sent secret warnings of imminent invasion to the governments in Norway, Denmark, Holland and Belgium), von Stulpnagel (ex-governor of Paris), von Tresckow (a key figure on the Russian front where he formed a circle of anti-Nazi officers) and thirty-five senior officers. Other names on the roll of honour were ex-ambassadors von Hassell and von der Schulenburg; several ecclesiastics, the Protestant pastor Dietrich Bonhoeffer and the Jesuit Père Delf; aristocrats, von Trott zu Stolz, Helmuth von Moltke and Otto von Bismarck; and Goerdeler, ex-Mayor of Leipzig, a central figure with special foreign contacts, including Winston Churchill (Bernard, 1976).

SOE's German Section X achieved little of note until the last months of the war when OSS were also active, especially on the SI side (Persico, 1979). From July 1944, after Overlord and Rastenburg, with growing confusion in the Third Reich and ever-increasing numbers of foreign workers to preoccupy the SD and Gestapo, it became possible to parachute in moderate numbers of specially trained agents of various nationalities. It is known that some of these German Section missions achieved their objectives; but in the last months of the Nazi régime and under mounting bombing, it was hard to identify damage clearly attributable to special operations. From November 1944 to May 1945, SOE's X Section was headed by Field-Marshal Sir Gerald Templer, an old friend of Gubbins, in his interval between the Italian campaign and heading the British sector in the western zone of occupied Germany.

From late 1943 the establishment of air bases in south Italy and the growth of the Jugoslav Partisan movement in Slovenia made it possible to consider penetrating Austria from the south and establishing courier lines in support of resistance groups. During 1943 a plan was developed to create one or more despatch posts in Slovenia, manned by British officers and located with Jugoslav Partisan units within striking distance of the 1937 Austrian frontier. This was the origin of Operation Clowder. Three SOE officers, Colonel Peter Wilkinson, Major Charles Villiers and Major A. Hesketh-Prichard, were dropped into Partisan areas further south. The project was explained to Tito at his Jajce headquarters in order to obtain his consent since Partisan support was needed. By summer of 1944 a chain of despatch posts was set up for some sixty miles along the 1937 frontier. The Germans, who were reading the

Partisan ciphers, were well aware of these activities and reacted vigorously.

Allied Forces Headquarters at Caserta in September 1944 had hopes of Allied armies reaching Vienna by the end of the year and were interested in the possibility of mobilising some Austrian resistance to support the advance of the Eighth Army. Partly with this in mind Hesketh-Prichard persuaded the local Partisans to cross the River Drau (Drava) with him and enter Austria in the hope of setting up a base among the scattered Slovene communities believed to exist in the Saualpen to the north-east of Klagenfurt. SOE parachuted rubber boats in to him and they crossed the river in mid-October, eighty strong. He radioed a week later that he had reached the Saualpen summit and asked for supplies. Bad weather delayed drops until late December, but Hesketh-Prichard after a radio transmission on 3 December went off the air and was not heard of again. Of the eighty men, only forty survivors remained when the Eighth Army arrived in May 1945.

After the surrender of the German Afrika Korps in May 1943, there was some hope of recruiting from amongst them some anti-Nazi Austrian agents, for up to then recruitment of suitable agents had been difficult. The shortage was a serious handicap, especially in radio operators, but by the winter of 1944–5 some thirty former prisoners-of-war, who had volunteered for special duties, were in training by SOE in southern Italy. In February/March 1945 four blind drops were made and in the last six weeks of the war over twenty SOE agents were dropped, but they had little time in which to achieve results of importance. There was one exception; a social democrat with underground experience in Styria, who had been conscripted into the Wehrmacht in 1944, deserted to the *maquis* in France and volunteered to return to Austria. He and his party organised an effective group at Bad Aussee; and when the US Army arrived he was able to hand over a purged and effective local administration, to help in the arrest of Kaltenbrunner and other top SD officials, and to recover the Austrian crown jewels and other property of great value.

12

Eastern Europe

At the outbreak of war, Czechoslovakia, Poland, Hungary, Rumania and Bulgaria, five countries of Eastern Europe, had been reduced to four by the Nazi occupation and break-up of Czechoslovakia in March 1939, when Hitler repudiated the Munich agreement of September 1938. Czechoslovakia had previously been the strongest of the five, both in a military and an industrial sense; nevertheless, it had been subjugated by Hitler in spite of having a formal military alliance with France. The remaining four countries thus had good cause to fear Nazi invasion or occupation in the near future. So it was an act of the highest collective courage by the Poles, even with the encouragement of the British guarantee to come to their aid, to resist Nazi threats through the summer of 1939 and to continue to do so even after the crushing news of the Nazi–Soviet pact in August. From then on it was clear that the countries of Eastern Europe would soon fall under the total domination of either Hitler or Stalin. It was not until 22 June 1941, when Hitler invaded the Soviet Union, that the answer to that question seemed to be revealed, only to be reversed four years later by the unconditional Nazi surrender to the Allies in May 1945.

In 1939, the four countries were underdeveloped industrially and generally, having agricultural economies mostly of a primitive peasant variety, but with many vast estates, with poor communications and with few major natural resources apart from the Ploesti oilfields in Rumania. On the political side, Poland and Hungary were governed by oligarchies, military and aristocratic, Rumania and Bulgaria by monarchies. All four were overshadowed by the two nightmares of Nazi military aggression or Soviet Communist subversion. No one in Eastern Europe, or indeed elsewhere, could read the future over the next four years, but probably in 1939 the majority were resigned, however much they detested it, to the victory of an efficient Nazi military machine backed by German industrial power.

The background and the prospects were not encouraging to potential organisers of resistance.

Poland

Nearly two centuries of foreign occupation by Austrians, Prussians
and Russians had taught the Poles many lessons. As a result they
were unsurpassed experts in clandestine resistance with immense
technical cipher proficiency and the highest standards of security.
Before the war had even begun, they had taken two remarkable
secret measures of far-reaching importance. From the spring of
1939, at the instigation of Gubbins who visited Warsaw twice that
year, first in the spring, then again in August as a member of a British
military mission, they started to draw up plans for underground
resistance in case Poland should be overrun by the Nazis. In July, the
Poles presented British and French deciphering experts with two
models of the commercial Enigma enciphering machine, which the
Germans had modified to carry their most secret signals and which
the Poles had succeeded in copying.

Enigma was a machine which could be used to decipher or en-
cipher several different codes, and was capable of almost infinite
mechanical variations. Changes could be made every month or week
or even day to defeat the would-be codebreaker. At that date the
Poles had begun to decipher one or two German codes for short
periods but had been defeated by the periodical variations. The
French decipherers had made little progress with one army code but
were reading the Luftwaffe code when the defeat of the French army
made the decrypts valueless. The British, more fortunate in timing,
had broken the main Luftwaffe codes by July 1940, just in time for
the aerial Battle of Britain, and later they succeeded in breaking most
of the German army and naval codes and some of the Italians'. Later
the Americans broke some of the Japanese naval codes with decisive
results for the Battle of the Pacific. The contribution which Polish
intellect and generosity in this field made to the ultimate Allied
victory was immense and should never be forgotten.

After September 1939, when Poland had been overrun, first by
Nazis from the west and then by the Red Army from the east, most of
the Polish deciphering team had managed to escape through the
Balkans to France where they started working for Major Bertrand,
head of the French D section (déchiffrement).

Many ministers and officials of the Polish government and

thousands of members of the armed services also managed to reach France. By the time of the French surrender in June 1940, there were nearly 500,000 Polish citizens on French soil of whom many had lived there for years, but over 80,000 were armed and trained. General Sikorski had become Prime Minister of a government which had been promptly recognised by France, Britain and America; one of the best military minds in Poland, he was a good democrat and for political reasons had been rejected by the pre-war Pilsudski–Beck oligarchy.

This Polish government-in-exile kept contact by radio and courier with the underground movement which had been formed from a mixture of the four major democratic parties, the socialists, peasant, national and Christian groups. These members of the resistance concentrated in 1939–41 on attacking trains transporting Russian grain and oil through Poland into Germany.

In June 1940, the French high command agreed with the Germans that Polish forces would surrender along with the French. Sikorski refused, in a stormy meeting with General Weygand, and flew to London to promise Churchill that Poland would continue to fight. By the beginning of 1941, some 24,000 Poles had reached London and became the nucleus of a force which later grew to nearly 250,000 and included several Polish naval vessels and many fighter pilots. Once in England, Mikolajczyk and his staff kept in touch with their homeland through their own efficient signals and cipher systems. They controlled their own signals traffic and developed their own radio sets which were at least as good as, if not better than, the British sets in the early war years. The Poles consequently established a measure of independence which no other London-based government-in-exile or any other resistance movement ever approached.

Sikorski was constantly pressing Churchill for more funds to support the Polish army which was being built up in Britain. On one occasion in December 1940, Churchill, who was accompanied by a Foreign Office friend of mine, replied to Sikorski, when he could not meet his demands for more and more funds, '*Mon général, quand je me trouve devant la vieille femme de Threadneedle Street, je suis impotent.*' Then turning to my friend he added with a twinkle, 'Or should I have said "*impuissant*"?' Nevertheless, when I arrived in Lisbon some three weeks later in January 1941, I soon found myself acting as a channel for funds from London for at least three Polish intelligence services run by Colonel Kovaleski, personal intelligence representative of General Sikorski, Colonel Mally and Captain Tomaszewski representing the Sixth Bureau of the army general staff, and a Lisbon representative of the Minister of the Interior, Kot. Each of the three was scrupulously separate from the others, certainly on security grounds and probably also for reasons of domestic politics. They were all engaged in receiving and forwarding Polish refugees and organising or operating lines of communication to and from Poland, and, of course, generally collecting intelligence from occupied Europe.

Poland geographically was at the extreme range for the aircraft of the 1940s – she was wholly out of range during the short summer when the hours of darkness were too few to allow pilots to avoid the enemy night-fighters over Denmark and Germany, both coming and going. These factors all combined to keep the Polish home army, Armia Krajowa, or AK, seriously short of external supplies. It was not until February 1941 that the first SOE air operation to Poland took place, and three Polish agents were dropped near Bielsko in western Poland and reached their destination. The home army was highly centralised and all Polish agents, wherever dropped, had to report to Warsaw.

Polish agents were trained at various SOE schools in England and Scotland in weapon training, security and parachuting. In demolitions and guerrilla warfare, including movement across country at night, most of the Poles were trained at Arisaig in north-west Scotland. I did my own training on my return from Lisbon along with the Poles at Arisaig, and found them to be a group of dedicated young men, most of whom, sadly, were destined to die two years later in the Warsaw rising. Others were being trained in Canadian camps, an arrangement which Sikorski had made on his visits to the USA and Canada. He had also arranged for Poland to be included in the Lease-Lend programme newly established by President Roosevelt, although Washington was still officially neutral in 1941.

Early that June, the Polish underground reported huge German troop movements, which foreshadowed the invasion of Russia on the 22 in Operation Barbarossa. This invasion transformed the Polish problem, but not to the extent hoped for by Sikorski who 'dreamed of the day when Polish armies reformed in Russia would fight at the side of Red Army men, and that in battle against a common foe, the two groups would be united as brothers' (Mikolajczyk, 1948).

[193]

At the end of July 1941 the Sikorski–Maisky pact was signed in London; the USSR renounced the territorial changes previously laid down in the Ribbentrop–Molotov pact of August 1939, restored diplomatic relations with the Polish government in London, agreed to help rebuild a Polish army in the USSR and to grant amnesty to all Polish citizens deprived of their freedom in Russian territory. Mikolajczyk's estimate was that 250,000 Polish soldiers and 1,500,000 Polish civilians had been forcibly transported from Poland into the USSR since September 1939. General Anders, a gallant officer who had been badly wounded, was made commander of the new Polish army in Russia, and became concerned at the small number of Polish officers reporting to him, less than four hundred. In December 1941, Sikorski personally took this matter up with Stalin, who was evasive. Two years later the Nazis announced the discovery of eight mass graves at Katyn, near Smolensk, which contained the corpses of thousands of Polish officers, none bearing any documents later than 1940. The Polish government-in-exile asked the International Red Cross to investigate, whereupon the Soviet Union served notice on the Polish ambassador in Moscow, severing diplomatic relations.

Another major blow to Polish morale at this period was the death of Sikorski with others, including Colonel Victor Cazalet, a British member of Parliament who had been attached to him as a liaison officer on Churchill's orders. They were all killed in an air crash on taking off from Gibraltar, a notoriously short runway. The crash was beyond question an accident, though both the Nazi propaganda minister, Goebbels, and a play written after the war advanced the theory that Churchill, a great admirer and supporter of Sikorski, ordered his death to please Stalin. His death was a great loss to Poland and to the Allied cause; he was succeeded as Prime Minister by Mikolajczyk.

Up to this time, Polish partisans had not been able to operate on any scale because they were so short of weapons. The RAF had tried to drop supplies operating out of bases in the United Kingdom, but the northern route involved crossing the flak and dodging the enemy fighters between Denmark and southern Belgium and then continuing over Germany and the Baltic; it was the most dangerous air route in Europe and losses were heavy. When six aircraft alone were lost on Polish sorties in two nights in September 1943, Bomber Command decided to stop using the northern route.

[194]

Instead, the Air Ministry in London decided that it would be best for the Polish Flight 1386 to operate out of Brindisi in southern Italy, where bases for supply-dropping operations (as well as bombing) were established after the Allied liberation of southern Italy in September 1943. The route to Poland was not easy so even although they dropped six hundred tons of stores between January and September 1944, the Polish flight and other British and South African units lost over seventy aircraft in so doing.

To organise the special operations side, the Polish Section of SOE decided, in December 1943, to set up an operational base at Latiano near Bari, with a training school at Ostuni and headquarters at Monopoli, attached for administrative purposes to Special Operations Mediterranean which came into existence in January 1944. Apart from Air Force operations, Force 139, an *ad hoc* unit made up out of SOE's Polish Section in London plus SOE's Mediterranean people, was responsible to SOE London, although the Polish army staff in London continued to have charge of intelligence and to maintain direct radio links with Poland.

Considerable changes had taken place in enemy-occupied Poland after the Soviet victory at Stalingrad at the beginning of 1943, when General von Paulus's army had been encircled and forced to surrender. The Russians then began their long advance to the west and, as they did so, the Soviet Government began to put more emphasis on the build-up of Communist resistance groups in Poland under the aegis of the NKVD. The Union of Polish Patriots was organised in Moscow and sponsored a small Polish army under General Berling. When the inter-Allied conferences took place at Teheran in November 1943 and at Yalta in January 1945 Stalin got his way and was allowed drastically to alter the frontiers of pre-war Poland despite strong objections from Churchill and Roosevelt. The USSR insisted on extending its frontiers westward to the so-called Curzon Line, which included the ancient Polish capital of Lwow, preferring to give compensation to Poland in the west at the expense of Germany. According to Polish sources, the Soviet partisans under General Ponomarenko were burning and destroying Polish villages and townships in eastern Poland and murdering the male inhabitants as early as May 1943.

As the Russians moved steadily westwards, the Royal Air Force under pressure from Force 139 tried to step up the number of sorties to Poland from Brindisi. Three were accomplished in

December 1943, but then the weather turned bad and only twenty-three were possible in the whole of the first quarter of 1944, of which only two succeeded, at the cost of two aircraft lost. This was most disappointing since the decision to switch to a Central European route had been based on the expectation of better weather conditions as well as avoiding the western night-fighter belt. But the second quarter showed a striking improvement. April had 132 sorties, of which 65 succeeded. In May, 192 tons of supplies were dropped as well as 104 men. The total of Force 139's Polish operations from December 1943 until they were discontinued at the beginning of 1945 was 620 sorties, of which 290 succeeded, dropping 152 men and 362 tons of supplies, at the cost of 48 aircraft. (These figures include sorties in connection with the Warsaw rising.)

There were three separate air routes from Brindisi to different areas of Poland. Route 3 went over Lake Balaton, west of Budapest, over the Tatra Mountains to Cracow (600m) or to Warsaw (900m). Route 4 went further east by way of Kotor, east of Budapest, and was then similar to route 3. Route 5 went still further east over Durazzo in Albania to Lwow (684m). The move to Brindisi had increased the area of Poland within reach of air sorties and over six hundred reception areas were organised. This led the Polish resistance to decentralise; they now permitted local districts to maintain and defend their own reception areas and allowed them to keep certain arms and supplies for their own use. But it continued to be the rule that all parachutists had to report to Warsaw, and all money had to be delivered to Warsaw to ensure central control.

Three remarkable pick-up operations were successfully carried out in south Poland by unarmed C47 Dakotas operating from Brindisi, known by the code name Wildhorn. These sorties in April, May and July 1944 enabled important political and military figures to be brought out of Poland so that they could talk to the Polish government-in-exile in London. In addition, Operation Wildhorn III on 25 July brought out as well as the future Prime Minister, Arciszewski, the key parts of a V2 rocket, which had been recovered by members of the resistance from some marshy land where it had fallen. The Wildhorn operations were made possible not only by the skill, daring and endurance of the air crews, but also by the achievements and high organisation of the local underground, who had to position strong detachments of troops to prevent any German patrols overrunning the airfield while the aircraft was on the ground.

Detailed planning of loading and landing drill was essential. In Wildhorn I and Wildhorn II the time on the ground was only three and seven minutes respectively; Wildhorn III took seventy minutes because the aircraft got bogged down as a result of recent heavy rains, but the local detachment were able to keep the enemy at bay for just long enough for the delayed take-off, helped by ropes and horses.

At the end of July 1944 the advance elements of the Red Army reached the banks of the Vistula opposite Warsaw and on the 29, Radio SWIT, run by Moscow-trained Poles, was calling on the Poles of Warsaw to rise and expel the German enemy. The text can be found in Mikolajczyk and is summarised in Churchill's *The Second World War* (1954). The Poles were ambitious to liberate their own capital and they thought they had a chance to do so, given maximum air supply from southern Italy. Their commander, General Bor-Komorowski, radioed his government-in-exile in London, and Churchill signalled Supreme Allied Commander Mediterranean requesting maximum supply drops to Warsaw. Churchill could only 'request' SACMED, for instructions could only come from the combined chiefs of staff in Washington. The short summer nights and the need for aircraft to descend to low levels over Warsaw's anti-aircraft defences, illuminated by burning ruins and searchlights, made heavy losses inevitable. In all, thirty-one aircraft were lost on eighty-seven sorties, delivering 130 tons of supplies to Warsaw. Churchill asked Stalin for Soviet aid, but this was refused until it was too late. On 16 August, General Bor signalled from Warsaw: 'Gallant efforts of your airmen have enabled us to continue struggle. We bow with deepest reverence before the fallen crews.'

On 17 August 1944 I was present with Colonel Threlfall of Force 139 at a meeting in Bari between Air Marshal Elliot, commander of the Balkan Air Force, who was in charge of the Polish sorties, General Ira C. Eaker and Marshal of the RAF Sir John Slessor, at that time Commander and Deputy Commander of MAAF, who had flown across the Apennines that morning from Caserta. All the evidence was reviewed, the losses of aircraft and crew were considered and Threlfall's vigorous and reasoned pleading of the Polish case was heard. In the end the air chiefs reluctantly came to the conclusion that we had exhausted the resources available in southern Italy, and so this was no longer a feasible operation of war and must be stopped despite Churchill's request, which up to now had been carried out to the utmost limit of capacity. To me, and to Threlfall, this was one of the most tragic moments of the war, but the decision was incontrovertible: no more flights to Warsaw and its immediate surroundings. On 18 August, Supreme Allied Command ruled that only the aircraft of the Polish Flight could continue to fly to Poland in view of the air supply needs of the Italian partisans.

Our losses over Warsaw were not made good for over six months, and as a result we were able to make fewer air sorties to northern Italy. The Italians were bitter about this as many of them thought we were deliberately refraining from supporting them. After the war I was asked by Dr Pizzoni, leader of the Italian partisan high command, to give a talk in Florence on this subject to dispel rumours that the Allies had lost interest in them in the second half of 1944 and to explain how our losses over Warsaw had affected air-supply dropping capacity.

Warsaw confirmed the lesson long learned by Gubbins and other experts that lightly armed urban guerrillas cannot be supplied by long-range air sorties on a scale which enables them to resist heavily armed regulars. General Bor's call for a mass uprising was a desperate and tragic move. No doubt he thought, as millions did elsewhere, that the attempted assassination of Hitler at Rastenburg a few days earlier was the beginning of the end of the Third Reich, and that that end would be quick. No doubt he also thought that as the Red Army had reached the Vistula in the eastern suburbs of Warsaw, it would soon continue its advance into the city itself. There may be good grounds for saying that the Red Army at this point had overreached itself and was bound to halt on the eastern banks of the Vistula to enable its supply lines to catch up, but there are signs that Stalin was well content to let the core of the Polish resistance be battered to annihilation in the ruins of Warsaw.

Churchill records how the British Cabinet considered the situation on 4 September: 'I do not remember any occasion on which such deep anger was shown by our members, Tory, Labour, Liberal, alike.' He also wrote that 'from September 14 onwards the Soviet Air Force dropped supplies but few of the parachutes opened and many of the containers were smashed and useless . . . [the Russians] wished to have the non-Communist Poles destroyed but also to keep alive the idea that they were going to their rescue . . . of the forty thousand men and women of the Polish underground army about fifteen thousand fell. Out of a population of a million nearly two hundred thousand had been stricken. The suppression of the revolt cost the German army ten thousand killed, seven thousand missing and nine thousand wounded. The proportions attest the hand to hand character of the fighting. When the Russians entered the city three months later they found little but shattered streets and unburied dead. Such was the liberation of Poland where they now rule' (Churchill, 1954, pp. 124–7).

Czechoslovakia

When the Nazis took over Czechoslovakia in March 1939, the leading members of the government, which included President Beneš and Foreign Minister Masaryk, fled to London. At the same time their chief of intelligence, Moravec, his senior staff and his essential files, were flown to London with the help of SIS. This government-in-exile was primarily interested in maintaining international recognition, looking after fellow countrymen in exile and planning for restoration after the war.

Moravec had, however, managed to make some preparations for a 'left behind' organisation which could become the nucleus of a resistance movement at the right time. It was called Obrana Naroda and had hidden about 100,000 rifles and 10,000 machine guns; it also had a sabotage section and several divisions under regular army officers, but it was slow to start operations and appeared to be insecure and unimpressive. The spirit may have been willing but the Nazi military and security apparatus seemed to fill the members of the resistance with fear.

The Czechs, having established in London a government-in-exile before the war began, preserved a great degree of autonomy in technical matters, kept their own codes and sets, and on security grounds restricted circulation of their telegrams so severely that they did not get much further than the hands of Gubbins. As a result, it was difficult for SOE to influence policy and operations and it was reduced to being virtually a supply and transport agent.

However, Gubbins and SOE were able to give operational and technical help to Moravec's project Anthropoid to eliminate Reinhard Heydrich, who was Number Two in the SS under Himmler and had been made governor of Bohemia and Moravia in 1941. In a book about strategic deception, A. Cave Brown suggests that Anthropoid was an SIS idea conceived by General Stewart Menzies to help his German opposite number, Admiral Canaris, by eliminating one of the heads of the Nazi party's intelligence service, which was destined to destroy the Abwehr by absorption; it was, however, entirely a Czech government-in-exile concept which had the approval of Beneš and technical help and training from SOE (Cave Brown, 1975).

Two highly trained agents, Kubis, a Czech, and Gabcik, a Slovak, threw a specially designed bomb into Heydrich's open car, which had been slowed down by one agent with a sten gun. Heydrich was mortally wounded and died a few days later. The two agents got away but were later cornered by Nazi troops and committed suicide after a gun battle. Savage reprisals predictably followed, and over 2000 victims were killed, including the entire population of the village of Lidice. When it became known that Heydrich's death had been planned in London, the government-in-exile's prestige was much enhanced. But the reprisals, coupled with tightened security measures, had a deadening effect on embryo resistance, especially in the Czech territories known in the Reich as the protectorate of Bohemia.

Slovakia, a separate territory since March 1939, was treated less oppressively until the rising in August 1944 which centred on Banska Bystrica, just as the Warsaw rising was being crushed in Poland. The Slovak independent army had two divisions fighting on the German side; they revolted during the retreat and the Slovaks got in touch with the Czech government-in-exile in London, where plans were made for an American OSS mission to go to Banska Bystrica and establish both liaison with the insurgents and an air rescue unit. Several American OSS officers flew in from Bari to the nearest airfield at Tri Duby. They were in uniform as part of a combined mission to bring in supplies to the Slovak army and to bring back stranded – mostly American – aircrews. Colonel Threlfall of Force 139 also flew in and came back to Bari on the return flight, but most of the OSS officers later died of exposure or were captured and executed. A Slovak airborne brigade was also flown in from Russia, but was poorly armed and equipped and contributed nothing. The rising was a failure, being geographically too remote from bases in southern Italy and from those in Russia. There were heavy casualties, though some escaped to the mountains and survived the winter. Two OSS officers eventually escaped through the Russian lines.

London and Italy continued to despatch intelligence missions, but the resistance movement in Czechoslovakia remained passive until the last days of the war. I recall one Force 139 operation from Bari when two British officers, Foster and Seymour, made three or four unsuccessful sorties in January 1945 without being able to find any trace of the planned reception committee.

From 1943 onwards it became progressively clearer and clearer that the Nazis would never defeat the Russians and that the Red Army would sooner or later overrun Eastern and Central Europe. The Communist-run branch of the Czech underground movement came under growing pressure from the Soviet Union to establish itself in eastern Slovakia as soon as the Red Army arrived in 1945, despite the presence of the government-in-exile in London under Beneš and Masaryk.

Hungary

Most of the Hungarian nobility were traditionally pro-British, but German influence was strong and became overwhelming by 1940. Admiral Horthy was then in control, acting theoretically as regent for the absent Habsburg monarch, and he finally decided to throw in his lot with the Germans and to declare war on Russia. He allowed free passage through to the eastern front for the Nazi armies bent on Operation Barbarossa, and sent a Hungarian army corps with them.

But in 1943 the destruction of the German armies in Stalingrad and North Africa followed by the Italian armistice and the Allied invasion of southern Italy caused the old Admiral to think again. He sent one of his ministers to Berne to contact Allen Dulles of the American OSS. OSS parachuted a mission of three officers into Hungary in March 1944; but this coincided with a German take-over of full control from the Hungarians, so these three men were handed straight over to the Germans and interrogated for six weeks. They were interned in Germany and eventually liberated.

SOE missions to Hungary were considered necessary probing operations, though the prospect of organising resistance or carrying out *coup de main* operations of substance seemed remote. Colonel Basil Davidson in August 1943 worked into the Backa area from Jugoslavia; Colonel Boughey landed near Lake Balaton with a cover story of searching for non-existent guerrillas but with the object of contacting Prime Minister Kallay, and was captured in 1944; Major Coates was also captured and roughly treated by the secret police in Budapest.

In 1943, a Hungarian diplomat, Laszlo Veres, made contact with the SOE mission in Lisbon and later with the SOE mission in Istanbul and the British Ambassador to Turkey. He took two B Mark II radio transmitters back with him to Budapest, which he operated with the aid of a couple of Hungarian secret police corporals from a building adjoining the office of the Prime Minister. He was secretly representing a group including the President, the Prime Minister, the Foreign Minister and the Chief of Staff. A good deal of traffic was passed on the subject of a possible Hungarian surrender to the Western Allies. Unfortunately, the Hungarians, like the Rumanians, never seem to have appreciated the impossibility of surrendering to the next country but one; you can only surrender to a country whose armed forces are in your own country or at least in territory immediately adjacent. When the Germans took control in March 1944, Veres escaped from Buda into Jugoslavia, where he got in touch with Tito's Partisans and was eventually brought out to Italy.

As late as September 1944, Admiral Horthy was still trying to come to terms with the Western Allies to save Hungary from Soviet domination, and the Archduke Otto von Habsburg even approached Churchill on this point during the Quebec Conference. But the Red Army rolled on and by March 1945 Hungary was under Soviet occupation and a Communist régime was progressively imposed on the unwilling Magyars.

Bulgaria

The Bulgarians are of central Asian origin and speak a Slavonic language which is closely allied to Russian, but in the Thirties they were a monarchy and were officially aligned against the USSR. Yet when it came to the point, they never declared war on Russia but did so only on Britain and America. As a result, there was a Soviet embassy in Sofia throughout the war which was no doubt extremely active in collecting intelligence information and organising resistance against the Germans, not only in Bulgaria, but in the adjoining countries of Jugoslavia and Rumania as well. Finally Russia declared war on Bulgaria on 2 September 1944 but peace was concluded a week later.

News that a Bulgarian patriotic front existed reached London late in 1943. It appeared to be a broadly based resistance movement, directed by a political committee which was Communist-controlled but not exclusively Communist. So when SOE in London were asked later that year whether it would be more effective to bomb Sofia or Budapest, they advised Sofia, for there was in Bulgaria, unlike Hungary, a growing resistance movement which the creation of disorder would encourage.

That SOE were correct in their appraisal is borne out by the German Leverkuehn of the Abwehr who wrote: 'With the bombing of Sofia and other towns from January 1944 onwards, the pace of internal lawlessness, rebellion and disruption began to accelerate, till it culminated in complete collapse in face of the approaching Russian front in September 1944' (Leverkuehn, 1954, p. 151).

SOE officers began to explore the Bulgarian scene from 1943, making use of other known guerrilla organisations in adjoining countries. When Mostyn Davies and Frank Thompson came through Serbian Macedonia, one was killed in action, the other captured and executed by Bulgarians although in uniform. Later in 1944, Ian MacPherson through Thrace joined forces with John Harrington, arriving in Sofia with their partisans, who had organised a *coup d'état* in early September 1944. Two OSS missions moved into Sofia at the same time and helped evacuate over three hundred American airmen. Sofia was taken over rapidly by Communists, who took over the levers of power, and Bulgarian troops, who joined forces with the advancing Red Army. The two British officers were soon ordered by the Red Army to leave and returned to Istanbul and Cairo. At the same time, at the end of September 1944, the American intelligence mission was also ordered out.

Rumania

In the 1920s Rumania had been a member of the Little Entente, associated with France, but the growing pressure of the Third Reich in the Thirties forced her to withdraw from it. King Carol, a spendthrift monarch, left the country for Western Europe in 1939 and the country came under a Fascist pro-Nazi government headed by Marshal Antonescu. The Nazi occupation of Austria and Czechoslovakia opened up the way for Germans to move eastwards, and in June 1941 the Rumanians joined forces with them for the invasion of Russia.

The oilfields of Ploesti (which had been partly sabotaged by British operatives in the First World War before the German occupation in 1916) were the most important sources of energy for the Reich. Section D and later SOE were constantly studying, with departments such as the Treasury and Economic Warfare, means of reducing the production of Rumanian oil and impeding its transportation to Germany up the Danube. Bearing in mind that Rumania was a neutral up to June 1941, physical sabotage of the oilfields was not merely difficult but could have been counter-productive, either by bringing Rumania into the war on the German side prematurely or by attracting Nazi counter-sabotage measures, such as German armed guards at all key points. Leverkuehn says that Canaris, head of the Abwehr, ' . . . had assumed that the British Secret Service would initiate sabotage acts against the production centres of oil and against its means of transportation. Why nothing of the sort was in fact attempted remains a mystery' (Leverkuehn, 1954, p. 138). Then the Germans moved in after June 1940, and protective measures were taken for the oilfields with security units and anti-aircraft artillery (Hinsley, 1979).

Various plans to interrupt transport of oil and other commodities by Danube shipping were considered: plans for major demolitions to block the Iron Gates; plans to sink a large steamer in the middle of the Narrows; the creation of a company to buy up Danube barges and deny their use to the Germans. But it was not until 1944 that the Allied acquisition of air bases in south Italy made it possible for effective action to be taken against Rumanian oil. Then USAAF daylight bombing of Ploesti seriously reduced oil production and the continued mining of the Danube disrupted river transportation of oil to Germany. Neither of these major air operations would have been possible from bases in the United Kingdom or North Africa.

The search for a Rumanian political leader to organise resistance led SOE to Juliu Maniu, head of the National Peasant Party. He was recommended by SOE's chief representative in Rumania, G. de Chastelain, who from 1941 headed the SOE office in Istanbul with success. He wanted to get Maniu out of Rumania to the Middle East, and in 1941 Maniu seemed willing to go. The Foreign Office had no enthusiasm for Maniu, preferring Dr Tilea, Rumanian Minister in London, a friend of King Carol, and so de Chastelain's plan was stillborn and no Rumanian resistance leader was ever found. Maniu helped maintain an SOE radio set up to 1941 for occasional contact with Cairo, but he was never able to make up his mind to take a decisive step, such as organising a resistance movement or coming to Cairo to help SOE organise it from outside. A left-wing leader,

Patrascanu, kept in touch with Moscow, but he too seems to have achieved little.

Force 133 in Cairo recognised the need to get in more direct touch with Maniu if any action were to be generated. They dropped Major Russell into Jugoslavia; he crossed the Danube and got in touch with one of Maniu's men, only to be murdered soon after by a local bandit. However, his radio operator escaped and passed messages to Cairo, which led to another mission, also unsuccessful. De Chastelain and Ivor Porter were dropped at the end of December 1943, but by accident ended up several miles from the reception committee; both were soon arrested and taken to police headquarters in Bucharest. Just before this event, Maniu had reported that Antonescu had almost reached the point of handing over power to the opposition. Early in 1944, Antonescu took the further step of authorising Prince Stirbei, a well-known political figure, to visit Cairo to explore terms with the Allies for an armistice. In August 1944 the young King Michael, who had succeeded his father Carol, dismissed the Antonescu government, and formed a new government including Maniu and Patrascanu. Soon after the armistice negotiations were shifted to Moscow, and de Chastelain and Porter were released and returned to Istanbul.

The result of special operations in Eastern Europe and the position at the end of the war may be briefly summarised. Czechoslovakia produced two major acts of resistance, first the execution of Heydrich in 1942, planned and carried out by the government-in-exile with technical help, advice and training from SOE; second, the rising of the Slovak army at Banska Bystrica in 1944, supported by the OSS, but a serious failure with heavy casualties. Poland, helped by SOE but with wholly inadequate numbers of aircraft, maintained a highly organised and disciplined underground army from 1940 to 1944, with a steady record of resistance activity, culminating in the tragic disaster of the Warsaw rising. Hungary and Rumania produced numerous personalities in official positions who had hopes and ambitions of detaching their countries from alliance with the Nazis and negotiating a surrender to the Allies; but geographical and military circumstances made this impossible, and although a few British and American officers penetrated these countries, most were captured and no major achievement occurred, apart from the rescue of many imprisoned Allied airmen, mostly

American. In Bulgaria, a country with strong Slavonic ties to Russia, an effective resistance movement developed spontaneously in 1943; two SOE officers were lost when trying to establish contact, and two others succeeded in reaching Sofia at about the same time as the Red Army. All five countries were occupied by the Red Army in 1945, and sooner or later Communist régimes were imposed, the latest being Czechoslovakia in March 1948.

13

The Secret Weapons: V1 and V2

Hitler's secret weapons, Vergeltungswaffe I, the flying bomb, and Vergeltungswaffe II, the rocket, might well have made it impossible for Britain to continue the war, or at least to act as an effective base for the cross-Channel invasion in June 1944. However, information and action from resistance movements in Denmark, Poland and France enabled measures both defensive and offensive to be taken in Britain whereby the damage inflicted by the V1 and V2, though still heavy, was greatly reduced. The measures taken delayed launching of the V1 weapons from sites in France and Belgium until shortly before they were overrun in August and September 1944, and delayed the V2s from being launched until September 1944 from sites in the Netherlands round The Hague.

Research on jet-propelled missiles was already beginning in Germany under Professor Werner von Braun and Major Dornberger, an army engineer, before the Nazis took power in 1933. While the Army Weapons Office under General Karl Becker in the 1930s controlled experimental work on jet-propelled rockets, the Luftwaffe sponsored the idea of a pilotless aircraft with an explosive warhead. In 1936, following a demonstration of a rocket at a proving ground not far from Berlin (an area obviously unacceptable on security grounds), an island site at Peenemuende near the mouth of the Oder on the Baltic was acquired by the Luftwaffe. It was, however, designated an army experimental station to be used by both armed services jointly.

The western side of the island was taken over for V1 by the air force and the eastern side for V2 by the army. An airfield was built on the northern edge. The V1 experiments and tests only required workshops and launching pads, but the V2 rocket was far more complex and needed a wind tunnel, production workshops, launching sites for the rockets and settlements and barracks for the scientists, soldiers and workmen. The Abwehr was responsible for security, but in October 1939, in spite of strict security precautions, the results of tests at Peenemuende for both weapons were delivered to the office of the British Naval Attaché in Oslo. Known as the 'Oslo Report', little attention was paid to it in British defence circles except by Dr R. V. Jones.

After easy victories against Poland, France and the Low Countries, Hitler took the view that he would win the war by conventional weapons without the need of the V1 and V2, so he moved them from the priority list. General Becker, the senior officer in charge, resisted him and then committed suicide. Later, after the defeat of the Luftwaffe in the Battle of Britain in September 1940, Hitler again changed his mind, recognising that when the V weapons were ready for operational use – obviously at least two or three years ahead – they would be invaluable for long-range bombardment of the British Isles from Continental bases, even though the Luftwaffe had lost control of the skies over Britain. In late 1940 he doubtless already had in mind Operation Barbarossa for 1941 and must have appreciated that these V weapons had no special advantage over conventional weapons in the vast land spaces of continental Russia. So with the support of General von Brauchitsch, the work at Peenemuende went on as a long-term project with the British Isles as the main target in mind.

As the war continued the labour shortage in the Third Reich became more acute. Forced foreign labour from occupied countries or from concentration camps began to be used even in the top-security compounds of Peenemuende. Among them, inevitably, were Poles, and early in 1943 the AK (Polish Home Army) began to get reports coming out of Peenemuende that small aircraft with short wings were flying into the Baltic. The news was relayed to the Sixth Bureau of the Polish general staff in London who liaised with AK and SOE, and passed it through their Second Intelligence Bureau to SIS. Later, on request, longer and fuller reports with maps were sent out from AK Warsaw by courier.

At the London end, Churchill's chief scientific adviser, Lord Cherwell (formerly Professor Lindemann of Oxford with a reputation for solving military–scientific problems in the First World War), was involved in studying these reports. He was sceptical, especially on the V2s. He refused to believe that Germany (whose universities and scientists he knew well) could be so far ahead of Britain in this experimental field. Fortunately, however, a young scientist introduced by him, Dr R.V. Jones, was head of the scientific section of Air Intelligence and also scientific adviser to SIS. Dr Jones had always borne in mind the 1939 Oslo Report and had been watching for evidence, especially from Ultra, to confirm the Oslo forecasts on the production of flying bombs and rockets, so he was quick to pick up the importance of a report from a Danish chemical engineer which reached London in December and to understand the implication in March 1943 of a transcript of a conversation in a British prisoner-of-war camp between two German generals, Cruewell and von Thoma who had been captured in North Africa; the latter referred to ' . . . this rocket business . . . huge things which go 15 kms into the stratosphere – and that there must have been a hold-up in the programme'. In April 1943 this well-informed and high-level warning was reported to the chiefs of staff and the Prime Minister, Churchill, and the War Cabinet then decided to make a politician of ministerial rank, Duncan Sandys, responsible for investigating the technical evidence of the German rocket programme, although he had no scientific qualifications, to the considerable vexation of both Lord Cherwell and Dr Jones (Jones, 1978).

At the request of Dr Jones, aerial photographs of Peenemuende were taken at discreet intervals and the Photographic Central Interpretation Unit at Medmenham was briefed on what to look for by Dr Jones. In June 1943 Jones spotted an apparent rocket about 35 feet long, and so advised Sandys. On 29 June a War Cabinet meeting was held to review the evidence, which after a sceptical introduction by Cherwell was presented mainly by Jones. It was decided that Bomber Command should attack Peenemuende on the heaviest possible scale as soon as conditions were favourable. The nights were not long enough for this raid, codenamed Operation Hydra, into eastern Germany until 17–18 August, when over six hundred bombers were despatched, forty-one being lost. Over one hundred German scientists and technicians were killed at Peenemuende, along with some six hundred of the foreign workmen. The chief of the German air staff, General Jeschonnek, committed suicide next day after furious reprimands from Field-Marshal Goering.

On 22 August, five days after the Hydra raid, a V1 pilotless aircraft went off course when launched from Peenemuende in an east-north-easterly direction and crashed on the Danish island of Bornholm. It was promptly photographed by a Danish naval officer, who also made a sketch. He forwarded it to the Danish resistance, who made several copies for transmission by several couriers through SOE's Stockholm office to SOE London. Another report reached SIS from a well-known French source, Amniarix, giving some details of activities at Peenemuende and information about possible launching sites in northern France, including sixteen anti-aircraft batteries under Colonel Wachtel near Amiens.

In London, arguments continued to rage as to the reality of the threat, the possibility that the Germans had produced simultaneously two competitive long-range weapons, the pilotless aircraft and the rocket, and the feasibility of a fuel having been invented which was sufficiently powerful and reliable to power them. At the same time skilful use of Ultra enabled Jones and others to intercept reports by two specialised German signals companies stationed on the Baltic coast, transmitting bearings and ranges on a series of moving objects taking off from Peenemuende and proceeding east-north-east at about 400 mph (600 kph). The reports sometimes quoted a reference FZG 76, which from other sources was found to be a codeword for the flying bomb project.

Within a week of Operation Hydra on 18 August, Himmler's SS took over security from the Abwehr and control of V2 firing tests was moved to Blizna in south Poland, which was out of range of Allied bombers. Development work was moved to mountain caves in Austria, and mass production to underground factories in the Harz Mountains. Here working conditions were appalling, and half-starved foreign workers, constantly spied on and ill-treated, were set production targets of nine hundred rockets a month, which were impossible to achieve.

In northern France, Colonel Wachtel had been put in command of building launching pads, and he soon found himself involved in a high-level controversy. Was it better to build a few big bunkers which could resist the heaviest bombing and provide shelter for V1 equipment and several thousand bombs or warheads, or to build numerous launching pads, say one hundred, with moderate bunkers? Eventually Goering pronounced in favour of the latter. Wachtel was ordered to select sites, to arrange the secret training of fifteen soldiers and several experts for each site, and to organise radio and telephone communications. He was shocked to hear that British Intelligence knew his name and appearance and would no doubt try to put him out of action, so he changed his name first to Wolf and then to Wagner.

By 1944 over 40,000 workers, mostly French or foreign, were working at the V1 launching sites. Detailed locations and progress reports continued to flow in from SIS agents and French resistance units, including the EU/P Section of SOE which worked with the large Polish community round Lille and other parts of northern France. One major bunker at Watten had only just been completed when it was destroyed by a USAF daylight raid at the end of August 1943. During the bombings, more than fifty launching sites were seriously damaged, but over 150 Allied aircraft were lost.

What follows is really more part of the history of the air defence of Great Britain than the history of any of the resistance movements in Poland, Denmark or France, but it completes the V1 saga. The first ten V1s were fired from French sites on the night of 12–13 June 1944, seven days after D-Day, but only one reached London. On 15 June, however, Wachtel launched over two hundred, of which 73 reached Greater London. Before Wachtel's French and Belgian sites were overrun by Allied invasion forces in September, some 10,000 V1 flying bombs were launched, of which 2300 reached the London Civil Defence Region, causing over 5000 deaths and 16,000 seriously injured. In addition, over 5000 were launched against Belgium, mainly against the port of Antwerp.

The wide arc of the French coast made it easy enough to launch the lethal flying bomb at London from within about a hundred miles on a massive scale. If, as Hitler wanted, it had been operationally ready in January 1944 instead of June, it could have had a disruptive and possibly disastrous effect on the launching of the invasion, Overlord. Alternatively, even if Overlord could still have gone ahead undisrupted, and the V1 launching sites had still been overrun during September, the Greater London area would have been under continuous bombardment for nine months instead of three. The six months' delay was caused by Royal Air Force bombing first of Peenemuende and then of the French launching sites made possible by the vital information provided by members of the Polish, Danish and French resistance movements. The six months' delay also made it possible for the specifications of V1 to be analysed, and for air defence measures, such as resiting of AA guns, and fighter tactics to be worked out.

In May 1944 a V2 rocket crashed on marshy ground near Blizna by the River Bug. It was first concealed from the Germans for a few days by the Polish AK and then dragged out by horses, and examined by the best technical team that the AK could assemble under Kocjan, a highly-qualified engineer. Over a period the team dismantled, photographed and described it in a four-thousand-word report, supplemented by photographs and drawings. This report, together with selected key parts of the rocket (which was composed of 25,000 parts in all), was sent to London in an unarmed C47 transport aircraft, which flew into an abandoned airfield near Tarnow, south Poland, from Brindisi on 25 July 1944 – Operation Wildhorn III. The report and exhibits relating to the V2 were delivered in London to the Polish Sixth Bureau, who translated it and passed it to the British, seven weeks before the first operational V2 landed in Britain (Garlinski, 1978).

Meanwhile, in London arguments raged on the size of the V2 rocket, the size of the warhead, the nature of the propellant, the range, the probable rate of production and rate of firing. In June 1944 a V2 rocket from Peenemuende went off course and landed in Sweden; once again some essential parts were brought to England. By the end of August 1944 Dr Jones, with the aid of the Polish and Swedish exhibits, produced a full report on V2, which was finally accepted and later proved to be correct, showing that the main features were: total weight thirteen tons, warhead one ton, fuel liquid oxygen, a range of 200 miles, rate of production 500 per month, rate of firing 800 per month. The V2 was a weapon which ascended 200 miles into the stratosphere; against it there was at that date no defence, except destruction on the ground before launching, capture of the launching sites, or very deep shelters.

There was a moment in London in the first week of September 1944 when, after the liberation of France and Belgium, the British Government appeared to believe that the battle of London was over. But in the very same week, on 7 September, the first V2 rockets landed in the Greater London area. This long-range bombardment continued until April 1945. By then over one thousand V2s had been launched and over 500 fell in the London Civil Defence Region. In addition, over 1500 rockets were launched against the port of Antwerp, which by late November 1944 was an important supply base for the Allied invasion forces. There were sites round The Hague which were within range of London, 200 miles, and these sites were not liberated until April 1945. Air Force attacks on some of these sites caused heavy civilian casualties on the long-suffering population, who at the time of the Arnhem raid had hoped to be liberated before the sixth winter of the war set in.

The severe damage created by V1s and V2s was mitigated by photo reconnaissance and interpretation which enabled the sites to be recognised and to be bombed, which in turn delayed their manufacture and distribution. The high quality of British scientific expertise also helped, but it was 'the superb collaboration of the Polish, Danish and French undergrounds' which was of exceptional importance (Lewin, 1978, p. 321). If they had not sent out from occupied territories the data and the details, neither the scientists nor the photographers would have had sufficient evidence and the sceptics would not have been convinced.

14

South-East Asia and the Far East

Over the centuries the countries of South-East Asia derived most of their cultures, religions and immigrant populations from China and India. From the nineteenth century onwards all except Siam had become colonies or dependent territories of other countries in Europe or America: Burma and Malaya had become British colonial possessions; Cambodia, Laos and Vietnam belonged to France; Sumatra, Java and the other Indonesian islands were run by the Netherlands, and the Philippines were controlled by the United States. After 1930, Japan became increasingly dominant, progressively taking control of vast areas of the Chinese mainland. The government of the Republic of China under General Chiang Kai-shek, harassed by internal strife from the Communists under Mao Tse-tung, as well as by the Japanese invaders, withdrew up the Yangtze River gorges, making Chungking their capital.

The Nazi invasion of the Netherlands and France in the summer of 1940 changed the balance of power in the Far East. The Dutch colonial government in the Netherlands East Indies became responsible for Java, Sumatra, Borneo and a thousand lesser islands to an exiled government in London with limited resources, instead of the well-organised and wealthy government in The Hague. The French colonial government in Indo-China became responsible to the Pétain government in Vichy, subservient in large measure to the Nazi Reich. Previously these colonial governments, admittedly incapable of resisting the imperial Japanese forces by themselves before 1940, had at least had the benefit of the deterrent power of two European countries, who could not be attacked by Japan without provoking a world war. But after June 1940 world war was already raging and the two European governments were virtually powerless. At the same time Britain was under air attack and under siege by U-boats, on the defensive in the Mediterranean and North Africa, and clearly incapable of reinforcing her thin positions in India, Burma and

Malaya. Moreover, the Soviet Union was still an ally of Nazi Germany and the prospects of the United States coming into the war seemed remote. In December 1941 the Japanese attacked Pearl Harbor, put out of action a large part of the American Pacific fleet, and gained naval supremacy in the western Pacific and for a time even in the Bay of Bengal, which opened the way to the swift invasion of the Philippines, the Netherlands East Indies and South-East Asia.

From 1942, when the Japanese invaded and occupied Burma, the Chinese Government was cut off from Britain and the United States, except by air to India over the mountain range, known to the air crews as the 'Hump'. The Americans were air-lifting quantities of supplies over the 'Hump' to Chungking and were pressing Britain and the British military command in India to reconquer northern Burma so that a motor road could be built through five hundred miles of jungle and mountain from Ledo on the Assam–Burma border to Chungking. The British naturally wished to recapture Burma and remove the Japanese threat to north-east India but were more keenly aware than the Americans of the formidable character of the mountainous country in northern Burma and the primitive communications which made it impossible to supply and transport a major invasion force.

The Americans from President Roosevelt downwards were pre-occupied by their primary targets: first, the support of the Chinese Government and the establishment of an overland supply route to Chungking to enable bomber bases to be built in China from which Japanese targets could be attacked; and secondly, further afield, amphibious assaults on Pacific islands leading up to the final invasion of the Japanese mainland. The British, however, in the early stages wished to contain the Japanese in Burma and break out instead to the great arc of islands in the Dutch East Indies using amphibious power at every stage.

It seemed clear in 1942 and 1943 that which ever way the Allied global strategy might develop, there would be great scope for guerrilla activities in Burma and Malaya designed to divert and tie down the Japanese forces. But South-East Asia was destined to play a role secondary to the two American theatre commands, General Douglas MacArthur's South-West Pacific Command based on Australia and the American Pacific fleet working east from Hawaii and Guam.

South-East Asia Command (SEAC) was established at the Quebec Conference in August 1943 with Admiral Lord Louis Mountbatten as its supreme Allied commander (SACSEA) and the American General Joseph Stilwell as his deputy. Under these two were the British service chiefs, Admiral Somerville, General Giffard and Air Chief Marshal Peirse. They were made responsible for Burma, Malaya and the Netherlands East Indies, and jointly with Generalissimo Chiang Kai-shek for Indo-China and Thailand. At first their headquarters were in New Delhi, but in April of 1944 Mountbatten decided to move them to Kandy in Ceylon (modern Sri Lanka).

Plans for major amphibious landings in SEAC's territories were put in hand although much of the preparatory work had already been organised by India Command under General Sir Claude Auchinleck. It had been decided to land on the Andaman Islands, in Burma, and in Malaya, and to organise an assault on the northern tip of Sumatra. Secret activities in this area were co-ordinated by a special unit called 'P' under Captain Garnons Williams, RN, who was directly responsible to Admiral Lord Louis Mountbatten. These secret activities, in addition to SOE's which were much the largest element, included those undertaken by SIS, MI9, Deception Group's D Force and Political Warfare Executive.

SOE London had sent out Colin Mackenzie in 1941 to establish SOE India, also named Force 136, at Meerut, later based at Kandy in Ceylon when SEAC moved its headquarters there. He remained the head of it from start to finish. This was both a tribute to his effectiveness, his sound judgement and to the quality of his relations with the authorities, military and civilian, British, American and Dutch, with whom he had to deal. He had been a director of the Scottish textile group J. P. Coats, a classical scholar and an economist as well as an experienced and much travelled man of affairs. He was also a friend of Lord Linlithgow, the Viceroy in Delhi, who had personally suggested the establishment of an SOE mission in India. The first object of the 1941 mission was post-occupational preparation in case the Japanese should invade.

SOE's Force 136 set up a unit called Group A to be responsible for special operations in Burma, with headquarters in Calcutta under Colonel Gavin Stewart. Subject to prior rights of the American OSS, this Group A also operated in Indo-China, Thailand and China. SOE Group B, with headquarters in Colombo under Colonel C. Hudson, operated in Malaya and the Netherlands East Indies. Each group had its own country sections, signals and administrative units; the financial services of Force 136 were, however, centred in New

Delhi. Three stores depots, two para-naval bases and training schools were established on the Indian sub-continent including parachute training at Rawalpindi; there was also a jungle training school in Ceylon. The first airfields were at Calcutta and Chittagong, but later two more were made available in Ceylon although submarines based on Colombo were the most important form of operational transport until 1945. During 1944, SOE's Force 136 developed into a widespread organisation with total strength around 6000, of all races, including large numbers of FANYS on the administrative, secretarial and cipher staff.

Goa

One useful operation was handled in Goa, on the west coast of India, which was at that time a Portuguese colony and therefore neutral, although it has since been incorporated into India. Three German ships, including *Ehrenfels*, had taken refuge in Marmagoa harbour; its radio transmitter provided valuable information to German U-boats about Allied shipping in the Indian Ocean. SOE Force 136 was asked to find a solution, and after an unsuccessful attempt to bribe the German captain, succeeded in kidnapping the radio operator; but after a short interval the transmissions resumed and it was clear that another radio operator had been found. Plans were then made for a boarding party to put the transmitter out of action and, with the aid of diversionary measures on shore in the form of entertainments organised for the evening in question, the raid was successfully carried out by a team under Lt-Colonel Pugh with virtually no opposition. The three ships were all set on fire and scuttled (Leasor, 1956).

Malaya

SOE put forward a scheme in August 1941 for organising, training and equipping Malayan 'stay behind' parties to be made up of European police and volunteers, with Chinese, Malays and Indians to provide intelligence and to attack lines of communications with other forms of sabotage. This scheme was at first turned down for 'the Malayan command had no belief in the ability of the Japanese to invade Malaya let alone overrun it', in the words of Lord Wavell (Spencer Chapman, 1948); moreover, it was thought that any Chinese guerrillas might belong to the Malayan Communist Party (MCP), which was illegal. However, on 8 December, the day before the Japanese invaded Malaya, it was at last agreed that SOE's scheme could proceed. Training schemes were started, but the pace of events was too great and time was too short for organising a resistance movement and for training key personnel to the standards needed for success.

SOE had similar plans for Singapore and some months before the invasion had sent a mission there under Major Valentine Killery, who had worked for ICI in Shanghai for many years. He had little time to produce results but the seed he sowed proved fertile. A special training school, 101, was set up near Singapore under Lt-Colonel J. M. L. Gavin, an experienced SOE instructor, to train 'stay behind' parties. The trainees included 345 Chinese recruited by the Malayan Communist Party who were infiltrated into the jungle by Captain Davis and Captain Broome and spread over selected areas. One of the instructors at training school 101 was Captain F. Spencer Chapman, DSO, an explorer of great prowess and endurance, specialising in fieldcraft. He entered the jungle in January 1942 in charge of stay behind parties, mostly Chinese Communists; he emerged by submarine after three years in May 1945, and later that year was parachuted back into Malaya. His outstanding achievement in organising and training the Chinese is recorded in his book *The Jungle is Neutral*; in Lord Wavell's words, 'a story of endurance and survival beyond the normal human capacity for survival' (Spencer Chapman, 1948). His short period as instructor at STS 101 had led to contacts with MCP trainees who later became leading figures in the guerrilla movements and enabled him to join up with them in the jungle at the Ulu Slim Camp at Perak. He found that many of them did not even know how to use the sights on a rifle or to fire a tommy gun, so he at once resumed his role as instructor. While Spencer Chapman's book is an authoritative source for the areas of occupied Malaya in which he operated, the main present source for SOE's Force 136's Malayan activities and operations into Malaya from Ceylon is Ian Trenowden's *Operations Most Secret, SOE, the Malayan Theatre* (1978), to which I am indebted.

Throughout 1942 the Japanese seemed invincible as they crept further and further south, invading each and every island on the way. In March they had captured the Andaman Islands and had bombed Ceylon, so in September the British occupied Madagascar to forestall Japanese control of the Indian Ocean. The British were unable to mount any major campaign against them by land, sea or air. But in

January 1943 one of the three Netherlands East Indies submarines based on Colombo carried out Operation Baldhead and landed a five-man party under Major McCarthy in the Andaman Islands, where he had had five years' service as a police officer. They were equipped with folboats, light collapsible craft each able to carry 800 lbs of personnel and stores. They radioed back details of bombing targets, which were duly attacked, and collected useful intelligence about enemy troop dispositions and habits. They were picked up by submarine as planned after sixty-five days. This was the first successful landing of an Allied operational party in this theatre. A follow-up party with stores for six months was landed shortly after. In January 1944, two further sorties to the Andamans took place and a large party of eighteen was landed in December 1944.

Starting in May 1943 a series of landing operations in Malaya was planned under the code name Gustavus. The SOE Malayan Country Section under Basil Goodfellow had been moved from Calcutta, where they had succeeded in recruiting some Malayan Chinese, to Ceylon. Gustavus I sailed on 11 May, with John Davis and five Chinese, with radio and folboats; Gustavus II sailed on 15 June; Gustavus III, with Fenner, on 4 August; Gustavus IV, with David Broome, on 12 September; Gustavus V, with Elim Bo Send, on 25 October, all in Netherlands East Indies submarines; Gustavus VI, with Harrison, on 2 December in the Royal Navy's *Tally Ho*; and Gustavus Emergency in January 1944. These and other operations resulted in SOE being represented by British liaison officers in Selangor, Negri Sembilan, North and South Johore, Perak, West Pahong and Kedah. These SOE officers made contact with the Malayan Peoples' Anti-Japanese Army, MPA-JA, a mainly Malayan Chinese organisation controlled by the MCP. They claimed to be favourable to the Allies and offered both personnel for operations and facilities for radio sets and operators. In return they needed arms and medical supplies. John Davis and David Broome, the leaders of Gustavus I and IV, had originally trained MCP personnel at SOE's training school 101 before the capture of Singapore. Chen Ping, second-in-command of the MCP, visited Davis and arranged for his whole party to move into the Perak mountain ranges: they were thus in direct contact with the Malayan People's Anti-Japanese Army.

Colonel Hudson's SOE Group B dropped British liaison officers into Malaya, one to every regiment of the Malayan People's Anti-Japanese army, to be in tactical control but never in direct command.

These well-disciplined and well-armed guerrillas now numbered about 5000 and they would be encouraged to plan road ambushes, cut railway lines and attack Japanese telecommunication centres at exactly the right moment to synchronise with Operation Zipper, when two divisions would land on the beaches between Port Swettenham and Port Dickson in Selangor on 9 September 1945. However, all these plans came to naught because in August the Americans dropped two atom bombs on Japan and General MacArthur received the Japanese surrender in Tokyo Bay on 2 September. Days later Mountbatten received in Singapore the surrender of Japanese troops in the SEAC area.

Burma

The Japanese conquest of Burma in 1942 was barely complete when General Wavell's staff began to prepare plans for its recapture. But resources both human and material were desperately short until 1944. The mountain belt between Assam and Burma was in places one hundred miles wide and running up to as high as 10,000 feet. General Stilwell, newly arrived US deputy to General Chiang Kai-shek, insisted that US aid to China demanded the reopening of the Burma Road, via Mandalay–Lashio–Chungking. The lack of land communications from Bengal by the coast or from Assam over the mountains to Burma forced the planners at first to conceive the reconquest as a series of amphibious operations. Later, however, the exploits of General Orde Wingate's Long-Range Penetration Groups or 'Chindits' put the emphasis more on airborne troops with supply by air. The Chindits' first operation began on 13 February 1943 and lasted for three months. The Japanese were surprised at this new demonstration of British troops' capacity for jungle warfare. Their reaction was to mount an offensive against Assam which ultimately exhausted their resources.

The outstanding British figure in Burma was Hugh Seagrim, an officer in the Burma Rifles, who conceived his own plans for organising guerrilla forces in the hills, especially amongst the Karens, who had been pro-British for generations. Seagrim contacted SOE's mission in Burma and then recruited and armed some two hundred Karens; he remained in the area for over two years, but lost touch with SOE until October 1943, when a new mission was parachuted in which established radio communication with base. Karen guerrilla activity led to severe Japanese reprisals and the capture and execution of two SOE officers. Seagrim later surrendered to the Japanese to plead for mercy for the Karens, but was executed in Rangoon, a heroic figure.

In the spring of 1944 the last Japanese attacks had been defeated by the Fourteenth Army under General Slim at Imphal and Kohima. Later in the year, Fourteenth Army launched an offensive to recapture Mandalay on the Irrawaddy River. Force 136's Group A at Calcutta run by Colonel Gavin Stewart was directed to give top priority to supporting this offensive. British SOE missions were sent to the Karens, Chins and other tribal groups in the Shan states bordering on China, and the American OSS sent missions to the Kachin tribes. Two squadrons of aircraft were allocated to these missions and the Karen resistance movement, recovering from its earlier reprisals, grew to a strength of over 15,000 and inflicted heavy casualties on the Japanese. Two major general uprisings were also planned to coincide with the final assault on Rangoon in co-operation with the Burma Defence Army.

The Burma Defence Army had first been raised by the Japanese in 1942 for security duties and over 5000 young Burmese had been trained, including Aung San, a leading Burmese military figure, who was eventually to become President of Burma. Later the Burma Defence Army came under the influence of an anti-Fascist organisation, a popular front with many left-wing sympathisers, and with remarkable flexibility the army decided to throw in its lot with the Allies and to turn against their former Japanese masters. The decision, first by South-East Asia Command and then by the chiefs of staff in London (see Appendix D), to support Force 136's proposal to make use of the Burma Defence Army, a Japanese-sponsored organisation, produced inevitably a violent reaction from the British colonial 'Burma government-in-exile'. Based remotely in Simla, they were appalled at the consequences which such a move might have after the war. However, as with Greece and Jugoslavia, it was decided to give priority to winning the war in the shortest possible time rather than to feel constrained by the political compli-cations which would have to be faced on the outbreak of peace. Burma, granted premature independence in 1947, has not yet become a successful country, politically or economically. Never-theless, the London decision was intrinsically correct. The BDA was rechristened and purified as the 'Burma National Army' and their records in killing the enemy and tying down forces, which could otherwise have opposed Fourteenth Army, were at least respectable.

Sumatra

It had early been agreed that special operations into Sumatra, the nearest and only accessible island of the Netherlands East Indies, would only be undertaken with the consent of the Netherlands mission which was supported by a bomber squadron manned by Dutchmen and by Dutch submarines and other naval craft based on Ceylon. But unfortunately for one reason or another no SOE operations into Sumatra were ever carried out. MI9 sent in a group, but the party disappeared without trace.

Indo-China

There had been a statesmanlike compromise over Indo-China, which came under both South-East Asia Command and Chiang Kai-shek: it was decided that each side would be free to operate there and any territory liberated by either command would come under the command which had liberated it. British relations with their American allies and the Free French were, of course, delicate. The Free French were reluctant to put men into Indo-China, in case they came under Chinese command if the territory were to be liberated by China. The USA were congenitally averse from doing anything to help a European colonial power re-establish control of a former colonial territory. Nevertheless, French influence in Indo-China remained strong up to 1945, because French officials of the Vichy government had continued, ever since 1941, to administer it in collaboration with the Japanese. At the request of Colonel Passy of the Gaullist BCRA organisation, SOE's Force 136 created a French section to operate into Indo-China, headed by Jean de Crevecour. Ten or more parties had been infiltrated into Indo-China and continued to be in radio contact with Force 136. In March 1945 the Japanese, conscious of loss of control in South-East Asia generally, dismissed the Vichy administration, which led inevitably to acts of French resistance and Japanese reprisals. Colonel Passy himself flew to Kandy to implore Sweet-Escott (whom he had known in his period as head of the French RF Section in London but was now Colonel General Staff in Force 136) to increase the volume of support to French groups in Indo-China. But American objection made

SEAC support difficult and no major increase was achieved before the war ended in September 1945.

Thailand

Thai means free; Muang Thai or Thailand, the 'land of the free', was the only nation in South-East Asia to retain its independence, when all others became colonial possessions. The dictator, Pibul Songgram, introduced the phrase Thailand; but the opposition, led by Nai Pridi Phan Amyong, preferred Siam, and spoke of the Free Siamese Movement, which Pridi secretly headed during the Japanese occupation. However, since contemporary usage since 1945 has been Thai or Thailand, it seems best to follow it.

In January 1942 Thailand, under Japanese pressure, declared war both on Britain and the USA; but the United States never recognised that state of war. The Thai Government in 1942 was headed by Pibul, who was genuinely hostile to Britain and the USA; but in July 1944 he was overthrown by the opposition under Pridi, who became Regent and combined the functions of official head of government and secret head of the Free Thai Movement (FTM).

Force 136 had tried in 1943 to contact the FTM by submarine sorties to the west coast; then in 1944 long-range four-engined US B24 bombers became available and two parties of Thais were dropped blind, but they were both soon captured. They were taken to Bangkok and kept in gaol by the police chief Adul, who was also a leading figure in the FTM. They were interrogated by the Japanese, who, however, were prepared to allow the Thai Government as their official ally to deal with their own citizens. Then Force 136 received via China a coded message from the head of one of their captured Thai missions reporting Pridi's remarkable situation. Understanding correctly that Pridi had a strong security sense and kept complete secrecy about his leadership of the FTM, Force 136 organised another radio link direct with him, not passing through the Bangkok gaol and unknown to the police chief Adul. This was a shrewd move.

The Thai country section of Force 136 preferred to call itself the Siamese Country Section; it was based in Calcutta and headed by Captain Pointon with two assistants, one of whom was Andrew Gilchrist, who had been in the British Embassy in Bangkok before the war. His book *Bangkok Top Secret* (Gilchrist, 1970) gives a detailed and vivid account of the paradoxical situation in Thailand where he had had the advantage of having known personally Pridi and other leading Thai personalities before war broke out.

At the end of 1944 Force 136 had made contact with the FTM; established regular radio communications with its head Pridi, who was also head of state; passed from the stage of initial contact to the stage of preparing active operations, and established its capacity to locate missions to meet the strategic requirements. The time was therefore ripe for action. SEAC was, however, unable then to give a general directive for Thailand. Suffering from hold-ups in manpower, shipping and supplies, SEAC was seriously inhibited in planning its regular operations apart from those in Burma. Force 136, however, did succeed in getting a directive for a supporting role in Operation Roger, a SEAC plan to seize Puket Island on the west coast of Thailand and adjacent areas of mainland. Roger was later cancelled and so Force 136's Siamese section was left without any clear strategic objective, and after the atom bomb was dropped on Japan, strategic objectives were overtaken by events. Force 136 and OSS provided help on a big scale for MI9, with the result (Sweet-Escott, 1965) that over 900 tons of stores, and over a hundred doctors and relief workers were flown into Thailand to areas nearest to prisoner-of-war camps, where many thousands of prisoners were located. By August 1945 Force 136 had thirty radio sets working from Thailand compared with only one set a year earlier.

In South-East Asia SOE had the benefit of several favourable factors: a supreme commander, Mountbatten, with a commando background who knew about irregular warfare and special operations, who appreciated their value and limitations and understood how to handle problems with political as well as military aspects; secondly, the same commander of Force 136 from start to finish, Colin Mackenzie, provided continuity of direction, together with balanced judgement and a flair for good personal relations; thirdly, availability during 1944 and 1945 of several senior SOE officers redeployed from Europe with first-class experience either in staff appointments, conspicuously Brigadier John Anstey, Colonel Sweet-Escott and the Air Ops expert Lt-Colonel Wigginton, or in the field; fourthly, the pro-Allied, anti-Japanese attitude of some, but by no means all, elements in the Asiatic population, such as the hill tribesmen of northern Burma, Karens and Kachins, the left-wing Chinese guerrillas of Malaya and the majority of the Thais, including some at the highest governmental level.

On the other side of the balance sheet, the conditions of the area and of the Allied theatre command imposed serious difficulties: European or American officers, because of their physical appearance, were always visibly at risk except in remote guerrilla areas and jungles; secondly, the collaboration of some anti-European elements, such as the Burma Defence Army, with the Japanese occupation forces for a time; thirdly, the strategic subordination of SEAC to other theatres of command which enjoyed higher priority for aircraft, landing craft and supplies; and fourthly, the great distances involved – from Ceylon to Malaya and back meant air sorties of over 2500 miles.

In Burma SOE achieved major successes, especially in the hill tribal areas, in co-operation with OSS and in the revolt of the Burma Defence Army. Helped by the co-ordination of P Division, established in Kandy by Mountbatten in agreement with Donovan, SOE and OSS co-operated well in the support of Burmese resistance groups. In Malaya the network of the Chinese guerrillas, known as the Malayan People's Anti-Japanese Army, supported by SOE liaison officers, was beginning to achieve results and was ready to co-operate with the Allied invasion plans in August 1945. Likewise, in Thailand there was remarkable progress in the development of Thai resistance, with support from leading figures in the Thai Government and with secret help from SOE and OSS, until this was overtaken by the Japanese surrender.

The Far East and Pacific

The supreme commander of the south-west Pacific, General Douglas MacArthur, refused to allow OSS to operate, doubtless objecting to having in his theatre of command an organisation which could communicate independently with Washington. SOE, under the OSS–SOE agreement of 1942, was not entitled to operate in any American theatre command where OSS was operating, but in the absence of OSS from the south-west Pacific, SOE was entitled to assist an organisation in Australia.

Special Operations Australia, or SOA, had been set up by two SOE officers, Egerton Mott and Chapman Walker, in 1942 under the operational control of General Blamey, the Australian army commander responsible to MacArthur.

SOE London had links with SOA and it was a British officer attached to SOA who carried out one of the greatest individual acts of sabotage of the war. Major Ivan Lyon had been a regular British army officer, stationed in Singapore in 1941. Convinced of the imminence of a Japanese invasion, he made use of his main hobby, sailing, to reconnoitre hide-outs on islands near the Singapore roads, where a raiding ship could establish itself for sabotage attacks on enemy shipping. After the fall of Singapore he escaped to Australia, joined up with SOA at Exmouth Sound in the north-west and there worked out his Project Jaywick in detail. In a converted fishing-boat he and three Australians successfully navigated enemy-controlled waters for over one thousand miles to Singapore, and with limpet mines sank 37,000 tons of Japanese shipping. The Japanese Navy were convinced that it was the work of the Allied submarines. Lyon and his crew then sailed back to Australia, where they had difficulty in convincing MacArthur's intelligence staff of their achievements, until confirmation came through decrypted Japanese signals from Singapore to Tokyo. Lyon then visited SOE London to secure equipment to repeat the operation on a larger scale. He and his colleagues were landed with their stores on one of the Singapore islands by submarine. Unfortunately, all were captured and executed.

SOA was active in Borneo, where Tom Harrison from SOE London, the explorer and anthropologist of Mass Observation fame, was parachuted into the interior in March 1945 and, in the absence of modern arms, organised an underground force equipped with blowpipes. This and other SOE missions provided much tactical intelligence for the invading Australian troops and were officially credited with killing over 1500 Japanese.

In China after 1942 OSS had prior rights to operate, but SOE, which had previously established a mission in Chungking, remained active when British interests were involved. Quinine, as a prophylactic or remedy for malaria, was badly needed by the Allied forces in tropical areas, including South-East Asia and the south-west Pacific, but at one time most of the world's supply was controlled by the Japanese. SOE organised the purchase of quinine in Japanese-occupied China and smuggled it out to India, where it was handled through normal official channels. Similar arrangements were made by SOE Chungking over certain currencies, especially the purchase at a discount of blocked rupees in China, which saved the British and Indian governments many millions of pounds.

15

Reflections

SOE was set up to encourage resistance movements, guerrilla warfare, partisans and secret armies in other countries either before they were occupied or afterwards: it could advise, equip and organise but it was not itself meant to direct or control. SOE could offer to equip those who wanted arms, ammunition, radios, agents, leaders and liaison officers; it could also offer to organise communications networks, pick-ups, parachute drops and acts of sabotage, but there were many variables which affected the value of this work of equipment and organisation.

Within Britain itself there were many facets and wartime shortages which affected SOE's early performance: initial slowness of recruiting and training agents for an unknown and nameless organisation, desperate shortage of aircraft with which to send in agents and supplies, shortage of parachutes and specialised equipment all of which held up progress. Over-enthusiasm first by Churchill and then by Dalton and opposition from other departments and services were also detrimental to efficiency. Governments-in-exile and the Foreign Office created political and strategic variables and a complex diversity of aims.

But ultimately it was the conditions within the different enemy-occupied countries which made or marred the value of the aid offered. The success of special operations and the prospects for resistance movements were largely determined by the geography of a country, its size, the sparsity or density of its population, the types and location of frontiers, the ruggedness or flatness of the terrain and whether landlocked or with access to the sea. Nearness to Britain or British bases affected the amount of help that could be sent.

The internal climate or spirit inside the occupied country was all-important: whether there were native aspirations to spur initial underground activities; how many and what kind of partisan movements had emerged and what, if any, were their allegiances; whether they wished to conserve their resources and passively to receive aid until liberation seemed imminent or whether they were part of an aggressive resistance force, or what was the standard of common sense in security matters. The paramount factor was the general level of morale. In 1940 and 1941 few in occupied Europe could see how the Nazi war machine could be defeated by a Britain which, even with the support of its empire, could never command the necessary manpower to reconquer Europe. It was only after 1941, when first the Soviet Union and then the United States joined the alliance, that reconquest was seen to be possible and the spirit of resistance began to glow.

Other problems which affected SOE's relationships with resistance movements arose from the behaviour of the enemy: their efficiency in probing and capturing agents; in penetrating movements and groups; whether measures of reprisal, execution and deportation proved effective deterrents. Civil strife or inter-partisan fighting and conflict of aims and goals could reduce or even nullify the value of aid, as could breaches of security and poor chains of command. Good leadership and individual initiative were vital in any resistance group but, however much the indigenous inhabitants of a country fought back against the enemy and however much aid SOE managed to send, guerrillas could only attack isolated enemy units; they could not by themselves overcome tank brigades and regular armies. Moreover, unless they were next door to a neutral or liberated country or had a free seaboard where landings could eventually take place, partisans could never entirely free their country on their own, whatever the aid sent by external agencies. Perhaps Mao Tse-tung in China was eventually in 1949 to prove a solitary exception.

Beset by all these problems SOE units were limited in the things that they could do to help underground movements: they could send in trained agents to organise and to guide; they could provide the materials and the technical know-how for sabotage, ambushes, cutting communications, for derailing and demolition; they could equip and direct partisan action so as to delay enemy reinforcements from arriving at the battle front or from moving to other tasks elsewhere; they could give moral support and equipment for local movements, mobilise and organise them against the enemy and also help them to plan counter-scorch policies. They could initiate and equip communication networks and facilitate travel and pick-ups, so that information and key personnel could be sent in and out and they could help guerrillas to mount operations which would tie down military divisions. But the size, scope and success of their actions would always be governed by the nature of each country's own resistance movements, its aspirations, power and size.

By their very nature resistance movements, being clandestine, are small in comparison to regular forces, even when they reach the point of being described as secret armies. Nor can their size be verified in the conditions in which they operate. Some of the larger figures which have been quoted elsewhere suggest that the size of the resistance movements between 1939 and 1945 in France reached 140,000; in Italy 90,000; in Jugoslavia 250,000 and in Poland 300,000 (ERM, 1960); but the American OSS *War Report* puts the French figure as high as 300,000 (Roosevelt, 1976).

Between 1942 and 1945, 6,700 men and women of eighteen nationalities were parachuted into Europe and 40,000 tons of material (ERM, 1960, p. 36). Taking France by itself the numbers of air sorties rose from a mere 22 in 1941 to 93 in 1942, to 615 in 1943, increasing to over 3000 in less than nine months in 1944 (ERM, 1960 and Foot, 1966, p. 473).

The nature of resistance movements is such that in order for one country to plan to promote or to support a resistance movement in another, it must first make a forward-looking detailed analysis of the enemy or enemy-occupied country before dropping in a single agent, let alone hundreds, and before setting up complex home organisations and training centres. Is it an enemy country where the vast majority of the population and the whole of the security apparatus must be assumed to be hostile? Or is it an enemy-occupied country whose population can be expected to favour and secretly to help agents of their prospective liberators? What are the national characteristics in terms of past resistance to foreign occupation, experience in underground activities and above all intelligence, discretion and courage? How is the country situated in terms of geography and strategy? Is it certain or likely or unlikely to be the scene of regular military or combined naval and military operations at a later stage of the war? Has it a record of political stability or is it exposed to racial, religious or political upheavals, which may be either a weakness to be exploited or a source of internal strife which may frustrate any national resistance movement? Finally how do geographical factors, coastlines, mountains, forests, climate and distance from available operational bases, bear on the feasibility of resistance activity? This analysis is vital to success; it needs continual revision in the light of new factors.

The commonest error is to underestimate the time needed to build up a national resistance or regional resistance group. Creating a clandestine network, whether in urban industrialised areas for *coups de main* or sabotage or in rural areas, preferably mountainous or wooded, for guerrilla warfare, is inevitably slow. Security measures by occupying forces involve elaborate documentation and a system of permits and police checks on civilian travel; they not only restrict mobility but also demand a constant expenditure of time and energy and ingenuity. Even where there is an indigenous underground, the result of past foreign domination such as occurred in Poland, Czechoslovakia or Jugoslavia, months of work are needed to appoint, test, replace and train up regional organisers, to establish a network of safe houses, a courier service and other means of communication, to arrange in key centres for supply depots, finance and propaganda and to build up a security service to guard against the ever-present risk of enemy penetration. In the democratic countries of Western Europe there was little or no tradition in this respect with the exception of Belgium and northern France resulting from the First World War. Certainly the absence of any such tradition in British circles led to unreal expectations of early results.

A resistance movement often comes into existence spontaneously through resentment at the brutalities of the occupying power. It can organise itself up to a point, especially in a country such as Poland, with a long history of foreign occupation. It can even try to equip itself by capturing pistols, rifles, ammunition and other equipment from the occupation forces. This can sometimes happen on a massive scale as was shown by the Balkan guerrillas at the Italian armistice of 1943. But, generally speaking, arms and radio sets must come from an external source, and most resistance movements need far more from outside; they need advice and training on how to receive supplies by air, on radio and cipher procedure, security measures and training in weapons and demolitions. The process of supply soon raises the important question of control and direction. There is always some divergence between the resister eager for independence and the demands of the external supplier for strategic control or direction. The solution is never easy, sometimes impossible. Tito

with all his independence based on building up his Partisan movement for two years before receiving British supplies, nevertheless had
meetings in Italy with Churchill and Alexander, when some measure
of agreement was reached on strategy. But the agreement fell short of
a solution on Trieste, which he sought to seize and would have seized
but for an Anglo-American show of force. De Gaulle originally
resented any British action in organising or aiding French resistance.
If he had succeeded in eliminating British control or influence, especially SOE's independent F Section, the whole of French resistance
could have disintegrated following the capture and death of Jean
Moulin, the President of the Council of National Resistance, in
1943. There was no simple prescription and never will be; but it
must be recognised that control and direction is an unavoidable
problem and that the facts of each case must be considered in a
realistic way.

It is well to remember two propositions which have already been
quoted but bear repetition. First, in the words of Leverkuehn of the
Abwehr: 'In war the perpetration of any considerable act of sabotage
is among the most difficult of any of the tasks of a secret service'
(Leverkuehn, 1954, p.52). Second, in the words of Sweet-Escott of
SOE: 'It is an elementary principle that a guerrilla movement is used
to the best advantage when its operations are combined with those of
regular troops' (Sweet-Escott, 1965, p. 257).

Supreme allied commanders and commanders-in-chief, including
General Eisenhower, Field-Marshal Alexander, Field-Marshal
Wavell and Admiral Mountbatten, officially welcomed the contributions of resistance movements and paid high tributes to their
achievements, including those of Allied liaison officers trained and
despatched by SOE and OSS. Some have expressed opinions as to
the number of months by which the activities of resistance movements shortened the duration of the war. Such opinions are by their
nature subjective and impossible to appraise in any logical way.
Certain appraisals of a different kind may, however, carry more
conviction.

The contribution of the French and Belgian resistance movements
to the success of Operation Overlord and the speed with which
France and Belgium were liberated is beyond dispute, particularly in
disrupting communications and delaying the movements of enemy
forces.

General Eisenhower wrote to Gubbins on 31 May 1945:

'Before the combined staff of Special Force HQ disperses, I wish to express my appreciation of its high achievements. Since I assumed Supreme Command in January 1944 until the present day, its work has been marked by patient and farsighted planning, flexible adaptation to the operational requirements of Supreme HQ and efficient executive action during operations. In no previous war and in no other theatre during this war have resistance forces been so closely harnessed to the main military effort.

'While no final assessment of the operation value of resistance action has yet been completed, I consider that the disruption of enemy rail communications, the harassing of German road works and the continual and increasing strain placed on the German War Economy and internal services throughout occupied Europe by the organised forces of resistance, played a very considerable part in our complete and final victory . . .'

(Foot, 1966, p. 442)

The guerrilla movements in Jugoslavia, Greece and Albania were a major factor in tying up around forty (at times over fifty) enemy divisions. On 22 June 1943 (Howard, 1972, Vol IV, p. 504) Churchill telegraphed to Alexander in the Mediterranean the numbers of enemy divisions tied up in the Balkans: Jugoslavia, 39 (17 Italian, 9 German, 5 Bulgarian and 8 Croatian), Greek mainland, 16 (8 Italian, 6 German, 2 Bulgarian), a total of 55 enemy divisions, exclusive of the Greek islands and Albania. Of these divisions, certainly some – and conspicuously some of the 15 German divisions – would otherwise have been available in 1943 and 1944 to reinforce the anti-invasion troops in northern France. This might have turned the scales against the success of Overlord; it would certainly have increased Allied casualties and increased Hitler's ability to defend his west German frontier and thus prolong the war.

The same must be true to a lesser degree of the resistance movements in Norway, Denmark and the Netherlands, whose combined contribution in immobilising enemy forces must be considered in its cumulative effect along with that of the Balkans. It is, however, obviously necessary to take into account the influence of strategic deception plans on the decisions of the enemy general staff in the distribution of enemy forces, an influence which can be – and in 1943–4 certainly was – a powerful factor, though almost impossible to quantify.

The contribution of the Polish, Danish and French resistance to the measures, defensive and offensive, against the V1 flying bombs and the V2 rockets have been described; they were certainly a factor of importance in postponing the launching of both missiles and in providing advance information. In addition, the Polish home army inflicted continuou. damage on German lines of communication, culminating in the Warsaw rising.

The contribution of the Italian partisans to the Allied armies in Italy and the surrender of Army Group South, some days before the final surrender on the western front, was described by Field-Marshal Alexander as of great importance. The German high command also expressed this view in the Bolzano telegrams of February and April 1945 (Appendix C).

In South-East Asia Mountbatten in a report to the combined chiefs of staff described some of S O E's Force 136 activities in Burma and the operational necessity of supporting the indigenous resistance movement (Appendix D). The value of resistance movements in other Asian countries could not be finally tested because of the sudden Japanese surrender after atom bombs had been dropped.

In Germany several idealistic opposition groups showed great courage in planning acts of resistance, all amounting to treachery against the Nazi régime. If the planned assassination of Hitler in July 1944 had not been accidentally frustrated, the group responsible would have been recognised by history as a resistance movement of the highest value accelerating the collapse of the régime and the ending of hostilities. But in the light of events, there was no true German resistance movement.

In four countries, Italy, Hungary, Rumania and Thailand, S O E played a useful and substantial role in the preliminary establishment of communications leading up to negotiations for an armistice or surrender. In Italy the final surrender of Army Group South was handled by OSS in Switzerland, where Allen Dulles was in charge of secret intelligence as well as special operations and was also personal representative of the President of the United States.

Resistance channels also proved useful to the organisations responsible for strategic deception, though many channels, including secret intelligence, were used for this purpose.

The mere threat which resistance movements pose to the occupying power has considerable strategic value. Prolonged and widespread sabotage coupled with other forms of resistance may tie up substantial enemy forces, even though the underground army is imperfectly organised and equipped. When the Balkan guerrillas had not yet even begun to receive large-scale supplies from Allied bases in southern Italy, Churchill's telegram to Alexander, quoted above, on the 22 June 1943 gave the number of enemy divisions tied up in the Balkans as fifty-five, though fifteen were Croatian or Bulgarian and were probably not mobile.

Undoubtedly resistance movements do have offensive, defensive and strategic as well as psychological value: they disrupt and harass, they tie up enemy divisions, immobilise his forces and threaten his lines of communication. They also hasten surrender and shorten the length of a war. To support, encourage, equip, supply and help organise them was clearly worthwhile in the Second World War 1939–45.

Finally there is a question of organisation of the external supporting service. We should ponder whether or not SOE would have been more effective had it been part of the Secret Intelligence Service. Should secret intelligence and special operations be combined in one secret organisation with one joint head? Or should they be separated into two organisations with two heads, possibly responsible to two separate government departments? There are strong arguments for and against each alternative, but their validity depends so much on the circumstances of each case and the background conditions of the epoch, that in my personal view it is unwise to be dogmatic. Anyone with genuine experience in this field will have his own convictions; but they are conditioned by the environment in which he worked. Let me first state mine, based solely on Britain during the Second World War.

Special operations are even more difficult and more dangerous, in the sense of exposure of agents and groups to risks of capture and penetration, than secret intelligence work. The long-term needs of secret intelligence for continuing sources of reliable intelligence will always be used as an argument for giving them priority over special operations. If this priority is given, the special operations' demand for air and sea transport, communications and other facilities, will be subordinated to the demands of secret intelligence and may be indefinitely postponed or seriously jeopardised. There is, therefore, a case for separate organisations under separate ministries, so that there can be free competition for transport and other essential facilities. In Britain in 1940 the SIS had been starved of facilities for two decades of peace, and was desperately trying to rebuild itself. If SOE had been a mere branch of SIS, its chances of growth in the conditions of 1940–5 would have been poor.

On the other hand, there are substantial arguments of economy and unified direction in favour of a single organisation with two branches, subject to external circumstances permitting it, such as adequate pre-war preparation. The Abwehr in Germany handled intelligence and operations, as well as counter-intelligence; and, in so far as its achievements went, they doubtless benefited from unified direction. Likewise the American OSS. There should in theory be a freer exchange of information and intelligence between two branches of a single organisation than between two organisations separately directed, although in practice it is not always so. It is noteworthy that in the USSR, which for over half a century has put the maximum resources that any country in history has ever put into secret organisations, there is still a GRU for military intelligence, separate from the KGB (formerly NKVD or MVD) for political and economic intelligence and subversion. Finally, I must refer with respect to the clear and authoritative opinion of General Sir Colin Gubbins in a paper published in 1970:

'Having been much involved and having seen at close quarters all these things happening for more than four years, I have come to the conclusion that to co-ordinate in wartime all these activities (secret intelligence, political warfare and SOE activities which are all subversive) the three departments must come under one minister . . . I would also advocate one executive head for the three departments, for only in this way can you enforce collaboration and co-ordination'   (Elliott Bateman, 1970).

Some Abbreviations

ABWEHR   Military intelligence and counter-intelligence service of the German General Staff.

AFHQ   Allied Force Headquarters in Algiers 1942–3, in Caserta, Italy 1944–5.

AK   Armia Krajowa: the Polish secret home army.

BCRA   Bureau Central de Renseignements et d'Action: General de Gaulle's secret services.

BK   Balli Kombetar: anti-Communist Albanian national front.

BMM   British military mission.

BRAL   Bureau de Renseignements et d'Action Londres: General de Gaulle's London section of BCRA when he moved to Algiers.

BSC   British Security Co-ordination for the western hemisphere based on New York.

CCS   Combined Chiefs of Staff both American and British.

CIB   Central Intelligence Bureau in London of the Dutch resistance.

CIGS   Chief of the Imperial General Staff (London).

CLNAI   Comitato di Liberazione Nazionale Dell'Alta Italia: co-ordinating committee for the contribution of the Italian resistance movement to the liberation of northern Italy.

CNR   Conseil National de la Resistance: co-ordinating council of French resistance (except for the Communist FTP).

COS   Chiefs of staff London, consisting of the Chief of the Imperial General Staff, the First Sea Lord and the Chief of the Air Staff.

COSSAC   Chief of Staff to the Supreme Allied Commander.

D	Formerly an offshoot of SIS and a precursor to SOE.
EAM	Ethnikon Apeleftherotikon Metopon: the Greek left-wing national liberation front.
EDES	Ethnikos Dimokraticos Ellenikos Sundesmos: the right-wing national republican Greek league.
ELAS	Ellenikos Laikos Apeleftherotikos Stratos: the Greek popular liberation army, the military branch of EAM.
EMFFI	Etat Major des Forces Françaises de l'Interieur: the main London headquarters of the French para-military resistance organisation FFI.
ENIGMA	Secret cipher machine used by the Nazi high command and the Japanese.
EU/P	Section of SOE London dealing with Poles in France.
F section	Independent French SOE section working from Baker Street, London.
FFI	Forces Françaises de l'Interieur: the French para-military resistance organisation.
FTP	Franc Tireurs et Partisans: French Communist resisters.
GC & CS	British government code and cipher school at Bletchley Park.
ISRB	Inter Service Research Bureau: the official cover name for SOE at Baker Street in London.
JCS	US joint chiefs of staff Washington.
JIC	Joint Intelligence Committee of the COS in London.
JPS	Joint Planning Staff of the COS in London.
KKE	Kommunistikon Komma Ellenikon: Greek Communist Party.
LNC	Levisiya Nacional Clirimtare: the national liberation movement in Albania.
MAAF	Mediterranean Allied Air Forces.
MCP	Malayan Communist Party.
MI5	British security service within the United Kingdom and British territories.
MI6	One of the many cover names for SIS, the Secret Intelligence Service responsible for security external to the United Kingdom.

MIR	Military Intelligence Research, a precursor to SOE.
MI9	British escapers and evaders organisation.
MO I SP	War Office cover name for SOE.
MPA-JA	Malayan Peoples' Anti-Japanese Army (Communist).
Milorg	Military network branch of Norwegian resistance.
MVT	Dutch resistance liaison unit.
NID(Q)	British Admiralty cover name for SOE.
OSS	American Office of Strategic Services covering secret intelligence and special operations.
RF	SOE country section for Gaullist France in London.
RSS	British Radio Security Service.
SACMED	Supreme Allied Commander in the Mediterranean.
SACSEA	Supreme Allied Commander in South-East Asia.
SEAC	South-East Asia Command.
SHAEF	Supreme Headquarters Allied Expeditionary Force.
Section D	Offshoot of SIS and precursor to SOE.
Section V	Counter intelligence section working for MI5 and SIS.
SD	Sicherheitsdienst: intelligence and security service of the Nazi party including counter-resistance.
SIS	British Secret Intelligence Service responsible for security external to the United Kingdom.
SIPO	Sicherheits polizei: German security police.
SOA	Special Operations in Australia.
SOE	Special Operations Executive, London.
SOE units	Force 133 stationed in Cairo.
	Force 136 stationed first at Meerut and then Ceylon for South-East Asia.
	Force 139 stationed at Monopoli for Poland.
	Force 266 stationed at Bari for Albania.
	Force 399 stationed at Bari for Jugoslavia.
	ISSU 6 stationed at Algiers for France.
	No. 1 Special Force stationed at Monopoli, later Siena, working with the Italian resistance.
	No. 6 Special Force stationed at Monopoli working into Austria.
	Special French SOE sections were F, RF, DF, and EU/P for which see above.

SO	American special operations department for physical subversion, part of OSS.
SOM	British special operations in the Mediterranean, a branch of SOE.
STS	Special training schools run by SOE.
ULTRA	Name given to British decrypting of enemy cipher traffic using Enigma.
USTASA	Croatian pro-Axis militia.

APPENDIX A

Bibliography

There is no published work by any former staff member on SOE as a whole, its achievements in support of resistance movements, its failures and controversies and its relations with British and Allied governments and services. However, there are six works which deserve special mention: *SOE in France* (HMSO 1966), the official history by Professor M. R. D. Foot, who worked for the Special Air Service in occupied France and who is a leading authority on the history of resistance movements in general and the author of another invaluable book, *Resistance* (1976); *Baker Street Irregular* (Methuen 1965) by Colonel B. Sweet-Escott, a senior staff member of SOE who stressed that it is a history of his own experience, not of the organisation; *The Secret War Report of the OSS* (Berkeley Publishing Corporation 1976) written by an American team headed by Kermit Roosevelt in 1948, declassified in 1976 by the US Administration and edited by A. Cave Brown for publication; *British Intelligence in the Second World War*, Vol. 1 (HMSO 1979) by Professor F. H. Hinsley and others. Volume 1 to June 1941 naturally has little to say about SOE but later volumes will no doubt have more; *Britain and European Resistance 1940–1945; A Survey of the SOE with Documents* (Macmillan 1980) by David Stafford, Professor of History at Vancouver University B.C., analysing the historical, military and political aspects of SOE and reproducing a number of important official documents which are publicly available; *History of SOE* (unpublished) by Professor W. J. M. Mackenzie, written 1946 to 1948, mentioned in the Official History of the War, Grand Strategy Volume IV (1972); not seen by the author and not publicly available.

(All books published in the United Kingdom unless specified otherwise)

Amery, Julian   *Sons of the Eagle* (Macmillan 1948)

Auty, Phyllis and Clogg, R.   *British Policy Towards Wartime Resistance in Yugoslavia and Greece* (report of a 1973 conference, Macmillan 1975)

Avon, Earl of   *The Eden Memoirs* (Cassell 1965)

Bailey, Colonel S. W.   *British Policy Towards General Mihajlovic* (a paper in Auty and Clogg)

Barker, Elizabeth   *British Policy in S.E. Europe* (Macmillan 1975)

——   *Churchill and Eden at War* (Macmillan 1978)

Barry, General R. H.   *European Resistance Movements* (Pergamon 1960)

Beasly, Patrick   *Very Special Admiral – J. H. Godfrey* (Hamish Hamilton 1980)

Bernard, Professor Henri   *L'Autre Allemagne, La Résistance à Hitler* (La Renaissance du Livre, Brussels, Belgium 1976)

Buckmaster, Maurice   *Specially Employed* (Batchworth Press 1952)

Castellano, General G.   *Come Firmai L'Armistizio* (Mondadori, Milan 1945)

Cave Brown, A.   *Bodyguard of Lies* (Harper & Row, New York 1975)

Chapman, F. Spenser   *The Jungle is Neutral* (Chatto & Windus 1948)

Churchill, Sir Winston   *The Second World War* (Cassell 1954)

Cookridge, E. H.   *Inside SOE* (Arthur Barker 1966)

Dalton, Dr Hugh   *The Fateful Years 1931–45* (Frederick Muller 1957)

Dansette, A.   *Histoire de la Liberation de Paris* (Fayard, Paris 1946)

Davidson, Basil   *Partisan Picture* (Bedford Books 1946)

——   *Special Operations Europe* (Gollancz 1980)

Deakin, Sir F. W. D.   *The Embattled Mountain* (Oxford University Press 1971)

——   *Myth of an Allied Landing in the Balkans* (a paper in Auty and Clogg)

De Wavrin, A.   see Passy: his wartime alias

Dulles, Allen   *The Secret Surrender* (Harper & Row, New York 1963)

Elliott Bateman, M. (ed.)   *Fourth Dimension of Warfare* (Manchester University Press 1970)

E.R.M.   see European Resistance Movements below

European Resistance Movements   Papers of International Conference in Belgium 1958 (Pergamon Press 1960)

Foot, M. R. D.   *SOE in France* (HM Stationery Office 1966)

——   *Resistance* (Eyre Methuen 1976)

——   *Six Faces of Courage* (Eyre Methuen 1978)

Foot, M. R. D. and Langley, J. M.   *MI9* (Bodley Head 1978)

Fourcade, M. M.   *L'Arche de Noë* (Fayard, Paris 1968)

Garlinski, J.   *Poland, SOE and the Allies* (Allen & Unwin 1969)

—— *Hitler's Last Stand* (Julian Friedman 1978)

Gilchrist, Sir Andrew *Bangkok Top Secret* (Hutchinson 1970)

Gisevius, Hans *To The Bitter End* (Jonathan Cape 1948)

Giskes, H. J. *London Calling North Pole* (Kimber 1953)

Gubbins, Sir Colin *Resistance Movements in the War* Journal of the Royal United Service Institute 1948

Hamilton-Hill, Donald *SOE Assignment* (Kimber 1973)

Hamson, A. *We Fell Among Greeks* (Jonathan Cape 1946)

Hinsley, F. H. *British Intelligence in the Second World War, Vol. I* (HM Stationery Office 1979)

Howard, Michael, and others *Grand Strategy* (HM Stationery Office 1972)

Howarth, P. *Special Operations* (Routledge 1955)

—— *Undercover* (Routledge 1980)

Johns, Lt-Commander Philip *Within Two Cloaks* (Kimber 1979)

Jones, R. V. *Most Secret War – British Scientific Intelligence 1939–45* (Hamish Hamilton 1978)

Langley, J. M. *Fight Another Day* (Collins 1974)

Leasor, James *Boarding Party* (Heinemann 1956)

Leverkuehn, Paul *German Military Intelligence* (Weidenfeld & Nicolson 1954)

Lewin, R. *Ultra goes to War* (Hutchinson 1978)

Macksey, Kenneth *The Partisans of Europe* (Hart-Davis & MacGibbon 1975)

Maclean, General Sir Fitzroy *Eastern Approaches* (Jonathan Cape 1949)

—— *Disputed Barricades* (Jonathan Cape 1958)

Manvell, R. & Fraenkel, H. *The Men Who Tried to Kill Hitler* (Coward McCann, New York 1964)

Marder, A. J. *From the Dardanelles to Oran* (Oxford University Press 1974)

Martin, David *Mihajlovic, Patriot or Traitor* (Hoover Institution, Stanford University, California 1978)

Masson, Madeleine *Christine: Krystyna Skarbek* (Hamish Hamilton 1975)

Michel, Henri *Histoire de Résistance* (Presse Unitaire de France, Paris, 1950)

—— *The Shadow War* (André Deutsch 1972)

—— *Rapport General* in E.R.M.

Mikolajczyk, Stanislas   *Pattern of Soviet Domination* (Sampson Low 1948)

Mountfield, D.   *The Partisans* (Hamlyn 1979)

Muggeridge, Malcolm   *Chronicles of Wasted Time, The Infernal Grove* (Collins 1972)

Murphy, Robert   *Diplomat among Warriors* (Doubleday, New York 1964)

Myers, Brigadier E. C. W.   *Greek Entanglement* (Hart-Davis 1955)

Passy, Colonel (André de Wavrin)   *Souvenirs* (Raoul Solar, Monte Carlo 1947)

Persico, Joseph   *Piercing the Reich* (Ballantyne Books, New York 1979)

Piquet-Wicks, Eric   *Four in the Shadows* (Jarrold 1957)

Public Records Office Kew   Files; PREM 3 184/6; CAB 69/6XP326

Roosevelt, Kermit   *The Secret War Report of the OSS* edited by A. Cave Brown, (Berkeley Publishing Corporation, New York 1976)

Rootham, Jasper   *Miss Fire* (Chatto & Windus 1946)

Shirer, W. I.   *The Rise and Fall of the Third Reich* (Fawcett Publications Inc, New York 1960)

Smith, R. Harris   *OSS* (University of California 1972)

Stafford, David   *Britain and European Resistance 1940–45* (Macmillan 1980)

Steinbeck, John   *The Moon is Down* (Heinemann 1942)

Stevenson, W.   *A Man Called Intrepid* (Macmillan 1976)

Strong, Sir Kenneth   *Intelligence at the Top* (Cassell 1968)

Sweet-Escott, B.   *Baker Street Irregular* (Methuen 1965)

——   *SOE in the Balkans* (paper in Auty and Clogg)

Tillon, C.   *Les F.T.P.* (Juillard, Paris 1962)

Trenowden, I.   *Operations Most Secret, SOE the Malayan Theatre* (Kimber 1978)

Verity, H. B.   *We Landed by Moonlight* (Ian Allan 1978)

War Report of OSS   see Roosevelt, Kermit *supra*

Winterbotham, F. W.   *The Ultra Secret* (Weidenfeld & Nicolson 1974)

Woodhouse, C. M.   *Apples of Discord* (Hutchinson 1948)

——   *Summer 1943 The Critical Months* (paper in Auty and Clogg)

APPENDIX B

Résumé of Lord Selborne's undated Memorandum about the Special Operations Executive, circulated within a limited official circle in November 1943

Origin of SOE

The Memorandum first explains that immediately after the fall of France the War Cabinet decided in July 1940 to create an organisation which was to co-ordinate all action by way of sabotage and subversion against the enemy overseas. This eventually became known as the Special Operations Executive which was under the Direction of the Minister of Economic Warfare who reported direct on SOE affairs to the War Cabinet.

SOE receives directives from the Chiefs of Staff Committee regarding strategic objectives on which it should concentrate and the countries to which priority should be given.

From the Foreign Office SOE receives guidance regarding objectives for underground political activity.

From the Dominions, Colonial and India Offices SOE receives guidance regarding activities in the respective territories which they administer.

In June 1942 the CIGS informed the various Allied governments that SOE was to be regarded as the co-ordinating authority for all activities relating to resistance movements in occupied territories.

SOE Main Functions

The main functions are:
(a) to promote revolt or guerrilla warfare in all enemy and enemy-occupied countries;
(b) to hamper the enemy's war effort by means of sabotage and subversive warfare;
(c) to combat enemy interests and fifth-column activities by unacknowledgeable means.

Examples of various types of special operations by SOE are quoted as:

Sabotage of railways, telecommunications, oil targets, enemy shipping, U-boat maintenance services and industrial installations. Guerrilla activities to divert German forces from the Russian front. The collection of intelligence is not a function of SOE.

The Memorandum then states that many of the main achievements of the underground movements are now a matter of public knowledge through press reports. Such reports also make it clear that underground activities are conspicuous in France, Norway, Denmark, Poland, Jugoslavia and Greece.

Communication System

The first essential for the effective work of SOE is the establishment of rapid and secret means of communication.

In consequence a large number of W/T operators have been dropped by SOE in occupied territories. The handling of the resulting traffic has necessitated the establishment of several highly specialised wireless stations at home and abroad which required the recruiting and training of considerable numbers of W/T operators and cypher personnel.

Training & Security

The resistance groups in occupied countries would be comparatively ineffective without British or Allied organisers fully trained in para-military warfare, demolition, communications and security. The training of such officers, including parachute drill, is of vital importance. The maintenance of the highest standards of security is essential.

Transport

The chief limiting factor in SOE operational activities is transport. Sea transport over long distances, though economical, is very slow; submarines or coastal craft for transport of personnel can seldom be spared from their normal duties. Air transport is the best method because men and stores can be dropped at a pre-arranged point, especially since navigation by night has been developed to a remarkable extent by the RAF.

Stores dropped include arms, ammunition, explosives, W/T sets, boots, clothing and funds. Air transport is not only the lifeline of many resistance groups but is the visible token of Allied support and encouragement without which they tend to disintegrate.

Scale of Operations

SOE estimates that the resistance groups in Europe potentially available for clandestine operations against the Axis exceeds a million men. The directing of such numbers, even if only lightly armed and operating in small detachments, should, if properly trained and controlled, be able to be of value in diverting enemy forces and facilitating Allied military operations.

Main Areas of Current Activity

It is generally realised and now apparent from press reports that much is being done to harass the enemy by subversive activity and sabotage or guerrilla warfare in many countries, especially in France, Norway, Denmark, Poland, Jugoslavia and Greece. Much of this activity has been organised and promoted by SOE in conjunction with the Allied governments concerned. In the Far East SOE preparatory operations into Japanese occupied territories have commenced.

Co-ordination with Military Forces

Arrangements are being made to direct and co-ordinate the action of resistance groups with projected military operations. These groups generally lack mobility and are usually organised to operate only in small parties. Resistance groups may be able to assist military forces in the following ways: railway demolitions to hamper enemy movements of reinforcements, widespread attacks on telecommunications. Attacks on enemy HQ's installations. Guerrilla warfare in the enemy rear areas. Prevention in favourable circumstances of enemy port demolitions.

So as to assist in this co-operation between resistance groups and the military formations SOE officers are to be attached to the staffs of higher formations of invading Allied forces.

United States

SOE maintains a mission in Washington which keeps in touch with the Office of Strategic Services (OSS).

APPENDIX C

Telegram from C-in-C, South-West (Translation). 26 February 1945

To: 1 Supreme SS and Police Chief in Italy.
    2 Commander, 14th Army.
    3 Commander, Army of Liguria.

Activity of partisan bands in the western Apennines, and along the Via Emilia, particularly in the areas of Modena, Reggio and Parma, and south-west of them, as well as near the neighbourhood of Piacenza, has spread like lightning in the last ten days. The concentration of the partisan groups of varying political tendencies into one organisation, as ordered by the Allied High Command, is beginning to show clear results. The execution of partisan operations shows considerably more commanding leadership. Up to now it has been possible for us, with a few exceptions, to keep our vital rear lines of communications open by means of our slight protective forces, but this situation threatens to change considerably for the worse in the immediate future. Speedy and radical counter measures must anticipate this development.

It is clear to me that the only remedy, and the one which is unavoidably necessary to meet the situation, is the concentration of all available forces, even if this means temporary weakening in other places. I request you therefore to combine with 14th Army and the Army of Liguria, in carrying out several large-scale operations which will nip in the bud the increasing activity of the partisan bands in northern Italy. Please let me have your proposals as to when these measures can be carried out, and with what forces.

(Signed) KESSELRING

Telegram to the German Supreme Command from C-in-C, South-West (Translation). 5 April 1945

The situation with regard to partisan bands in northern Italy has been visibly deteriorating for several weeks. Wide areas are occupied, or endangered by partisan bands, particularly in the western Apennines and in the western Alps. A large number of vital supply routes are now only usable in convoy, and are to some extent completely in partisan hands. In addition to these numerical increases, it is easy to see that there has been a reorganisation of the Italian partisan bands, which are grouping themselves into military formations, taking military titles and uniforms, and appearing as formed bodies of troops. To an increasing extent leaders of the bands are recruited from Anglo-American officers and NCOs, and members of the bands from well-trained soldiers, keen to fight. Their armament and supply by air is proceeding continuously and, so far as can be seen, on a considerable scale.

The reasons for the reconstruction of the whole partisan group organisation are primarily the better weather, the military success of the Allies, the continuous increase in numbers of Italian deserters, and clear Anglo-American influence.

It is true that the activity of partisan bands is still limited to relatively small attacks and hold-ups, but more recently planned attacks on a larger scale have occurred. For example, on 10 March there was a planned infantry attack with the support of heavy weapons, and with the support of English aircraft. Prisoners have confirmed co-operation with the Allied air force. It can be safely assumed that the majority of the partisan formations are holding back as the result of instructions from the Allied Command with the intention of co-operating with the expected operations, and fighting in the rear of large German front-line formations. The danger which this presents, and which cannot be avoided, owing to our shortage in manpower, should not be under-estimated.

(Signed) ROETTIGER, General,
for C-in-C, South-West

APPENDIX D

Admiral Lord Louis Mountbatten, Supreme Allied Commander South-East Asia, Report of 1946 to Combined Chiefs of Staff, Washington DC, USA (Extracts)

On the 18 February, the Commander of Force 136 had requested that I should review an order by Lieut-General Leese forbidding any further distribution of arms to the Burma Defence Army (BDA), which was the military component of the 'Anti-Fascist Organisation' (AFO), the main Resistance movement in Burma. The AFO was a loosely co-ordinated 'popular front' of the active Resistance Parties, mainly of the Left; which included the Burmese Communist Party (though this was later expelled). Many of its members had engaged in active, and even illegal, opposition to the Government of Burma before the war; and some had collaborated with the Japanese during the occupation. The BDA, originally raised and equipped by the Japanese in the invasion of 1942 as the 'Burma Independence' Army, had been led by 30 young Burmans who had received military training from the Japanese in Siam and Hainan. After the British withdrawal it had been disbanded owing to the indiscipline of its members; but in August 1942 elements of it had been re-organised, again by the Japanese, under its new name. An officers' training school had been set up, with 300 cadet officers, of whom the 30 best graduates had subsequently been sent to Japan in June, 1943, for further training at the Military Academy. The BDA had been used for maintaining internal security, and had been debarred from all political activities.

488.   The leaders of the AFO had contacted an officer of Force 136 as early as December, 1943 – though this had not been known at the time, because the officer had had no wireless link with the world outside Burma. A year later the leaders of the AFO had again approached officers of Force 136, this time to inform them that an armed rising of the BDA against the Japanese was contemplated. Although well equipped with a considerable quantity of modern arms which they had either picked up on the battlefields after the fighting of 1942, or else received from the Japanese, the BDA were not sufficiently well armed to undertake military operations against fully-equipped regular troops; and, in view of their professed

intention to take part in the campaign on our side, at the appropriate moment. Force 136 had since then been supplying them with additional arms.

489. Major-General C. F. B. Pearce, Chief Civil Affairs Officer (Burma), had advised Lieut-General Leese that the further issue of arms to the BDA would imperil the present and future security of Burma; and Lieut-General Leese, who did not at this time consider that a rising of the BDA would be operationally valuable to us, had therefore ordered that no more arms were to be issued. The Commander of Force 136, argued, however, that a strengthened guerrilla movement in Burma would greatly assist his own operations behind the enemy lines. He linked the question, also with that of supporting the main Resistance movement in Malaya – the 'Anti-Japanese Union and Forces' (AJUF), which was also predominantly Left-wing – claiming that it would not be justifiable to continue providing arms and other material assistance to the AJUF if it was likely that similar political considerations would restrict its activities also, when Malaya in its turn became a battle-field.

490. We had already armed Kachin, Karen, Naga, and Lushai scouts as guerrillas among the hill tribes. If I now discouraged the only Resistance movement in Burma (apart from the hill tribes), I would not only be losing what military assistance the guerrillas might provide; but I would be increasing our operational difficulties by throwing away a chance of fighting over territory in which elements of the local population were actively engaged in fighting on our side. As a matter of fact, I might find myself placed – as a logical consequence of having discouraged Resistance activities – in the predicament of having to suppress the BDA by force, and to divert to this task troops who should be fighting the Japanese. Moreover, I considered that armed intervention on our part, to prevent the Burmese from fighting the common enemy and helping to liberate their own country, could not fail to have unfavourable repercussions in the United Kingdom, in the United States, and in other parts of the world.

491. The operational necessity to support the indigenous Resistance movement was clear. On the 24 February, therefore, I reviewed Lieut-General Leese's decision and directed that the issue of arms by Force 136 should continue. I gave orders, however, that arms were not to be distributed to the AFO as an organisation; but that only such limited numbers of individual members should be

armed as were required for our approved Intelligence and para-military operations. On the 5 March, I issued a directive outlining my policy with regard to bringing guerrillas, of whatever nature, into active participation in our operations. I laid down that, in its military aspects, the decision whether or not to do this would rest with the responsible commander on the spot, who must however keep me fully informed; and that, where there was a difference of opinion between two or more commanders, the matter was to be referred to me. In making this military decision commanders were to be guided by whatever directions I might have issued on the political aspect.

492. In its political aspects, the matter would be one for decision by me; and commanders in the field, or their advisers, were to present any views they might hold on the subject in detail for my consideration. When a decision to call a guerrilla band or sabotage party into active participation had been taken, it would be the responsibility of the British liaison unit concerned to supervise the arming, and to take subsequent command and control, of the band – subject to operational direction from the commander in the field. The unit responsible for the arming would also be made responsible for the subsequent disarming, when the guerrillas had completed their task – and experience on a limited scale with AFO representatives in Arakan had already shown that it was practicable to call in such arms when the operations were concluded.

493. Soon after this it became known, through officers of Force 136, that units of the BDA would leave Rangoon for the front on the 16 March; but that this was a cover-plan, to enable them to take up their positions before showing their hands. Their departure took place, as announced, with a great send-off from the Japanese; and on the 25, Lieut-General Leese informed me that the rebellion was imminent, and that the BDA had at their disposal at least 5000 armed men, most of whom were in the Pyinmana, Toungoo and Prome areas. He said he considered that the rising could assist his operations, and that now was the psychological moment for such action, adding that Lieut-General Slim welcomed this development and urged that the rebellion should be given the maximum support by Force 136. At the same time he warned me that the Civil Affairs officers at his Headquarters were still of the opinion that the arming of the guerrillas and the support of this rebellion would seriously increase internal security problems in Burma.

494. It seemed clear that the rising would take place before the end

of the month, whether we supported it or not; and Lieut-General Leese requested that, if it was to be supported, a decision to that effect might be made immediately. After careful consideration I ordered that the rising should be given maximum support, and authorised Lieut-General Leese to arm – in accordance with the terms of my directive of the 5 March – as many guerrillas as he considered necessary. I urged that every effort must be made, even at this late hour, to control and co-ordinate the rising through British liaison officers; and I left Lieut-General Leese a free hand to decide in detail how to ensure that it was not made prematurely, and to synchronise its phases with our overall plans for the drive to Rangoon. It seemed unlikely that the BDA (though an establishment of between 7000 and 10,000 men was claimed for it) would be able to inflict serious losses on the Japanese. The value of the rising would be psychological rather than military, for not only would this action prove a great surprise and embarrassment to the Japanese but it would provide a stimulus to pro-British sentiment in Burma by providing the local population with a stake in the actual fighting.

495.   On the 27 March I informed the British Chiefs of Staff of the whole position: telling them what action I had taken, and the considerations which had governed my decision. In asking for permission to support the rising, I pointed out that the movement, which was backed by a Left-wing nationalist group, the Anti-Fascist Organisation, was spontaneous and widespread; and that the rising itself would probably be led by Major-General Aung San, Commander of the Burmese Army which had been raised under the Japanese occupation. While the assistance we might expect from such a rising was not part of my plans, it would undoubtedly provide an acceptable bonus; and since the areas affected would be in the south, it might help to hasten the capture of Rangoon. But above all, I considered that it was operationally essential to avoid finding ourselves in a position where we were obliged to commit any of our troops to suppressing the movement by force.

496.   I made it clear that I fully realised the political implications of supporting this rising; and that, since the AFO were known to have been guilty of treason in the past by collaborating with the Japanese, I had issued a directive to Force 136 officers, to which they must strictly adhere in their dealings with the AFO. The leaders were to be informed that their assistance was appreciated, but that their past offences were not forgotten; that no general amnesty would be

given, and that offenders might consequently be required to stand trial in due course – though any service to the Allied cause would be taken into account. They were to be further informed that their movement would be expected to disarm voluntarily when instructed, though opportunity would be offered for suitable volunteers to be enrolled in the regular Burma armed forces; and that members of the movement would be enabled, and expected, to take part in the civil reconstruction of their country.

497. The Chiefs of Staff immediately referred the matter to the War Cabinet, who telegraphed me their approval on the 30. On the military side, the Chiefs of Staff instructed me that the rising should be supported, subject to the proviso that I make no additional demands for transport aircraft, and that no additional air support be given to the movement other than what I might wish to provide out of my own resources. On the political side, the War Cabinet approved the above points in my directive, stressing that it should be made abundantly clear to the AFO leaders that we did not attach any great importance to their contribution; and that they should be reminded that they had a lot of leeway to make up as collaborators with the Japanese. If Major-General Aung San, or other leaders of the movement, should ask our intentions for the future government of Burma, or our future policy, it should be made clear that we were not prepared to discuss political issues with them, or with any isolated section of the community.

498. The War Cabinet instructed me to publicise, by means of my Psychological Warfare Division, the fact that we considered the British and Indian forces, assisted by the Americans and the Chinese, to be the true liberators of Burma; to stress that the policy of His Majesty's Government for Burmese political development within the British Commonwealth had already been stated; and finally, that unity and discipline within the country, under British leadership, were essential for the immediate task of completing the liberation of Burma and for the next task of restoring the well-being of its people. On the 28 March, the BDA – re-named the 'Burma National Army', to symbolise the break-away from the Japanese – rose in armed revolt against the Japanese in many parts of Central and Southern Burma.

(This extract is reproduced with the permission of the Controller of Her Majesty's Stationery Office.)

APPENDIX E1

SOE MTO[1] 1942–5 Results[2]

1 AIR   Total
(a) No. of Air Sorties (incl. Poland & Czechoslovakia)   21,657
                                                          Successful 15,319
(b) Tons of Stores dropped or landed   20,436.5 tons
(c) Number of personnel dropped or landed   4,058
(d) Number of personnel evacuated   18,577

2 SEA
(a) Tons of stores landed   62,500
(b) Personnel landed   822
(c) Personnel evacuated   2,098

3 STORES
(a) No. of small arms delivered (air and sea)   259,653
(b) SAA rounds delivered (air and sea)   225,388,131
(c) Pairs of boots delivered (air and sea)   528,874
(d) Number of containers   83,780
            and packages   271,742

4 CASUALTIES BRITISH PERSONNEL ONLY

	Killed	Missing	Wounded
Officers	32	7	8
OR's	33	23	6

5 AWARDS

GC	1	MBE	49	GM	2
CBE	3	DCM	11	DSM	1
DSO	37	MM	47	DFC	1
MC	69	BEM	18	DFM	1
OBE	19	DSC	2		

Notes 1 MTO = Mediterranean Theatre of Operations
       2 This list was prepared in August 1945 at the author's request by the 'Q ops'
       department of SOE MTO

APPENDIX E2

Headquarters 2677th Regiment
Office of Strategic Services (Prov.)
APO 512

28 July 1945

Dear Colonel Beevor:

In reading the final report of the Operational Supply Officer on the Partisan supply program, I am particularly conscious, as I have been on many occasions in the past, of the extent to which the success of that joint venture was the result of the happy choice of personnel by our partners.

That our combined efforts were successful was readily apparent in the end result and I think I need not dwell on that point. However, I do want to express to you my appreciation of the spirit, and admiration of the abilities with which Lt-Colonel W. H. S. Byng, Lt-Colonel A. B. Flinn, Major Derek Crosthwaite and a host of others attacked our mutual problem of packing and delivering vitally needed arms and equipment to the Partisans in North Italy. OSS is indebted not alone for the material aid which these and other officers of Q (Ops) SOM were instrumental in providing and which were substantial, especially in the critical days when we were bending every effort to get the joint program under way. At least equally important was the spirit of true cooperation which we quickly learned to count on from the British 'side of the house.'

I hope you will express to Colonel Flinn and all of the Q (Ops) personnel associated with him the appreciation and thanks of our Operational Supply personnel, in which I heartily concur. With warmest personal regards, I am

Sincerely yours,

EDWARD J. F. GLAVIN
Colonel, Infantry
Commanding

Lt-Colonel John G. Beevor
Officer Commanding, Special Operations (Mediterranean)
CMF

APPENDIX E3

S.O.(M) Liaison Staff,
A.F.H.Q.,
C.H.P.

Ref: G/1454
2nd August, 1945

To: Colonel E. J. F. Glavin,
H.Q. 2677th Regt. O.S.S. (Prov),
APO 512, US Army.

Dear Colonel Glavin,

It was very good of you to write your kind and cordial letter of 28 July on the subject of the work of our supply department. I am passing on your letter to the Officers concerned to whom the credit is due and I would like in return to say how much all of us on our side have appreciated the spirit of co-operation which we have met.

In particular I feel that the remarkable success of the joint working arrangement of the packing station up at Cecina was only made possible by the mutual good will and confidence which existed between our supply Officers and those of your organisation; conspicuously Lt-Col. James F. Lawrence, Capt. Joan Matthews and Capt. Boh.

As Finance was an important item in the supply programme I think it is also appropriate to say here how grateful we were for the assistance of your Finance Officer, Capt. Crockett, who in all the complicated arrangements about Italian finance could not have been more helpful and co-operative. We all had a great admiration for his work.

I am returning to England in a few days myself for release from the Army and so take this opportunity of sending you our best thanks for the cordial relations which have existed between the two organisations in this theatre.

Yours sincerely,

Lt-Col.
(J. G. BEEVOR)
Commander S.O.(M)

APPENDIX F

Allocations of Special Duty Aircraft

Allocations of aircraft were made by the air staffs in the theatre concerned within the limits of any directives from the theatre commander, if any. For France, Germany, the Low Countries and Scandinavia by the Air Ministry in London, until January 1944, when France, Germany and the Low Countries came under the Supreme Allied Commander, General Eisenhower, whose Air Commander became responsible for allocation: for the Balkans by Air Commander in Chief Middle East until January 1944 when Commander Mediterranean Allied Air Forces (MAAF) became responsible, following the unification of command under Supreme Allied Commander Mediterranean (SACMED): for Italy and south of France by MAAF: for Poland, Czechoslovakia and Austria by the Air Ministry in London (in agreement with MAAF from 1944): for South-East Asia, mainly Burma, Malaya and Thailand, by Air Commander in Chief South-East Asia Command (SEAC). In the early period 1940–41 allocations related to individual aircraft, e.g. three Whitley bombers, two Lysander single-engined reconnaissance, one Hudson twin-engined. But obviously it soon became necessary to deal in terms of air force units, namely flights or squadrons.

In England RAF 161 Squadron (Whitley or Halifax bombers and Lysanders) operated partly at Tempsford in Bedfordshire and partly at Tangmere in Sussex, as an advanced base for Lysander pick-up operations in France. In the Middle East an RAF Halifax squadron and for a time long-range US B 24s Liberator bombers operated from Derna in Libya in 1942–3 into the Balkans; later, from the end of 1943 when south Italian bases became available after the Italian armistice, RAF and US bomber squadrons and the 1386 Polish Flight operated from Brindisi into Jugoslavia, Albania, Greece and northern Italy and sometimes to Poland. Other RAF and US Army Air Force squadrons, mostly with C47 Dakota transports, operated from Bari to Jugoslavia or elsewhere. In Algiers RAF and USAAF squadrons operated into southern France.

In South-East Asia Burma was served from Jessore near Calcutta by RAF 357 Squadron of B24 Liberators and USAAF Squadron of C47 Dakotas; Thailand and Malaya were served from two airfields in Ceylon (Sri Lanka) by RAF 357 and 358 squadrons of B24s.

At each base serving two or more countries aircraft were switched from one country to another at the discretion of the air force commander concerned, as required by weather and operational needs. This flexibility was essential in order to get the maximum use out of available aircraft. The SD (Special Duty) aircraft, as the Allied air forces called them, were shared between SOE and SIS and later with OSS as well.

INDEX